HOME
BAKING

Elizabeth Pomeroy

Note

1. All spoon measurements are level.
2. All eggs are sizes 3, 4, 5 (standard) unless otherwise stated.
3. Metric and imperial measurements have been calculated separately. Use one set of measurements only as they are not exact equivalents.
4. Cooking times may vary slightly depending on the individual oven. Dishes should be placed in the centre of the oven unless otherwise specified.
5. All flour is plain and all sugar is granulated (unless otherwise stated).
6. Always preheat the oven or grill to the specified temperature.
7. Spoon measures can be bought in both imperial and metric sizes to give accurate measurement of small quantities.

Helpful Hints
for Home Bakers

1. When starting a new recipe, first measure out all the ingredients in the sequence given, as they will be required in that order.

2. Read through the method and assemble the necessary utensils that you will need.

3. Before lighting the oven, check the position of the oven shelves as it is easier and safer to move them while they are cold.

4. Bread and cake dough tends to stick to the cooking utensils and hot water will 'cook' and harden it. If first soaked for a short time in cold water the dough is easily removed and the equipment can then be washed in hot water to remove any grease.

All colour
HOME BAKING

Elizabeth Pomeroy

OCTOPUS

**First published in 1979 by
Sundial Publications Limited**

This edition published in 1983
by Octopus Books Limited
59 Grosvenor Street
London W1

© 1979 Hennerwood Publications Limited

ISBN 0 7064 2012 8

Printed in Hong Kong

Contents

Introduction

Baking has a fascination for young and old alike — there is a feeling of absorbed interest and contentment in handling dough and a blissful satisfaction when it emerges from the oven, golden coloured and wafting around a delicious aroma.

Many home cooks find baking a welcome change from stewing, roasting and frying. There are no bulky loaves filling up the shopping bag, or squashy cake boxes which have to be shielded from disaster in the bus. There is no need to worry about bread strikes or long bank holiday weekends.

Above all, there is the positive enjoyment of creating something which is welcomed with such evident delight by family and friends.

How to use this book

The words 'Home Baking' immediately conjure up a picture of crusty golden loaves and hot rolls, so this book starts with yeasted breads.

There is no need to worry if you have never used yeast before. When you understand how it works — and this is not at all difficult — you will find it easy to master the basics of bread-making and you can then enjoy experimenting with different flours and a variety of shapes.

Yeast baking is followed by scone doughs, cakes and biscuits, and pastries. Each section starts by explaining the basic method and how to get the best results, and then gives a selection of recipes made by that method.

When you come to the collection of traditional recipes from the different regions of the British Isles, if you need a helpful reminder about kneading and proving, mixing a cake mixture or making pastry, you will find a reference back to the relevant page for detailed instructions.

Nowadays there is a lively interest in the cooking of our grandmother's day and the authentic regional recipes have been selected to give as wide a variety as possible. Scottish, Irish and Welsh recipes include a number baked in the traditional way on a bakestone or griddle — no longer over the glowing peat on an open hearth, but still on top of the stove and not in the oven.

There is also a wide variety of recipes for American and continental breads, pastries and cakes.

About ovens

For baking bread, the ovens in the Aga or similar fuel-storage cookers are ideal, as the steam from the loaves does not escape during cooking. The moisture is retained in the body of the loaves and they will still have splendid crusty tops if you glaze them.

The electric oven produces a dry heat which is excellent for pastry, but some cooks put a shallow tin of water on the oven base when baking yeast dough. The electric fan-assisted oven distributes the heat evenly over all the shelves and this is very practical for batch cooking as you can, for instance, bake six small or four large loaves, or eight medium flan cases at one time.

The heat in a gas oven is not so drying, but it rises from the open flames up to the top of the oven so the temperature is very hot on the top shelf, cooler in the centre and low near the bottom. This is useful when cooking recipes like rich pastries which need a high temperature to start with and then a lower one for the remainder of the cooking time. Instead of turning down the regulo, if you move the pastry to a lower shelf it will leave the top one available for the next batch, which you can start cooking at the same time.

A reliable oven is essential for good results when baking. Although in theory the temperature control of modern ovens is standardized, in practice it can vary. It may be because the thermostat is wearing and the oven needs recalibrating. Sometimes the gas pressure or electric power is reduced because a temporary upsurge in demand is too heavy. The answer is to invest in a reliable oven thermometer, which is not expensive.

Measuring ingredients

Level off spoonfuls of solid ingredients with the back of a
knife. If using treacle and similar sticky substances, see
the suggestion on page 47.

When mixing bread or pastry dough, it is not advisable to
give exact measures for liquid as the quantity required
will vary according to the type of flour used. Fine, soft
flours absorb much less water than the strong and coarse
meals, so approximate measures are given for guidance.
You will soon learn how to judge the quantity needed to
produce dough of the right consistency.

Baking with yeast

Many home cooks unfamiliar with yeast baking are surprised to find that once they start, it is not as complicated and time consuming as they imagined, but most enjoyable and rewarding. Both cook and family derive great pleasure from the aroma rising from freshly baked bread and the sight of crusty golden loaves emerging from the oven. However, before you start on your first bread recipe, it is well worth finding out how yeast works, how to choose it and the other basic ingredients you need for the best results, and how to knead and use the dough.

Yeast breads

What is yeast and how it works

The fascinating thing about yeast, which makes it different from chemical raising agents like baking powder, is that it is a living plant belonging to the fungi family. It grows when it has gentle warmth, moisture and food in the form of carbohydrates, such as flour and sugar. In favourable conditions it grows very rapidly, the sugar breaking down into alcohol and producing a gas — carbon dioxide. This fermentation rises the dough, giving it its spongy texture and characteristic sharp yeasty smell and flavour. To hasten the activity of yeast, the flour for the dough should be warmed in the mixing bowl in a very low oven or plate warmer for 5 to 6 minutes. The liquid should also be just above blood heat (warm to the hand) — 37°C/98°F for fresh yeast. (For dried yeast, see below.) Working with ingredients and equipment which has not been warmed will not prevent the yeast from working eventually, but it will take longer.

Sugar: yeast produces sugar, so it is not wise to add too much sugar to yeast dough, as it will over-activate and eventually destroy the yeast cells.

Salt: salt also affects the action of yeast, slowing down the rising. Too much produces a hard crust, but a certain amount of salt is essential to the taste of good bread. 25 g (1 oz) salt to 1½ kg (3 lb) of white flour is usual, but you can increase this for wholemeal bread. Add the salt to the flour, never to the yeast. A little salt also brings out the flavours in sweet and spiced doughs.

Dried granular yeast; fresh yeast

How to buy yeast

Fresh yeast

This should be bought as fresh as possible in small quantities. It is compressed into cakes which should be smooth, not dry and crumbly, a light putty colour and with a fresh smell. It is readily available in the northern counties, Scotland, Wales and the west country, where many housewives often make their own bread, and due to the increasing interest in home baking it is becoming easier to obtain in the south from bakers, delicatessens and whole and health food shops.

Storage of fresh yeast: if you are obliged to buy more than you need, you can store yeast in the refrigerator for several days in the same type of plastic container you use for bacon or cheese (not completely airtight) or a polythene bag. Yeast can be stored in the freezer for several months, but it is advisable to divide a large block into 25 g (1 oz) portions, wrap them individually in freezer film and seal in a container. In this way small quantities will be easy to thaw out as required. Unwrap the yeast and thaw slowly at room temperature, or for about 15 minutes in the tepid water used in the recipe — not hot as this will kill the yeast. If fresh yeast fails to froth in warm water, this indicates that it is no longer active and should be discarded.

Ascorbic acid

Ascorbic acid can be used with fresh yeast to produce a speeded up bread dough. It is sold by chemists in tablets of 25 or 50 mg. The baking heat kills the vitamin value, but the chemical reaction with fresh yeast (dried is not recommended) results in a very quick rise which can be convenient if you are in a hurry.

Dried granular yeast

This is obtainable at most food shops and supermarkets and some chemists. It is sold in small sachets from 15 g (½ oz) to 25 g (1 oz) or in 100 g (4 oz) tins. It is highly concentrated and 15 g (½ oz) of the dried granules will do the work of 25 g (1 oz) of fresh yeast. The granules must be thoroughly dissolved in a little hot water — (38°-43°C/100°-115°F) and reactivated with a pinch of sugar. It is best left for 15 to 20 minutes to froth before making the dough. Instructions are given by the manufacturer on the packet or tin.

Storage of dried yeast: dried yeast will keep for up to 6 months, if stored sealed in a cool, dry place. If granules do not froth within 15 minutes, this means the yeast is too stale to give satisfactory results.

Other ingredients

Choice of flour

It is important to choose the right type of flour when baking with yeast. For good bread dough you need strong plain flour. It has a high protein content so absorbs more liquid than the soft pastry flour and gives a high rise. Because of its strong gluten content, strong plain flour kneads into a firm elastic dough which, when baked, produces a large volume and light open textured bread. This is because gluten is the substance in dough which supports the gas bubbles and prevents the risen bread from collapsing. Strong plain flour is also excellent for flaky and puff pastry.

There is a wide choice of strong flours — *white, unbleached,* which is creamy coloured and has a good flavour, *brown wholemeal,* which contains 100 per cent of the wheat bran and wheatgerm, and *wheatmeal* which is also brown, but contains 85 to 90 per cent bran. There are also specialized flours such as *stone ground,* which is the whole grain ground between stones in the old fashioned way, from which nothing has been extracted. It is rather expensive and makes a rather solid loaf. *Granary meal* contains malted wheat and rye, and there are a number of proprietary blends like Hovis and Scofa. Strong white flour can be mixed in varying proportions with wholemeal to give a lighter texture to loaves. White (household) flour can be used for yeast baking provided it is not self-raising, but it will absorb less water and produce less volume and a closer texture. Blended fifty-fifty with a brown flour, it makes a good loaf.

Storage of flour: white flour keeps well, but brown flour should be used up quickly as the oil in the wheatgerm can turn rancid and affect the flavour.

Flour bins should be made preferably of metal — stainless steel, aluminium or enamelled metal, with straight sides, easy to clean and with a tight over-fitting lid. They should be kept in a cool dry place and frequently cleaned out as flour attracts pests.

Suitable fats

Fat enriches dough and makes a moister loaf which keeps better. Only a very small amount of butter or lard is rubbed into the flour for plain doughs, about 15 g (½ oz) to 450 g (1 lb) flour. For richer doughs a larger quantity of softened or melted butter or cream is added. As this slows down the action of the yeast, you may need a little more yeast and proving time to get a good rise. Oil is used for some continental doughs.

Sweeteners and flavours for yeast breads

Brown sugar, treacle, honey and malt extract will add flavour as well as sweetness to yeast doughs. Herbs, spices, dried and fresh fruit are also used in a variety of breads and buns.

Choice of liquids and mixing

Plain yeast doughs are mixed with water, slightly richer doughs with milk and water in equal quantities, and still richer doughs with all milk and sometimes beaten eggs. You need about 300 ml (½ pint) liquid to 450 g (1 lb) strong white flour, a little more for wholemeal and a little less for plain white flour. Add all the specified liquid at once and then work in extra flour if the dough is too soft to handle. Mix vigorously with the hand or a wooden spoon until the dough leaves the sides of the bowl clean.

If you add too little liquid at the beginning and the dough is too tight, you cannot add more liquid at this stage. It is easier to correct a dough which is too slack by adding more flour than the other way round, so it is better not to skimp the liquid at the start.

Choice of flours for bread-making. From the front, clockwise: granary meal; brown wholemeal; wheatmeal; unbleached white; strong white

How to add yeast to flour

1. Straight dough method with dissolved yeast

This is the most usual method used for bread doughs. Fresh yeast is blended with a cupful of the warm liquid, then added to the flour, salt and fat with the remaining liquid.

Dried yeast is dissolved in a cupful of hot water (44°C/110°F) and sweetened with a teaspoon of sugar to speed up its action. It should be left in a warm place for 15 minutes until frothy, then added to the dry ingredients with remaining liquid.

2. Sponge batter method

This method is used for rich doughs like fancy loaves, rolls and buns, containing extra fat, sugar and eggs, which otherwise would slow down the rising process. Put one third of the flour in a mixing bowl with the yeast and a teaspoon of the sugar, but no salt at this stage. Mix into a batter with the warm liquid. Set aside in a warm place for 20 to 30 minutes until frothy. Then mix in the remaining flour, salt and other ingredients to form a firm dough.

3. Rubbed-in method

This is the simplest method but is suitable only for fresh yeast, for soft doughs, quick breads and some sweet doughs. The yeast is rubbed into the flour and the liquid added to make a soft dough which must be well mixed.

From the front, clockwise: Sponge batter method; Rubbed-in method; Straight dough method

Kneading

All yeast doughs must be kneaded after mixing to strengthen the dough and get a good rise. Gather the dough into a ball, turn it on to a well floured board and flatten it slightly. Hold down the front of the dough with one hand and with the other stretch out the further edge, then fold it over towards you. Press down firmly, then using the heel of your hand, push the dough away from you with a punching movement. Give the dough a quarter turn and repeat the stretching, folding, punching and turning for about 10 minutes, developing a rocking rhythm, until the dough is firm, elastic and smooth. Keep your hands floured to prevent the dough sticking to them or to the board. If using dough hooks on an electric mixer, turn to lowest speed and follow the maker's instructions. The mixer saves time, but many people find a unique satisfaction in hand-kneading the dough.

Stretching the dough

Punching the dough

Rising (proving) and knocking back

Yeast dough must be risen at least once before baking, often twice, before and after shaping, to allow the yeast to work. Dough can be shaped immediately after one kneading and left to rise in the tin before baking. Better results are obtained if the kneaded dough is allowed to rise before shaping, then 'knocked back', shaped and left to rise or 'prove' again before baking. To knock back the risen dough, turn it onto a board and knead it with your knuckles. This knocks out the air bubbles producing a more even texture.

The rising time varies according to the temperature and quantity of dough and yeast. Dried yeast is slower working than fresh yeast, and strong flour slower than soft flour. The dough should never be subjected to more than gentle heat. A slow rise produces the best bread, but you can time the rise to suit your convenience.

Knocking back the dough

Proving the dough

Unrisen dough

Risen dough

If the dough is refrigerated overnight, allow it to return to room temperature again and rise before shaping and baking.

The dough must be covered during rising to prevent a skin forming and loss of heat; an oiled plastic bag or container is the most convenient. Leave plenty of room for the dough to double its bulk. An easy way to measure this is to put the dough into a straight-sided plastic container instead of a bowl, flatten it slightly and put an elastic band round the outside to mark the dough level. Cover with a transparent lid or clingfilm and you can measure the rise to double height without difficulty.

RISING TIMES FOR YEAST BREAD DOUGHS	
In a warm place (quick rise)	40 to 60 minutes
Room temperature (21°C, 70°F)	1½ to 2 hours
Cold room or larder	8 to 12 hours
Refrigerator	12 to 14 hours

To bake yeast doughs

Yeast doughs should be put into an oven preheated to a high temperature to halt the rising (220°-230°C /425°-450°F, Gas Mark 7-8) which in some cases is modified after the first 20 minutes. The yeast is killed at 54°C/130°F, otherwise the dough would continue to rise. Bread is cooked when it sounds hollow if tapped on the bottom.

Storage of dough before baking

Unrisen dough can be stored for 24 hours in the refrigerator, or in the freezer for up to 8 weeks for a plain dough and up to 5 weeks for an enriched white dough. Be sure to protect it with a greased polythene bag, leaving space for expansion and allow it to return to room temperature before preparing for baking. If you intend to store the dough for a lengthy period, it is advisable to make it with cold ingredients. Risen bread dough, both before and after shaping, does not usually freeze satisfactorily.

Storing bread

When storing bread, make sure it is quite cold before wrapping it or putting it in a container. This can be a crock of porous earthenware, a roll-top bread box or a ventilated enamelled bread bin. Bread will keep well in an airtight tin for one or two days and then the moisture in the loaf starts to condense and mould will form on the crust. Stale breadcrumbs also generate mould, so it is important to keep the crock or bin very clean and free from crumbs.

A crusty loaf or rolls should not be wrapped as the crust will soften. Soft bread and rolls can be wrapped in a clean cloth for storage instead of putting them in a container. Large loaves keep better than small ones, and rolls tend to dry out quickly, so are usually best re-heated.

Freezing

Baked yeast products freeze very satisfactorily. Plain bread loaves and soft rolls can be stored for up to a year provided they are thoroughly cooled, carefully wrapped in foil or freezer film and sealed to prevent dehydration. Loaves can be defrosted by placing in a hot oven (200°C/400°F, Gas Mark 6), for up to 20 to 30 minutes depending on size, rolls for about 15 minutes, and served hot or cooled. Slices of frozen bread can be placed directly under the grill for toast.

Richer yeast products, like tea breads which contain eggs and extra sugar, store well in the freezer for up to 3 months, but it is inadvisable to keep baked yeast pastries for longer than 2 to 3 weeks.

Tips for top baking

1. Choose the right flour.
2. Mix in the correct amount of yeast the right way.
3. Add all the liquid at once.
4. Knead the dough thoroughly.
5. Prove before baking until doubled in bulk.
6. Cover rising dough to prevent a skin forming.
7. Bake in a preheated oven at a high temperature:
   Plain doughs: 230°C/450°F, Gas Mark 8
   Richer doughs: 200°C/400°F, Gas Mark 6 to
   220°C/425°F, Gas Mark 7

Common mistakes in bread making

A flying top: the top crust breaks away from the loaf because the dough was not kneaded until elastic, or under-proved, so the crust bakes hard before the loaf expands.

White spots on top crust: skin has formed while dough was proving because it was not covered with a cloth or polythene.

Lack of volume and uneven texture: dough under-kneaded or under-proved, or the oven too hot.

Lack of volume and open crumbly texture: dough over-proved or oven not hot enough.

Sour or bitter taste: yeast not fresh enough or dough over-proved.

Finishes and glazes

Soft finish: rub or brush with flour.
Crusty finish: brush with salted water.
Shiny glaze: brush with milk or cream.
Golden glaze: brush with *Egg Wash;* 1 egg beaten with 1 to 2 tablespoons water or milk.
Sweet glaze: brush with *Sugar Syrup;* 2 tablespoons sugar dissolved in 2 tablespoons hot water or milk.

Basic white bread dough

METRIC	IMPERIAL
750 g strong white or unbleached flour	*1½ lb strong white or unbleached flour*
2 teaspoons salt	*2 teaspoons salt*
15 g lard	*½ oz lard*
15 g fresh yeast	*½ oz fresh yeast*
450 ml water	*¾ pint water*
or	*or*
1½ teaspoons dried yeast with 1 teaspoon caster sugar	*1½ teaspoons dried yeast with 1 teaspoon caster sugar*

To make the dough with fresh yeast: sift the flour and salt into a mixing bowl and warm gently for 5 to 6 minutes. Rub in the lard lightly. Warm the water until tepid and blend in the yeast. Add all the water at once to the dry ingredients. Mix into a soft dough and beat well with a wooden spoon, or by hand, until the dough leaves the sides of the bowl clean, adding a little extra flour if sticky, or leave this until kneading.

To make the dough with dried yeast: heat a cupful of the measured water until hand-hot (40°C/110°F) and add the sugar. Sprinkle the dried yeast on top, swirl it around and leave for about 10 minutes or until frothy. Add with remaining water to the warm dry ingredients and mix to a dough as for fresh yeast.

Kneading: gather the dough into a ball (add more flour if sticky), turn it on to a floured board, and knead it for about 10 minutes (p.14) until firm, elastic and smooth to touch.

Rising and knocking back the dough: round up the dough into a ball and place it in an oiled container or polythene bag (p.15) and leave to rise until doubled in bulk. When risen, turn the dough on to a board and knock it back with your knuckles before shaping (p.15), to ensure the baked dough will have an even texture with no large holes. Do not work in extra flour at this stage.

Proving the shaped dough: mould the dough according to the type of loaf required, taking care not to work in extra flour as this will affect the colour and finish of the crust. Place the shaped dough in tins or hand mould on a baking sheet, cover with polythene and leave to rise until doubled in bulk — it will be springy to the touch when sufficiently proved. Glaze according to recipe instructions.

Baking: remove the polythene and bake the loaves in the centre of a preheated hot oven at 230°C/450°F, Gas Mark 8 for 30 to 40 minutes according to size. The bread is ready when the crust is well browned and the loaf begins to shrink from the sides of the tin. Remove from the oven, turn out of the tin or turn upside down if hand-moulded and tap the bottom. The loaf will sound hollow when cooked. If not ready, or a specially crisp crust is desired, return to the oven without the tin for a little longer. When cooked, cool by placing the loaf across the tin or on a wire tray.

Stages in bread-making, from left to right: dough mixture in bowl; after first kneading; half risen dough in container; first rising (proving); second rising (proving); finished breads

Shaping and slashing loaves

Loaves can be shaped to fit rectangular or round tins, earthenware moulds or free formed, without a tin and placed on a baking sheet. These require care in making because if the dough is too slack or over-proved they will spread and lose shape. Slashing the top with a sharp knife or making cuts with scissors will make the crust crisper and more varied in colour and texture. Whether this is done before or after the final proving is important and it is advisable to follow the recipe instructions carefully.

Tin loaves

After knocking back the dough, round it up into a ball and leave for 10 minutes. Flatten the ball with your floured hands into an oval shape. Fold the two curved ends over towards the centre to give straight sides. Now fold in three lengthwise into a cylinder shape or roll up fairly tightly like a Swiss roll. The roll should be slightly shorter than the tin so that as it expands, it domes evenly. Place the roll in a 23 × 12cm/9 × 5 inch warmed and greased tin. For 2 small loaves, halve the risen dough before shaping and use two 18 × 10cm/7 × 4 inch loaf tins. Cover with polythene and set aside to prove (see page 15). Brush with salted water before baking.

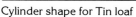
Cylinder shape for Tin loaf   Swiss roll shape for Tin loaf

Split tin or Farmhouse loaf

After the dough, shaped as above, has proved for about 10 minutes, sprinkle with water and make a deep cut lengthwise down the centre of the loaf. As the dough expands in the tin, the cut opens with it. Continue proving and bake as above.

Bloomer

This loaf is baked without a tin. For 2 small loaves divide the risen dough in half before shaping into cylinders. Place the roll (or rolls) on a baking sheet, cover and leave for 10 minutes to prove. Brush with Egg Wash (p.16) and with a sharp knife make 5 deep gashes diagonally across the top at regular intervals. (It is easier if you make the centre cut first and then two on either side.) Continue proving for a further 5 to 10 minutes and as the cuts open, sprinkle in some water from a pastry brush. Bake immediately in a preheated hot oven at 230°C/450°F, Gas Mark 8 for 30 minutes. Reduce the heat to 220°C/425°F, Gas Mark 7 for a further 15 minutes or until cooked. The basic white dough can be mixed with half milk and half water if preferred.

Short baton

The Basic White Bread Dough recipe (p.16) will make 2 or 3 of these loaves. Divide the risen dough accordingly, and shape into cylinders. Place on a board and gently roll each cylinder to and fro with your hands, working from the centre outwards, so that the ends taper. Place on the baking sheet and prove for 10 minutes. Sprinkle with flour and with a sharp knife make a deep cut lengthwise down the centre of the dough. You can also make smaller diagonal cuts each side of the slit. Continue proving for a further 10 minutes and as the cut or gashes open, sprinkle in a little water from the pastry brush. Continue proving and bake as for Bloomer. Cooking times will vary slightly from 30 minutes according to the thickness of the loaf.

Coburg (free-form)

This is a crusty version of the simple Cob Loaf (p.20). You can make it with white or brown flour or a combination of both.

To make a small loaf, use half the quantity of kneaded dough in the Basic White Bread recipe.
The remainder may be used for a Crown Loaf (p.21).
If making a large loaf, use two thirds quantity and make the remainder into rolls (p.22).
Shape the kneaded dough into a ball and prove until doubled in bulk. Knock back very thoroughly. Work in some extra flour if the dough is at all slack, or it will spread out flat during proving and baking.
Shape the dough into a ball and place it on a floured baking sheet. Push in the bottom edges of the dough all round, tucking it in under the ball and plumping it up well so it will rise in a dome and not flatten out. This is important and may require a little practice. Cover with polythene and prove for a second time until nearly doubled in bulk — be careful not to over-prove. Cut a fairly deep gash across the top of the loaf. Now cut from the outside towards the centre so as to form a cross. Do not cut too near the edge of the loaf. As soon as the cuts open, bake the loaf in a preheated hot oven at 230°C/450°F, Gas Mark 8 for 15 minutes. Reduce the heat to 200°C/400°F, Gas Mark 6, and bake for a further 20 minutes. Then switch off the oven, invert the loaf and leave in the oven for 15 to 20 minutes. Remove from the oven and cool on a wire tray.

Making gashes across the top of a Bloomer

Cottage loaf

This is quite a tricky loaf to make as the dough must be stiff enough to hold its form, but not stodgy. The top-knot also tends to slide off the bottom part during baking unless carefully moulded and firmly fixed.

METRIC	IMPERIAL
450 g strong white flour	*1 lb strong white flour*
2 teaspoons salt	*2 teaspoons salt*
15 g butter or lard	*½ oz butter or lard*
15 g fresh yeast	*½ oz fresh yeast*
or	*or*
1 teaspoon dried yeast with 1 teaspoon caster sugar	*1 teaspoon dried yeast with 1 teaspoon caster sugar*
300 ml warm water	*½ pint warm water*

MAKES 1 LOAF

Make the dough following the recipe for Basic White Bread Dough (p.16). When knocking back the dough after the first rise, work in a little extra flour if the dough seems slack. Cut off a third of the dough and round up into one large and one small ball. Place the large ball on a floured baking sheet and flatten the top. Place the small ball beside it, leaving room for both to expand. It is best to

Prove the rounds separately   Press together before baking

prove the parts separately, as the weight of the top knot tends to flatten out the base. Cover and prove until nearly doubled in bulk — it is safe to under-prove slightly rather than over-prove, which would cause the loaf to spread and collapse in the oven.

Move the large round to the middle of the baking sheet, flatten the top again if necessary, cut a cross in the centre and brush with water. Damp the bottom of the small round and place it on top of the large round, centring it carefully.

Fix the two pieces firmly by pinching the dough together round the base of the top knot. Put your middle finger over your index finger, dip them together into the flour bag and then into the centre of the top-knot, pressing firmly down into the lower part of the loaf. Withdraw your fingers carefully and make sure both parts of the loaf are nicely rounded. Brush the loaf all over with salted water for a crisp crust, or dust with flour for a soft crust.

Bake in the centre of a preheated hot oven at 220°C/450°F, Gas Mark 8 for 20 minutes, then reduce the heat to 200°C/400°F, Gas Mark 6 for a further 20 to 25 minutes. Test by turning upside down and tapping the bottom of the loaf. If it does not sound hollow, return it to the oven for a little longer. Cool on a wire tray.

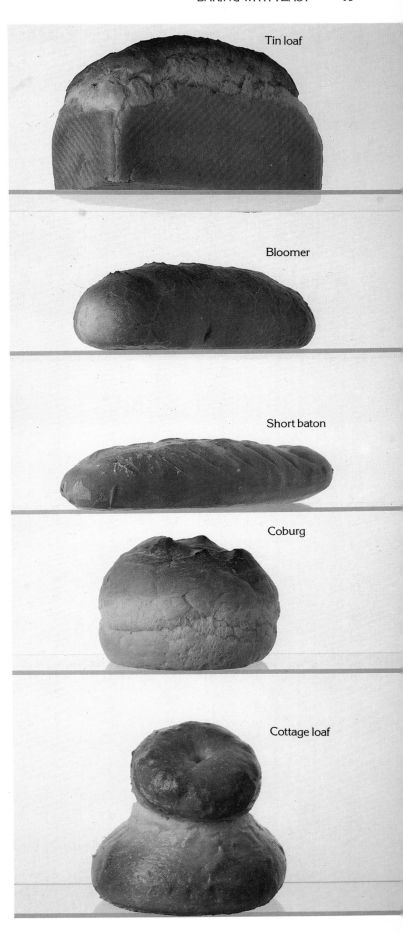

Tin loaf

Bloomer

Short baton

Coburg

Cottage loaf

Tin loaf

Cob loaf

Granary cob

Basic brown bread dough

METRIC	IMPERIAL
750 g strong wheatmeal flour	*1½ lb strong wheatmeal flour*
15 g salt	*½ oz salt*
15 g lard or butter	*½ oz lard or butter*
15 g fresh yeast	*½ oz fresh yeast*
or	*or*
2 teaspoons dried yeast with 1 teaspoon caster sugar	*2 teaspoons dried yeast with 1 teaspoon caster sugar*
500 ml warm water	*18 fl oz warm water*

Make the dough with fresh or dried yeast according to the instructions for Basic White Bread Dough (p.16). Brown flour usually absorbs more liquid than white, hence the extra quantity of water. Knead, rise, knock back and prove the dough as in the basic white bread recipe.

Tin loaves

Shape and bake as for white Tin Loaves (p.18). Allow 30 minutes baking time for smaller loaves, 40 minutes for a large loaf. For a soft crust, dust with flour before baking. For a crisp crust, brush with salted water.

Brown cob loaf

This is a simple round loaf baked without a tin. Divide the Basic Brown Bread Dough in half after the first rising and knocking back. Shape each piece into a round and place on a floured baking sheet. Cover and prove until doubled in bulk. Sprinkle with cracked wheat or sesame seeds, or dust with flour. Bake in a preheated hot oven at 230°C/450°F, Gas Mark 8 for 30 minutes or until cooked. This loaf can also be made with all wholemeal, or half brown and half strong white flour.

Crown loaf

Crown loaf

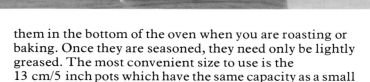

Flowerpot loaves

Granary bread

This is made in the same way as Basic Brown Bread Dough, but using granary meal instead of brown flour; it is a mixture of wheat kernels and flakes, rye and wheatmeal. The bread has a nutty texture and some mixtures have a pleasant malty flavour. If preferred, vegetable oil can be substituted for the lard. Add it to the warm liquid as it does not rub in like solid fat. Shape and bake as Tin Loaves or Cob Loaf, or for a change use clean, tempered flower pots (see below).

METRIC	IMPERIAL
750 g granary meal	*1½ lb granary meal*
2 teaspoons salt	*2 teaspoons salt*
15 g fresh yeast	*½ oz fresh yeast*
or	*or*
2 teaspoons dried yeast with 1 teaspoon sugar	*2 teaspoons dried yeast with 1 teaspoon sugar*
approx. 500 ml warm water	*approx. 18 fl oz warm water*
1 tablespoon vegetable oil or melted lard	*1 tablespoon vegetable oil or melted lard*

MAKES 2 LOAVES AND ROLLS, OR 3 LOAVES

Put the granary meal and salt into a warm bowl — it is too coarse to put through a flour sieve, so just aerate it with the fingers. Blend the yeast with 300 ml/½ pint warm water, adding the sugar if using dried yeast. Leave to froth. Add the oil or fat to the remaining water, and mix with the yeast liquid. Stir into the flour and mix into a soft dough, adding a little more warm water if necessary. Do not skimp the liquid when using coarse meals or the bread will be hard. Beat well with a wooden spoon, turn on to a floured board and knead for about 10 minutes until firm and elastic. Round up the dough into a ball and put in an oiled bag or a container and leave to prove until doubled in bulk (p.15). Knock back the dough. Shape and bake as for Tin Loaves or Cob Loaf, or break off two pieces of dough for flower pots (each should weigh about 400 g/14 oz). You will have sufficient dough over to make a Crown Loaf (opposite) or Brown Rolls (p.22).

Flower pot loaves

These are baked in earthenware flower pots, *not* plastic. They should be well scrubbed, outside and in, oiled inside and tempered in a warm oven two or three times before they are used for the first time. The easiest way is to leave them in the bottom of the oven when you are roasting or baking. Once they are seasoned, they need only be lightly greased. The most convenient size to use is the 13 cm/5 inch pots which have the same capacity as a small loaf tin.

Make up the Granary Bread dough as described.

Round up each portion of dough and shape smoothly to fit into the bottom half of the warmed and greased flower pot. If you like a nutty crust, sprinkle the inside of the pot with coarse oatmeal. Put the dough into the pots and sprinkle with more oatmeal. For a soft crust, omit the oatmeal and flour the outside of the dough.

Cover the filled pots and put in a warm place to prove. When the dough has risen to 2.5 cm/1 inch below the top of the pot, put the pots on a baking sheet in the centre of a preheated hot oven at 230°C/450°F, Gas Mark 8 for 30 minutes. Reduce the heat to 180°C/350°F, Gas Mark 4. Unmould the loaves, stand them upside down on the baking sheet and bake for a further 15 to 20 minutes. If you prefer your loaves to have a flat top instead of domed, bake them upside down. The dough will expand in the oven and fill the pot, and because the earthenware is porous the bread, though covered, will have a good open texture and a crisp crust. Use the handle of a wooden spoon to release the crust which rises through the hole in the base of the flower pot. Bake unmoulded at the lower temperature for the last 15 to 20 minutes.

Flower pot loaves can be made with wheatmeal or wholemeal flour and the Quick Brown Bread recipe (p.24) can also be used.

Crown loaf

Use 500 g/1¼ lb Granary Bread dough (or wheatmeal or wholemeal Brown Bread Dough), weighed after proving and knocking back.

Grease a 20 cm/8 inch cake tin. Divide the dough into 10 equal portions of 50 g/2 oz each. Flour your hands and roll each portion into a ball in the palms of your hands. Arrange 7 balls round the edge of the tin and fit 3 into the centre. Cover and prove for 30 to 35 minutes, until risen. Dust with flour for a soft crust. If you prefer a crisp crust, brush with milk, or Egg and Milk Wash (p.16) and sprinkle with poppy or sesame seeds. Bake in a preheated hot oven at 200°C/400°F, Gas Mark 6 for 30 to 35 minutes. Allow to shrink before turning out.

The loaf can be cut into wedges or broken up into portions.

Plain crusty rolls

You can make these with the Basic White Bread Dough (p.16) or Basic Brown Bread Dough (p.20). The recipe will make 18 to 24 rolls according to size, so you may find it more convenient to divide the dough in half and use one half for rolls and the rest for a small loaf or to stock up your freezer with unrisen dough. For the rolls, knock back the dough after the first rising and weigh off 50 g/2 oz portions for small round dinner rolls or 65 g - 75 g/2½ - 3 oz portions for large breakfast rolls, knots or small cottage loaves.

Crusty rolls should be served as fresh as possible. If kept overnight in a tin, reheat in a preheated moderate oven at 180°C/350°F, Gas Mark 4 just before serving.

Round rolls

Roll each piece of dough into a ball between the floured palms of your hands. Press down on the pastry board and then release. Place the rolls on a lightly greased baking sheet. Cover with polythene and leave to rise. When ready the dough will spring back when pressed with a floured finger.

Remove the polythene, brush the tops of the rolls with lightly salted water. Bake in the centre of a preheated hot oven at 230°C/450°F, Gas Mark 8 for 20 minutes or until they sound hollow when tapped. Remove from the baking sheet and cool on a wire tray.

Knots

Roll each portion of dough into a thin sausage shape and twist into a knot. Prove, glaze and bake as for Round Rolls. Be careful not to over-prove before baking or the dough will spread and lose shape.

Small cottage loaves

Divide the dough into 75 g/3 oz portions. Then divide each portion into two-thirds and one-third. Roll each piece into a ball. Damp the top of the larger ball and place the smaller one on top. Push your floured forefinger or the handle of a small wooden spoon through the centre to secure the two pieces together. Prove, glaze and bake as for Round Rolls.

From the left: Knots; Small cottage loaves and Round rolls; Soft wholemeal rolls; Scots baps

Soft rolls

These are normally made with milk, or at least half milk and half water, in order to produce a soft texture. To get a soft crust, dust with flour just before baking, instead of glazing with salted water.

Scots baps

These soft rolls have long been traditionally served for breakfast in Scotland where they are known as morning rolls. This popularity has now spread well beyond the borders. They are delicious served freshly baked and hot from the oven with butter and honey or marmalade, but they can be reheated in a preheated moderate oven at 180°C/350°F, Gas Mark 4, or split and toasted.

METRIC	IMPERIAL
450 g strong white flour	*1 lb strong white flour*
2 teaspoons salt	*2 teaspoons salt*
150 ml warm milk	*¼ pint warm milk*
150 ml warm water	*¼ pint warm water*
15 g fresh yeast	*½ oz fresh yeast*
milk and flour for glazing	*milk and flour for glazing*

MAKES 12

Sift the flour and salt into a mixing bowl and leave in a warm place. Mix the milk and water together and blend in the yeast. Leave for 10 minutes to froth, then stir into the flour. Mix well to a soft slack dough, adding a little more warm water if necessary.
If using dried yeast, put 2 teaspoons yeast and 1 teaspoon sugar into 150 ml/¼ pint warm water to froth. Pour into warmed flour, add the milk and continue as above.
Turn on to a floured board and knead for 4 to 5 minutes (p.14), until the dough no longer sticks. Cover the bowl with a damp cloth or put the dough into an oiled polythene bag and leave to rise for 1½ hours or until the dough springs back when pressed.
Knock back the dough (p.15). Press it out by hand or use a floured rolling pin, until 1.5 cm/½ inch thick and divide into 8 or 10 equal sized pieces. With floured fingers shape into ovals. Place on a floured baking sheet, leaving room between them for expansion. Cover and prove for 15 minutes. Brush tops and sides with milk and sprinkle with flour. Press 3 floured fingers firmly into the centre of each bap to prevent blistering in the oven.
Bake in the centre of a preheated hot oven at 220°C/425°F, Gas Mark 7 for 15 to 20 minutes, until well risen and golden brown. Remove from the oven and dust with flour. Serve hot wrapped in a napkin, or cool on a wire tray covered with a cloth.

Soft wholemeal rolls

METRIC	IMPERIAL
225 g wholemeal flour	*8 oz wholemeal flour*
1 teaspoon salt	*1 teaspoon salt*
25 g margarine or lard	*1 oz margarine or lard*
15 g fresh yeast	*½ oz fresh yeast*
or	*or*
1½ teaspoons dried yeast with 1 teaspoon sugar	*1½ teaspoons dried yeast with 1 teaspoon sugar*
approx. 150 ml warm milk	*approx. ¼ pint warm milk*

MAKES 8 ROLLS

Sift the flour with the salt into a mixing bowl and warm. Rub in the fat. Blend the fresh yeast with the warm milk and leave for 10 minutes to froth.
If using dried yeast, dissolve the sugar in the warm milk, sprinkle in the dried yeast and leave for 15 to 20 minutes until frothy.
Pour the yeast liquid into the flour, and mix, adding a little more milk if necessary. Beat until the dough leaves the sides of the bowl clean, turn on to a floured board and knead for 10 minutes (p.14). Put the dough into an oiled polythene bag and leave to rise until doubled in bulk. Knock back the dough (p.15), make a fat sausage shape and cut across into 8 equal-sized pieces. Shape into rounds or ovals. Press down firmly with the heel of your hand and release. Place on a floured baking sheet, leaving space between them for expansion. Cover and prove for 15 minutes or until doubled in size. Dust with flour and bake in the centre of a preheated hot oven at 230°C/450°F, Gas Mark 8 for 15 to 20 minutes. When cooked, remove to a wire tray and cover with a tea cloth.

Quick yeast doughs

The making of yeast dough can be speeded up by eliminating one rising period — by adding ascorbic acid and/or increasing the amount of yeast and sugar.

It enables you to make and bake one large or two small loaves in about 1¾ hours. Although satisfactory with fresh yeast, this method is not recommended for dried, which takes longer to rise and tends to give the bread too strong a yeasty flavour.

Plain soft flour can be used instead of strong flour, but it will absorb less water and produce a smaller loaf with a rather close texture.

Ascorbic acid is readily available in chemist shops in tablet form of 25 mg or 50 mg.

Quick white bread

This dough is made using ascorbic acid.

METRIC	IMPERIAL
750 g strong white flour	1½ lb strong white flour
15 g salt	½ oz salt
1 teaspoon sugar	1 teaspoon sugar
15 g lard	½ oz lard
25 g fresh yeast	1 oz fresh yeast
450 ml warm water	¾ pint warm water
25 mg ascorbic acid tablet	25 mg ascorbic acid tablet

MAKES 1 LARGE OR 2 SMALL LOAVES, OR 18 ROLLS

An electric mixer with dough hooks saves kneading time

Sift the flour and salt into a mixing bowl and leave in a warm place. Mix in the sugar and rub in the fat.

Blend the yeast into the warm water, then add the ascorbic acid tablet and dissolve it. Add to the dry ingredients all at once and beat with a wooden spoon into a stiff dough, adding extra flour if necessary. When the dough leaves the sides of the bowl clean, turn on to a floured board. Knead thoroughly for 10 minutes (p.14).

If using an electric mixer and dough hooks, pour the yeast liquid into the mixer bowl and add the mixed dry ingredients. Mix for 1 minute on speed 1, then raise to speed 2 and knead for a further 3 minutes. Remove the dough from the mixer bowl, shape into a ball and put into an oiled polythene bag. Leave to rest for 5 minutes.

Grease 1 large or 2 small loaf tins.

Stretch the dough to fit the tin or tins, fold in 3 and fit into tins. Place in a lightly oiled polythene bag. Leave for 45 to 50 minutes at room temperature to rise to the top of the tin. When ready, the dough will spring back when pressed. Remove the polythene and bake in the centre of a preheated hot oven at 230°C/450°F, Gas Mark 8 for 30 to 35 minutes until well risen and golden brown. When cooked, the loaf will shrink slightly from the tin. Turn out, test by tapping the bottom, and cool across the tin or on a wire tray.

Quick brown bread

In this one-rise bread fresh or dried yeast may be used with the quantity slightly increased and a little extra sugar added to the mixture.

METRIC	IMPERIAL
450 g wholemeal flour or	1 lb wholemeal flour or
225 g wholemeal and	8 oz wholemeal and
225 g strong white flour	8 oz strong white flour
2 teaspoons salt	2 teaspoons salt
1 teaspoon caster sugar	1 teaspoon caster sugar
25 g lard or butter	1 oz lard or butter
15 g fresh yeast	½ oz fresh yeast
or	or
2 teaspoons dried yeast with	2 teaspoons dried yeast with
1 teaspoon caster sugar	1 teaspoon caster sugar
approx. 350 ml warm water	approx. 12 fl oz warm water

MAKES 1 LARGE OR 2 SMALL LOAVES

Sift the flour and salt into a mixing bowl and rub in the fat. Prepare the yeast liquid by Method 1 (p.14) and add to the flour all at once. Beat with a wooden spoon into a fairly soft dough, adding more water if necessary.

Turn on to a floured board and knead well for 10 minutes (p.14). Stretch the dough to fit 1 large tin or divide in half to fit 2 small tins. Fold in three or roll up and put into the warmed and greased tins. Place in an oiled polythene bag and leave to rise in a warm place until it reaches the top edge of the tin. Brush with slightly salted water and bake in the centre of a preheated hot oven at 230°C/450°F, Gas Mark 8, for 15 minutes. Reduce the heat to 200°C/400°F, Gas Mark 6, and cook for a further 30 to 40 minutes according to size. When cooked the loaf will shrink slightly from the tin. Turn out and tap the base to see if it sounds hollow. Remove from the oven and cool.

Grant stone ground loaf

Mrs. Doris Grant's recipe, which bears her name, was published in 1944 and is favoured by health food enthusiasts who like a very substantial, some would say solid, wholemeal loaf. A single slice of Grant loaf is as satisfying and nourishing as two slices of ordinary bread. In the original recipe Mrs. Grant advocates a high proportion of yeast 'for extra food value' and sufficient water to make the dough 'wet and slippery' (600 ml/1 pint water to 750 g/1½ lb stone ground flour). In this recipe the amount of water has been modified, but you may like to experiment with a more liquid dough.

It is made by an unusual and easy method requiring no kneading and only a single rising. It is rather crumbly when freshly baked and is best kept uncut for 24 hours. It then remains moist for 4 or 5 days and also toasts satisfactorily. It can be made with strong wholemeal flour and ordinary salt and soft brown sugar.

METRIC	IMPERIAL
750 g stone ground flour	*1½ lb stone ground flour*
15 g sea salt	*½ oz sea salt*
25 g margarine or butter	*1 oz margarine or butter*
15 g Barbados sugar	*½ oz Barbados sugar*
approx. 450 ml warm water	*approx. ¾ pint warm water*
15 g fresh yeast	*½ oz fresh yeast*

MAKES 1 LARGE AND 1 SMALL LOAF, OR 3 SMALL LOAVES

Sift the flour and salt into a mixing bowl and warm for 5 minutes. Rub in the fat. Crumble the yeast into 150 ml/¼ pint of the warm water and add the sugar. Stir until dissolved and leave for 10 minutes to froth up. Pour the yeast liquid into the flour and stir in the rest of the water. Mix well and if necessary add more warm water.

Pour or spoon the dough into the warmed and greased tins — 3 small tins or 1 large and 1 small. They should be only half-filled. Put the tins in a polythene bag, place on a plate warmer or similar warm place, and leave to rise until doubled in bulk. This should take about 30 minutes. If under-proved, the loaf will have too close a texture; if over-proved, the bread will be spongy. Remove the polythene and bake in a preheated moderately hot oven at 200°C/400°F, Gas Mark 6 for 45 minutes to 1 hour according to size. Test by tapping the top crust with the knuckles to see if it sounds hollow. Allow to cool and shrink slightly before turning out to cool on a wire tray.

From the front: Grant stone ground loaf; Quick brown bread

Enriched doughs

Enriched doughs can be varied in richness according to the proportion of fat and eggs added to the dough. The basic recipe is made by the Sponge Batter Method (p.14).

Basic enriched dough

METRIC	IMPERIAL
450 g strong white flour	*1 lb strong white flour*
15 g fresh yeast	*½ oz fresh yeast*
or	*or*
2 teaspoons dried yeast with 1 teaspoon sugar	*2 teaspoons dried yeast with 1 teaspoon sugar*
scant 300 ml warm milk and water	*scant ½ pint warm milk and water*
50 g butter or margarine	*2 oz butter or margarine*
1 egg, beaten	*1 egg, beaten*

Sift 150 g/5 oz of the flour into a warm bowl. Add the yeast to the warm milk and water (with the sugar if using dried yeast).

Mix with the flour into a batter and leave in a warm place for about 20 minutes until frothy. Sift the remaining flour and salt into a warm mixing bowl and rub in the fat. Add the yeast batter and beaten egg, then mix well into a soft dough, adding a little warm water if necessary. Turn on to a floured board and knead for about 10 minutes by hand to stretch and develop the dough (p.14). When smooth and elastic, cover and leave to rise until doubled in bulk. Knock back (p.15) and shape into 2 lemon-shaped loaves, or make into plaits or fancy rolls or use as a pizza base.

Vienna loaves and rolls

Lemon shaped loaf

Knock back the risen dough and divide in half. Form one half into a large lemon shape. Put on a greased baking sheet. Brush with milk or thin cream and with a sharp knife cut a slit lengthwise down the centre of the loaf. Cover and prove until the dough is springy. Glaze with milk. Bake the loaf in the centre of a preheated hot oven at 230°C/450°F, Gas Mark 8 for 30 to 40 minutes or until it sounds hollow when tapped on the bottom. Cool on a wire tray.

French shaped loaf; Lemon shaped loaf; Crescents; Twists; Snails

French shaped loaf

Form the other half of the dough into a slightly longer shape, tapered at each end, and make four or five diagonal slits across the top. Glaze with milk or cream, set in a warm place to prove until the dough is springy when pressed. Bake as for Lemon Shape.

Crescent rolls

Divide the risen dough in half. Pat or roll out one half into a circle about 1 cm/½ inch thick. Cut across into triangles. Brush lightly with water. Roll up each triangle from the wide end to the point. Curl the ends towards each other, to form a crescent. Place on a greased baking sheet. Cover and prove in a warm place for about 10 minutes, or until the dough is springy. Brush with Egg and Milk Wash (p.16), sprinkle with poppy or sesame seeds, and bake in a preheated hot oven at 220°C/425°F, Gas Mark 7 for 20 minutes or until well risen and golden brown.

Twists

Pinch off pieces of dough from the second half of the dough, roll into finger-thick rolls 23-25 cm/9-10 inches in length, tie each one into a loose knot and twist in the ends neatly to make a braided circle. Prove, glaze and bake as for Crescents.

Snails

Make the dough into thin rolls as for Twists and twist each one round and round into a snail shell shape. Prove, glaze and bake as for Twists.

Bridge rolls

METRIC	IMPERIAL
225 g strong white flour	*8 oz strong white flour*
1 teaspoon salt	*1 teaspoon salt*
50 g butter or margarine	*2 oz butter or margarine*
15 g fresh yeast	*½ oz fresh yeast*
or	*or*
1½ teaspoons dried yeast with 1 teaspoon sugar	*1½ teaspoons dried yeast with 1 teaspoon sugar*
1 egg, beaten	*1 egg, beaten*
approx. 100 ml warm milk	*approx. 4 fl oz warm milk*
cream or Egg and Milk Wash (p.16) for glazing	*cream or Egg and Milk Wash (p.16) for glazing*

MAKES 12 TO 16 ROLLS

Sift the flour and salt into a mixing bowl and leave in a warm place. Cut the fat into the flour and rub in to a breadcrumb consistency. Blend the fresh yeast with the warm milk.

For dried yeast, make the milk slightly warmer, dissolve the sugar in it and sprinkle on the yeast.

When the yeast liquid is frothy, add the beaten egg and mix into the flour to a fairly soft dough, adding extra milk if necessary. Turn on to a floured board and knead until smooth (p.14). Put into an oiled polythene bag and leave in a warm place until doubled in bulk.

Knock back the dough on a floured board (p.15). Shape into a sausage and divide into 12 or 16 equal-sized pieces. With floured fingers, roll each piece into a torpedo shape and place fairly close together in rows on a lightly greased baking sheet. Cover with polythene and leave to rise for 15 to 20 minutes until the dough springs back when pressed. Brush with cream or egg wash. Bake in the centre of a preheated hot oven at 220°C/425°F, Gas Mark 7 for 15 to 20 minutes according to size. Remove from the oven and if they have baked together, separate carefully. Cool on a wire tray.

Serve with a savoury filling such as mayonnaise mixed with chopped hard-boiled egg and/or minced ham, chicken, cooked salmon or tuna fish, boned and crushed sardines or grated cheese.

From the left: French shaped loaf; Snails; Crescents; Twists; Bridge rolls

Bun loaf

Bun loaf

Weigh off the chosen dough after the first rising.

METRIC	IMPERIAL
50 g butter or margarine	*2 oz butter or margarine*
50 g sugar	*2 oz sugar*
¼ teaspoon mixed spice	*¼ teaspoon mixed spice*
2 teaspoons grated lemon rind	*2 teaspoons grated lemon rind*
1 egg, beaten	*1 egg, beaten*
100 g mixed dried fruit	*4 oz mixed dried fruit*
25 g chopped mixed peel	*1 oz chopped mixed peel*
450 g risen Basic White Bread Dough (p.16) or Basic Enriched Dough (opposite page)	*1 lb risen Basic White Bread Dough (p.16) or Basic Enriched Dough (opposite page)*
TO GLAZE:	*TO GLAZE:*
milk	*milk*
demerara sugar	*demerara sugar*

MAKES 1 LARGE LOAF

Cream together the fat, sugar, spice and lemon rind and beat in the egg, dried fruit and mixed peel. Work this into the dough in a warm mixing bowl. Turn on to a floured board and knead for a few minutes (p.14). Round up the dough and put it into a 15 cm/6 inch round cake tin or a large loaf tin. Cover and prove in a warm place for 10 minutes, or until the dough has doubled in bulk. Brush with milk and sprinkle with sugar. Bake in a preheated moderately hot oven at 200°C/400°F, Gas Mark 6 for 40 minutes or until cooked. Remove from tin and tap the bottom to see if it sounds hollow. Cool on a wire tray.

Shaping Parker house rolls

Parker house rolls

These are traditional American bread rolls, which are reputed to have originated in the famous eighteenth century hostelry in Boston, called The Parker House. They should be golden outside, but soft and light and slightly sweet inside. They are delicious served fresh from the oven with butter and/or preserves. They can also be refrigerated and reheated, and will freeze successfully.

METRIC	IMPERIAL
350 g strong white flour	12 oz strong white flour
1 teaspoon salt	1 teaspoon salt
15 g fresh yeast	½ oz fresh yeast
or	or
2 teaspoons dried yeast	2 teaspoons dried yeast
2 teaspoons sugar	2 teaspoons sugar
120 ml warm water	4 fl oz warm water
250 ml milk	8 fl oz milk
25 g butter, cut up	1 oz butter, cut up
melted butter for coating	melted butter for coating
Egg and Water Wash (p.16) for glazing	Egg and Water Wash (p.16) for glazing

MAKES 8 ROLLS

Sift the flour and salt into a bowl and leave in a warm place. Blend the yeast and sugar into the warm water then leave to froth. Heat the milk gently. Add the butter to the milk and when dissolved pour into the yeast mixture. Stir this liquid into half the flour and beat vigorously with a wooden spoon into a smooth batter. Cover with a damp cloth and leave in a warm place for 1 hour or until doubled in bulk. Break it down with a wooden spoon, then gradually add the rest of the flour and beat into a soft dough.

Turn out on to a floured board and knead until smooth and elastic (p.14). Shape the dough into a ball and put it into a warm bowl. Brush with melted butter and leave to rise again until doubled in bulk. Knock back the dough on a lightly floured board (p.15) and roll out to about 1 cm/½ inch thick. Cut into 8 rounds with a 6 cm/2½ inch floured cutter or a tumbler. Brush the rounds with melted butter.

Press a knife handle or pencil firmly across the centre of each round to make a deep crease, fold the dough over at the crease, and press firmly down to seal.

Place the folded rolls on a greased baking sheet leaving room for expansion. Cover and leave to prove. When springy, brush with Egg and Water Wash and bake in a preheated hot oven at 220°C/425°F, Gas Mark 7 for 20 minutes or until puffed and golden. Serve hot straight from the oven, or reheat.

The foldover is the traditional Parker House shape, but the dough remaining can be shaped into Crescents (p.26) or Butterflake Rolls, and the trimmings into Cloverleaf Rolls (below).

Butterflake rolls

Roll the remaining dough out thinly to 5 mm/¼ inch thick. Brush with melted butter and cut into strips about 25 cm/10 inches long and 3 cm/1¼ inches wide. Stack 5 strips on top of each other and cut into 4 cm/1½ inch lengths. Place the stacks on their sides in greased muffin tins. Brush with butter, prove, glaze and bake as for Parker House Rolls. Serve hot from the oven or reheated. Pull the layers slightly apart and insert flakes of butter.

Cloverleaf rolls

Work up the trimmings and pinch off pieces of dough the size of walnuts. Roll these into smooth little balls and place in threes in well buttered muffin tins. Prove, glaze and bake as for Parker House Rolls.

Making Butterflake rolls

Shaping Cloverleaf rolls

Parker house rolls; Butterflake rolls; Cloverleaf rolls; Bread sticks;
Vienna plait

Rich continental dough

This recipe, which uses a higher proportion of eggs and
yeast than the preceding one, makes a lighter dough. It
can also be used for Vienna loaves and rolls, as a base for
pizzas and, with the addition of sugar and dried fruit, for
continental coffee cakes. It can be made with either strong
or soft plain flour.

METRIC	IMPERIAL
225 g strong white flour	8 oz strong white flour
1 teaspoon salt	1 teaspoon salt
15 g fresh yeast	½ oz fresh yeast
1 teaspoon sugar	1 teaspoon sugar
75 ml warm milk	3 fl oz warm milk
2 eggs, beaten	2 eggs, beaten
50 g butter, softened	2 oz butter, softened
TO GLAZE:	TO GLAZE:
beaten egg or Egg and Milk Wash (p.16)	beaten egg or Egg and Milk Wash (p.16)
poppy seeds	poppy seeds

MAKES 1 LARGE OR 2 SMALL LOAVES

Sift the flour and salt into a mixing bowl, and leave in a
warm place. Cream the sugar and yeast together, add the
warm milk and beaten eggs. Make a well in the flour, stir
in the liquid ingredients and with a wooden spoon beat
into a stiff dough, adding a little more warm water if
necessary. Gradually beat in the softened butter. Cover
the bowl with a damp cloth and put in a warm place to
prove for about 40 to 45 minutes or until doubled in bulk.
Flour the pastry board thickly and pour the dough into the
centre. Flour your hands and sprinkle flour over the
dough, and knead until it is no longer sticky but still soft
(p.14). The dough is now ready for use.

Vienna plait

For 2 small loaves, divide the dough in half, and each half
into 3 equal portions. For the first loaf, roll each portion
into a sausage shape about 25 cm/10 inches long. Lay the
three rolls side by side and starting from the middle, plait
loosely down to one end. Pinch the three ends together.

Turn the dough over and plait from the centre down to the
other end, then pinch the three other ends together.
Make another plait with the other half of the dough. Put
the plaits on a greased baking sheet, cover, and leave in a
warm place to prove until the dough feels springy. Brush
with milk or Egg and Milk Wash (p.16) and sprinkle with
poppy seeds if desired. Bake in the centre of a preheated
hot oven at 220°C/425°F, Gas Mark 7 for 30 minutes or
until the loaves sound hollow when tapped on the bottom.
Cool on a wire tray.
If you use the whole of the dough to make 1 large loaf, it
will require about 15 minutes longer in the oven.

Bread sticks

These crisp bread sticks are like the Italian grissini and
store well in an airtight tin. You can also make them with
brown wheatmeal flour.

METRIC	IMPERIAL
225 g strong white flour	8 oz strong white flour
½ teaspoon salt	½ teaspoon salt
10 g fresh yeast	¼ oz fresh yeast
1 teaspoon sugar	1 teaspoon sugar
25 g butter or margarine	1 oz butter or margarine
150 ml warm milk	¼ pint warm milk
TO FINISH:	TO FINISH:
milk	milk
sea salt	sea salt

Sift the flour and salt into a mixing bowl and leave in a
warm place. Dissolve the sugar in half the warm milk,
blend in the yeast and leave for 10 minutes.
Make a well in the centre of the flour, pour in the yeast
liquid and cover with some of the flour. Leave to rise for 20
minutes or until frothy. Melt the fat in the remaining
milk, add to the flour and mix into a fairly firm dough.
Cover with a damp cloth and leave to rise for a further 10
minutes or until springy to the touch. Turn on to a lightly
floured board and knead for 3 to 4 minutes (p.14). Roll into
a sausage shape. Cut into slices weighing about 15 g/½ oz.
Roll each one into a stick the thickness of your little finger
and about 20 cm/8 inches long. Place on a greased baking
sheet and prove for 10 minutes. Brush with milk and
sprinkle with sea salt crystals. Bake in a preheated
moderate oven at 180°C/350°F, Gas Mark 4 for 20
minutes. Turn down to the lowest setting and leave the
sticks to crisp, so they will snap when broken. When cold,
store in an airtight container.

Plaiting Vienna plait

Rolling Bread sticks

Sweet tea breads and buns

Sweet tea breads, which are enriched with butter, egg, and frequently fruit, are favourites mainly for tea or high tea whether plain or toasted.

Currant loaf

METRIC	IMPERIAL
15 g fresh yeast	*½ oz fresh yeast*
or	*or*
1½ teaspoons dried yeast	*1½ teaspoons dried yeast*
1 teaspoon sugar	*1 teaspoon sugar*
approx. 450 ml warm milk	*approx. ¾ pint warm milk*
750 g strong white flour	*1½ lb strong white flour*
1 teaspoon salt	*1 teaspoon salt*
50 g butter or margarine, cut up	*2 oz butter or margarine, cut up*
225 g currants	*8 oz currants*
Sugar Syrup (p.16) to glaze	*Sugar Syrup (p.16) to glaze*

MAKES 2 SMALL LOAVES, OR 1 LOAF AND 8 BUNS

Add the yeast with the sugar to 150 ml/¼ pint of the warm milk and leave to froth. Sift the flour and salt into a warm bowl and rub in the fat to a breadcrumb consistency. Mix in the currants, make a well in the centre and add the yeast liquid. Stir into a fairly soft dough with as much remaining milk as necessary. Turn out on to a floured board and knead until smooth and elastic. Cover and leave to rise in a warm place until doubled in bulk. Knock back and shape into 2 small loaves as for Tin Loaves (p.18) or use half for Currant Buns. Prove for about 20 minutes or until the dough rises to the top of the tin.

Bake in the centre of a preheated hot oven at 230°C/450°F, Gas Mark 8 for 15 to 20 minutes. Reduce the heat to 190°C/375°F, Gas Mark 5, and continue cooking for 30 minutes or until the loaves sound hollow when tapped on the bottom. Brush the top with sweetened milk or sugar syrup and return to the oven for two minutes for the glaze to set. Cool on a wire tray. Serve freshly baked or toasted and buttered.

Currant buns

Pinch off pieces of the Currant Loaf dough after it has risen and been knocked back. They should weigh about 50 g/2 oz each. Shape, prove, bake and glaze as for Penny Buns in the following recipe. Serve freshly baked or split, toasted and buttered.

Penny buns

These currant buns can no longer be bought for a penny each, but they are still inexpensive to make.

METRIC	IMPERIAL
500 g strong white flour	*1¼ lb strong white flour*
15 g fresh yeast	*½ oz fresh yeast*
1 teaspoon sugar	*1 teaspoon sugar*
approx. 600 ml warm milk	*approx. 1 pint warm milk*
50 g butter, cut up	*2 oz butter, cut up*
1 egg, beaten	*1 egg, beaten*
75 g currants	*3 oz currants*
50 g sugar	*2 oz sugar*
Sugar Syrup (p.16) to glaze	*Sugar Syrup (p.16) to glaze*

MAKES ABOUT 16 BUNS

Sift half the flour into a warm bowl. Blend the yeast with the sugar, and add 150 ml/¼ pint of the warm milk. Mix into a firm dough, adding a little more milk if necessary. Beat well with your hand or a wooden spoon. Cover and leave to rise for 30 to 40 minutes. Dissolve the butter in the remaining milk. Pour this into the beaten egg and stir well.

Mix the liquid into the risen dough with the remaining flour, the currants and the sugar. Beat well and leave to rise in a warm place until doubled in bulk. Knock back (p.15), and scoop off pieces of dough weighing about 50 g/2 oz each.

Shape each piece into a smooth ball, place on a greased baking sheet and flatten slightly; alternatively, half-fill well greased bun tins. Cover and prove until springy to the touch. Bake in a preheated hot oven at 220°C/425°F, Gas Mark 7 for about 15 minutes or until cooked. Remove and brush with sweetened milk or sugar syrup, then replace in the oven for a few moments for the glaze to dry. Cool on a wire tray. Serve freshly baked, or split, toasted and buttered if preferred.

Honey twist; Penny buns; Currant buns; Currant loaf; Malt loaf

Malt loaf

This is a sweet loaf with a distinctive malt flavour. The dough is rather sticky to handle and dough hooks on the mixer are helpful for kneading if used at the lowest speed.

METRIC	IMPERIAL
25 g fresh yeast	*1 oz fresh yeast*
or	*or*
15 g dried yeast with 1 teaspoon sugar	*½ oz dried yeast with 1 teaspoon sugar*
150 ml warm water	*¼ pint warm water*
450 g soft white flour	*1 lb soft white flour*
1 teaspoon salt	*1 teaspoon salt*
50-75 g sultanas (optional)	*2-3 oz sultanas (optional)*
100 g malt extract	*4 oz malt extract*
1 tablespoon black treacle	*1 tablespoon black treacle*
25 g butter or margarine	*1 oz butter or margarine*
Sugar Syrup (p.16) to glaze	*Sugar Syrup (p.16) to glaze*

MAKES 2 SMALL LOAVES

Dissolve the yeast in the warm water, adding the sugar if using dried yeast. Leave for 10 minutes or until frothy. Sift the flour and salt into a warm bowl and mix in the sultanas, if using. Heat the malt, treacle and fat gently in a small pan until liquid, then cool slightly. Stir the yeast liquid and malt mixture into the dry ingredients and mix to a soft, sticky dough, adding more warm water if necessary. Turn the dough on to a floured board and knead until firm and elastic (p.14).

Divide the dough in half, shape and put into 2 greased 500 g/1 lb loaf tins (p.18). Cover and leave to prove until the dough rises to the top of the tins. Malt dough rises slowly so this may take up to 2 hours. Bake in the centre of a preheated moderately hot oven at 200°C/400°F, Gas Mark 6 for 30 to 40 minutes. When cooked, remove the loaves, brush the tops with sugar syrup and return to the oven for two minutes. Cool on a wire tray.

Honey twist

This is a rich sweet dough which is slow in rising. It has a delicious honey and butter topping.

METRIC	IMPERIAL
15 g fresh yeast	*½ oz fresh yeast*
or	*or*
10 g dried yeast with 1 teaspoon sugar	*¼ oz dried yeast with 1 teaspoon sugar*
50 ml warm water	*2 fl oz warm water*
150 ml warm milk	*¼ pint warm milk*
50 g butter or margarine	*2 oz butter or margarine*
40 g sugar	*1½ oz sugar*
1 egg yolk, beaten	*1 egg yolk, beaten*
350 g strong white flour	*12 oz strong white flour*
1 teaspoon salt	*1 teaspoon salt*
50 g chopped mixed peel	*2 oz chopped mixed peel*
50 g sultanas	*2 oz sultanas*
TOPPING:	*TOPPING:*
50 g butter or margarine	*2 oz butter or margarine*
25 g sugar	*1 oz sugar*
3 tablespoons honey	*3 tablespoons honey*
1 egg white	*1 egg white*

Dissolve the yeast in the warm water, adding the sugar if using dried yeast. Leave for 10 minutes or until frothy. Put the butter or margarine and sugar in a bowl. Pour in the milk and stir until dissolved. Cool slightly and add the yeast liquid. Stir in the beaten egg yolk. Sift and stir in the flour and salt. Add the peel and sultanas. Beat until smooth. Turn on to a floured board and knead lightly, adding more flour if necessary. Put into a warm bowl, cover and prove until doubled in bulk.

Meanwhile cream the fat and sugar together for the topping. Mix in the honey and finally the unbeaten egg white. Turn the risen dough on to a floured board and knead for 4 to 5 minutes (p.14). Roll out into a long sausage shape not more than 4 cm/1½ inches thick. Take care not to twist or break it. Coil this loosely into a warmed and greased 25 cm/10 inch sandwich tin, working from the outside into the centre. Cover and prove in a warm place until springy to the touch. Pour over the topping and spread it evenly.

Bake in a preheated moderately hot oven at 200°C/400°F, Gas Mark 6 for 15 minutes. Reduce the heat to 180°C/350°F, Gas Mark 4 for a further 30 minutes or until cooked. Test with a skewer which will come out clean when the bread is ready. Cool on a wire tray. Serve with butter.

Coiling in Honey twist dough   Spreading on the topping

Apricot and walnut loaf

This fruit loaf recipe can be varied in a number of ways by using different fruit and nuts and adding grated lemon or orange rind for flavouring. When using dried apricots or prunes, it is easier to snip them with scissors instead of chopping with a knife.

METRIC	IMPERIAL
225 g wholemeal flour	*8 oz wholemeal flour*
225 g strong white flour	*8 oz strong white flour*
25 g sugar	*1 oz sugar*
100 g dried apricots, snipped	*4 oz dried apricots, snipped*
50 g walnuts, chopped	*2 oz walnuts, chopped*
15 g fresh yeast	*½ oz fresh yeast*
or	*or*
1½ teaspoons dried yeast with 1 teaspoon sugar	*1½ teaspoons dried yeast with 1 teaspoon sugar*
300 ml warm milk and water	*½ pint warm milk and water*
50 g butter, cut up	*2 oz butter, cut up*
1 egg, beaten	*1 egg, beaten*
warm honey or Sugar Syrup (p.16) for glazing	*warm honey or Sugar Syrup (p.16) for glazing*

MAKES 2 SMALL LOAVES

Sift the flours into a warm mixing bowl. Mix in the sugar, apricots and walnuts.

Dissolve the yeast in half the warm milk and water, adding the sugar if using dried yeast. Leave for 10 minutes or until frothy.

Dissolve the butter in the remaining warm milk and water. Stir in the beaten egg. Add all the liquids to the dry ingredients and mix to a smooth dough. Knead well (p.14), cover and put into a warm place to prove until doubled in bulk.

Turn on to a floured board, knock back the dough (p.15) and divide in half. Put into 2 small warmed and greased loaf tins. Cover and prove in a warm place until the dough fills the tins.

Bake in a preheated hot oven at 230°C/450°F, Gas Mark 8 for 20 minutes. Reduce the heat to 200°C/400°F, Gas Mark 6 and cook for a further 15 to 20 minutes. Brush with warm honey or sugar glaze and return to the oven for 4 to 5 minutes for the glaze to set. Allow to shrink slightly, unmould and cool on a wire tray.

Serve sliced and buttered or with cream cheese.

Oatmeal bread; Soft oatmeal rolls; Apricot and walnut loaf; Prune and nut loaf

Prune and nut loaf

Follow the recipe for Apricot and Walnut Loaf replacing the apricots with 100 g/4 oz snipped dried prunes. Chopped cashews or almonds can replace the walnuts, or nuts can be omitted and 2 teaspoons grated lemon or orange rind added for flavouring.

Oatmeal bread

White wheat flour was a luxury in the remote highlands and islands of Scotland until after the last war. Oatmeal from locally grown crops was the staple meal, used in cooking of all kinds. The following recipe uses about 50 per cent wheat flour which can be strong white or plain unbleached flour. It produces a delightful loaf of good flavour and delicious soft rolls. The secret is to soak the oatmeal in the milk over night, and be prepared for the yeasted dough to rise rather slowly, or you will have a 'flying top' (p.16). The dough requires care in handling as it is very soft.

Serve sliced and buttered with cream cheese or preserves.

METRIC	IMPERIAL
225 g medium oatmeal	8 oz medium oatmeal
450 ml milk	¾ pint milk
15 g fresh yeast	½ oz fresh yeast
or	or
1½ teaspoons dried yeast with 1 teaspoon sugar	1½ teaspoons dried yeast with 1 teaspoon sugar
4 tablespoons warm water	4 tablespoons warm water
2-3 teaspoons salt	2-3 teaspoons salt
50 g butter or lard, melted	2 oz butter or lard, melted
225 g strong white or unbleached flour	8 oz strong white or unbleached flour
TO FINISH	TO FINISH
milk	milk
coarse oatmeal	coarse oatmeal

MAKES 1 SMALL LOAF AND 8 ROLLS OR 2 SMALL LOAVES

Put the oatmeal in a mixing bowl and add the milk. Leave to soak overnight for the oatmeal to absorb the milk. Dissolve the yeast in the warm water, adding the sugar if using dried yeast, and leave to froth. Mix the yeast liquid into the oatmeal which will be of porridge consistency, with the salt and melted fat.

Sift and beat in sufficient white flour to make a smooth, very soft dough. Knead thoroughly on a thickly floured board, adding more flour if necessary (p.14). (Dough hooks on a mixer at lowest speed will cut the kneading time to about 5 minutes.) Replace in a warm bowl, cover with a damp cloth and leave in a warm place to prove for 1½ to 2 hours or until the dough has doubled in bulk. Knock back the dough (p.15) on a board sprinkled with medium oatmeal. Divide in two and put one half into a small warmed and greased tin. It should half-fill the tin. Cover and prove for about 45 minutes or until the dough rises to the top of the tin.

Brush with milk and sprinkle with coarse oatmeal. Bake in a preheated hot oven at 220°C/425°F, Gas Mark 7 for 20 to 30 minutes. Lower the heat to 160°C/325°F, Gas Mark 3 and bake for a further 15 to 20 minutes. Remove from tin and tap the bottom to see if it sounds hollow. Cool on a wire tray.

Soft oatmeal rolls

Round up the remaining dough after knocking back, and divide into 8 equal portions. Roll into smooth balls and put into warmed and greased bun or muffin tins. They should be only half-filled. Cover and prove until doubled in bulk. Brush with milk and sprinkle with coarse oatmeal. Bake in a preheated hot oven at 220°C/425°F, Gas Mark 7 for 20 to 30 minutes with the Oatmeal Bread. Cool on a wire tray.

Crumpets and muffins

Hot buttered crumpets and muffins for tea are a traditional treat and compensation on cold, damp English winter evenings. They are as popular now as in Dickens' time. They are made with yeast batter or dough and are cooked on a griddle (see page 44).

A griddle heats beautifully evenly on the large hot plate of an Aga or Raeburn cooker. If using a gas or electric cooker the heat is highest in the centre of the griddle, so move the crumpets, muffins or pikelets around so they brown evenly.

English crumpets

The distinguishing features of real crumpets are their pliable texture and the characteristic holes all over the top surface, into which the generously spread butter melts so enticingly.

They are made with a rather thin yeast batter and are cooked on a griddle in crumpet rings which are about 2.5 cm/1 inch deep. Metal scone or pastry cutters make a good substitute.

METRIC	IMPERIAL
100 g strong white flour	*4 oz strong white flour*
100 g plain flour	*4 oz plain flour*
2 teaspoons salt	*2 teaspoons salt*
12 g fresh yeast	*¼ oz fresh yeast*
1 teaspoon sugar	*1 teaspoon sugar*
300 ml warm milk and water	*½ pint warm milk and water*
1 tablespoon vegetable oil	*1 tablespoon vegetable oil*
½ teaspoon bicarbonate of soda	*½ teaspoon bicarbonate of soda*
150 ml warm water	*¼ pint warm water*

MAKES 12 TO 14

Sift the flours and salt into a warm bowl. Cream the yeast with the sugar. Add the warmed milk and water, then the oil. Stir into the flour to make a batter and beat vigorously until smooth and elastic. Cover the bowl, put in a warm place and leave until the mixture rises and the surface is full of bubbles (about 1½ hours). Break it down by beating with a wooden spoon.

Dissolve the bicarbonate of soda in the warm water and stir into the batter. Cover and leave in a warm place to prove for about 30 minutes.

To cook the crumpets, heat and grease the griddle lightly. Grease 5 to 6 crumpet rings 8-9 cm/3-3½ inches or scone cutters and put them on the griddle to heat. Cook as many crumpets as possible at a time as the batter will not remain bubbly for long.

Put 1 cm/½ inch of batter into each ring. Cook gently for 7 to 10 minutes or until the surface sets and is full of tiny bubbles. Using an oven glove for protection, lift off the ring and if the base of the crumpet is pale gold, flip it over and cook for another 3 minutes until the other side is just coloured. If the crumpet batter is set but sticks slightly in the ring, push it out gently with the back of a wooden spoon. Wipe, grease and heat the rings for each batch of crumpets.

If serving immediately, wrap the crumpets in a cloth, and keep warm between batches. Butter generously and serve at once. If reheating, toast the crumpets under the grill, cooking the smooth surface first and then the top, so the butter will melt into the holes.

Pikelets

These are similar to crumpets and in different parts of the country they are called variously Welsh crumpets, griddle cakes and yeast pancakes. They are made with a yeast batter and are cooked on the griddle, but without rings.

METRIC	IMPERIAL
225 g plain or unbleached flour	8 oz plain or unbleached flour
1 teaspoon salt	1 teaspoon salt
15 g fresh yeast	½ oz fresh yeast
or	or
1½ teaspoons dried yeast	1½ teaspoons dried yeast
1 teaspoon sugar	1 teaspoon sugar
150 ml warm water	¼ pint warm water
1 teaspoon butter	1 teaspoon butter
150 ml warm milk	¼ pint warm milk
1 egg, beaten	1 egg, beaten
MAKES 20 TO 24	

Sift the flour and salt into a warm bowl. Dissolve the yeast and the sugar in the warm water. Melt the butter in the warm milk and beat in the egg. Stir the yeast liquid and then the milk mixture into the flour. Mix into a smooth batter and beat well. Cover and leave in a warm place for 1 to 1½ hours until the batter is thick and bubbling. Warm the griddle and grease with a piece of lard on a fork. When a drop of water splutters on the griddle, it is hot enough. Stir the batter, then use a ladle or jug to pour it on to the griddle in round 'puddles', leaving space in between so they are easy to turn. The yeast batter does not spread as much as pancake batter.

Cook over moderate heat until bubbles break the top surface and the underneath is pale gold. Using a palette knife, flip over the pikelets and cook the other side until honey coloured. Keep each batch warm in a folded cloth in a low oven. Serve hot with butter, honey or preserves, or for a savoury dish with cream cheese or grilled bacon or little sausages. To reheat, crisp under the grill.

Below: English crumpets; Pikelets
Above right: English muffins

English muffins

These are also cooked on the griddle like crumpets, but are made with a yeast dough instead of a batter. They should be served very hot, generously buttered, in a hot dish with a cover — the Victorians produced very attractive silver or decorative china muffin dishes.

METRIC	IMPERIAL
450 g strong white flour	1 lb strong white flour
1 tablespoon salt	1 tablespoon salt
15 g fresh yeast	½ oz fresh yeast
or	or
1½ teaspoons dried yeast	1½ teaspoons dried yeast
1 teaspoon sugar	1 teaspoon sugar
250 ml warm milk and water	8 fl oz warm milk and water
50 g butter, melted	2 oz butter, melted
MAKES 8 TO 10	

Sift the flour and salt into a bowl and leave in a warm place. Dissolve the yeast and sugar in 150 ml/¼ pint of the warm milk and water. Leave to froth, then mix in the fat. Stir all the liquid into the warm flour and beat well until smooth and elastic. Cover and prove in a warm place for 50 minutes or until doubled in bulk. Turn on to a well floured board and knead (p.14), working in a little more flour if necessary to make the dough easy to shape. Round up the dough, roll into a thick sausage shape and divide into 8 to 10 portions, about 1-2 cm/½-¾ inch thick. Shape each one into a round with straight sides. Put on to a greased baking sheet. Cover and put in a warm place to prove for 30 to 40 minutes or until springy to the touch. Leave room for expansion and be careful not to over-prove as the muffins will lose their shape. Warm the griddle gently and grease lightly with a small piece of lard on a fork. Lift the muffins carefully on to the griddle and cook over very moderate heat for 8 to 10 minutes until pale gold underneath. Turn and cook the other side. Wrap in a cloth and keep warm in a low oven if cooking in batches. To serve insert a knife in the side, then with fingers, pull the top and bottom apart and insert thin slices of butter. If reheating from cold, toast the top and bottom, then pull apart and butter.

Soda breads & scones

Soda breads and scones are popular all over Britain and in the remoter parts of Ireland and Scotland are often preferred to yeast breads. They are quickly mixed and baked and delicious when fresh, but those containing little or no fat go dry very quickly. They can be warmed up in the oven, but are much better sliced and toasted. Fresh soda bread and scones freeze most successfully. Unlike yeast bread, which requires vigorous kneading and time for the yeast to work and rise the dough slowly before baking, scone dough needs quick, light handling. The chemical raising agents will not start raising the dough until it is put into a hot oven or on a heated griddle.

Raising agents

The raising agent is a mixture of bicarbonate of soda, an alkali, and cream of tartar, which is acid. When liquid is added, this produces a chemical reaction releasing carbonic gas which rises the dough when heated. If the liquid added is water or fresh milk, the proportions are usually 2 teaspoons cream of tartar to 1 teaspoon bicarbonate of soda. If buttermilk or sour cream, which are acid, are used, the cream of tartar is reduced. Baking powder consists of ready-mixed bicarbonate of soda and cream of tartar with the addition of rice flour, or similar fine starch, as a stabilizer. The raising agent should be sifted with the flour so that it is evenly distributed. Self-raising flour contains raising agents but for some recipes, additional baking powder is required.

Liquids

Buttermilk makes a particularly light dough; cultured buttermilk and soured cream is available at most supermarkets. Alternatively fresh milk or cream can be soured by the addition of 2-3 teaspoons lemon juice or white vinegar to 300 ml/½ pint milk.

For plain doughs, milk and water mixed in equal quantities is used, and for richer doughs, cream or beaten eggs are added. Always add sufficient liquid to the dry ingredients to make a really soft dough or the bread or scones will bake hard. About 400 ml/⅔ pint to each 450 g/1 lb flour is a rough guide, but the quantity depends on the type of flour used, as coarse meals require extra liquid. Use a palette knife for mixing as it has a rounded end and is flexible.

Flour

Plain white or brown flours are equally satisfactory for scone doughs. Strong flour is not necessary, but it can be used and will require extra liquid. A little salt should always be added to all flour for flavour.

Fats

Any hard fat may be used — butter, margarine, lard or clarified dripping — and it is rubbed into the flour until the mixture resembles breadcrumbs. Beaten egg is added to the richer doughs and cream instead of, or in addition to, the rubbed in fat.

Baking powder bread

This is a similar scone dough to the Irish Buttermilk Soda Bread, but using baking powder. The texture is closer and not so light.

METRIC	IMPERIAL
450 g plain flour	*1 lb plain flour*
1 teaspoon salt	*1 teaspoon salt*
4 teaspoons baking powder	*4 teaspoons baking powder*
25 g butter or margarine	*1 oz butter or margarine*
300 ml fresh or soured milk	*½ pint fresh or soured milk*
little water	*little water*
MAKES 1 LOAF	

Sift the flour, salt and baking powder into a mixing bowl. Rub in the fat to a breadcrumb consistency. Stir in the milk, adding a little water if necessary to produce a soft manageable dough. Knead, shape and bake as for Irish Buttermilk Soda Bread.

American baking powder biscuits

Make the dough as for Baking Powder Bread. Roll out to 1.5 cm/¾ inch thick. Cut into 6 cm/2½ inch rounds. Place on a warmed and floured baking sheet and bake near the top of a preheated hot oven at 230°C/450°F, Gas Mark 8 for 15 minutes.

Irish buttermilk soda bread

This traditional recipe is popular because it is quick and easy to make, delicious when fresh and any left over makes excellent toast. If no buttermilk is available, curdle some fresh milk by adding 3 teaspoons of lemon juice or white wine vinegar and stir well.

METRIC	IMPERIAL
450 g plain or wheatmeal flour	*1 lb plain or wheatmeal flour*
1-2 teaspoons salt	*1-2 teaspoons salt*
1 teaspoon bicarbonate of soda	*1 teaspoon bicarbonate of soda*
300 ml buttermilk	*½ pint buttermilk*
3-4 tablespoons water	*3-4 tablespoons water*
MAKES 1 LOAF	

Sift the flour, salt and bicarbonate of soda into a mixing bowl. Stir in the buttermilk and add a little water if necessary to make a soft dough. Turn out on to a floured board, knead lightly and quickly and shape into a smooth round bun.

Cut a deep cross right across the top of the loaf so that when baked it can be divided into 4 'farls', as they are called. Place on a warmed and floured baking sheet. Bake just above the centre of a preheated moderately hot oven at 200°C/400°F, Gas Mark 6 for 30 to 35 minutes or until well risen and nicely browned. For a soft crust, wrap in a teacloth, for a crisp crust, cool on a wire tray.

Irish buttermilk soda bread; Baking powder bread; American baking powder biscuits; Apple and walnut loaf; American banana loaf

Sweet soda breads

These are sweetened with white or brown sugar, golden syrup or treacle. Beaten egg, as well as a raising agent, is added to lighten the dough. They are normally baked in a loaf tin. This must be well greased and partially lined. Cut a strip of baking parchment or greaseproof paper long enough to cover the base and ends of the tin and extend 5 cm/2 inches at each end. This will enable you to lift out the cooked loaf easily.

Apple and walnut loaf

METRIC	IMPERIAL
175 g granary or wholemeal flour	6 oz granary or wholemeal flour
175 g plain flour	6 oz plain flour
½ teaspoon salt	½ teaspoon salt
2 teaspoons bicarbonate of soda	2 teaspoons bicarbonate of soda
½ teaspoon cream of tartar	½ teaspoon cream of tartar
75 g butter or margarine	3 oz butter or margarine
50 g caster sugar	2 oz caster sugar
225 g cooking or dessert apples, peeled, cored and finely chopped	8 oz cooking or dessert apples, peeled, cored and finely chopped
50 g walnuts, chopped	2 oz walnuts, chopped
100 g honey	4 oz honey
75 ml buttermilk or soured milk	2½ fl oz buttermilk or soured milk
1 egg	1 egg

MAKES 1 LOAF

Sift the flours, salt, bicarbonate of soda and cream of tartar into a mixing bowl. Cut the fat into the flour and rub in to a breadcrumb consistency. Mix in the sugar with the chopped apples and walnuts, reserving 2 tablespoons of nuts. Mix thoroughly. Dissolve the honey in the buttermilk or soured milk and beat in the egg.

Stir the liquid into the dry ingredients and mix well. Turn the mixture into a prepared 23 × 13 cm/9 × 5 inch loaf tin. Scatter the remaining nuts over the top. Bake in the centre of a preheated moderate oven at 180°C/350°F, Gas Mark 4 for 1¼ hours or until a skewer inserted comes out clean. Leave to shrink slightly before lifting out on to a wire tray to cool. Keeps well.

American banana loaf

METRIC	IMPERIAL
225 g plain flour	8 oz plain flour
1 teaspoon bicarbonate of soda	1 teaspoon bicarbonate of soda
½ teaspoon cream of tartar	½ teaspoon cream of tartar
pinch of salt	pinch of salt
100 g butter or margarine	4 oz butter or margarine
175 g caster sugar	6 oz caster sugar
1 teaspoon lemon juice	1 teaspoon lemon juice
3 tablespoons milk	3 tablespoons milk
2 bananas, mashed	2 bananas, mashed
1 teaspoon grated lemon rind	1 teaspoon grated lemon rind
2 eggs, beaten	2 eggs, beaten
granulated sugar to finish	granulated sugar to finish

MAKES 1 LOAF

Sift the flour, bicarbonate of soda, cream of tartar and salt into a mixing bowl. Cut the fat into the flour and rub in to a breadcrumb consistency. Mix in the sugar thoroughly. Add the lemon juice to the milk. In a small bowl mix the mashed banana with the lemon rind. Stir in the curdled milk and beaten eggs. Make a well in the flour and mix in the banana mixture. Turn into a prepared 23 × 13 cm/9 × 5 inch loaf tin, smooth the top, and dredge with granulated sugar. Bake in the centre of a preheated moderate oven at 180°C/350°F, Gas Mark 4 for 1¼ hours or until a skewer inserted comes out clean.

Savoury soda breads

These are excellent when freshly baked for snacks and packed lunches or served hot with a hearty soup. When stale, serve toasted with cheese topping or fried with bacon, eggs, sausages and mushrooms.

Herb soda bread

This is particularly good made with fresh herbs but if only parsley is available, a teaspoon of dried herbs can be substituted for the mint or chervil. Garlic fanciers can add one or two cloves of garlic, either pressed or very finely chopped, according to personal taste.

METRIC	IMPERIAL
225 g wholemeal flour	8 oz wholemeal flour
225 g plain flour	8 oz plain flour
2 teaspoons salt	2 teaspoons salt
1 teaspoon bicarbonate of soda	1 teaspoon bicarbonate of soda
50 g butter or margarine	2 oz butter or margarine
100 g grated onion	4 oz grated onion
100 g grated celery	4 oz grated celery
2 tablespoons chopped fresh parsley	2 tablespoons chopped fresh parsley
1 tablespoon chopped fresh mint or chervil	1 tablespoon chopped fresh mint or chervil
275 ml milk	9 fl oz milk
3 teaspoons lemon juice	3 teaspoons lemon juice
TO FINISH:	TO FINISH:
milk and sesame or poppy seeds	milk and sesame or poppy seeds
MAKES 1 LOAF	

Sift the flours, salt and bicarbonate of soda into a mixing bowl. Cut the fat into the flour and rub in to a breadcrumb consistency. Add the grated onion, celery and herbs, rubbing in with the finger tips until thoroughly mixed. Stir the lemon juice into the milk and mix into a soft dough with the dry ingredients. Turn on to a well floured board and knead lightly into a smooth round ball. Place on a floured baking sheet and flatten into a circle of about 20 cm/8 inches. Brush with milk and cover with the seeds. With a sharp knife slash the top into 4 equal portions. Bake near the top of a preheated moderately hot oven at 200°C/400°F, Gas Mark 6 for 35 to 40 minutes until well risen and golden brown. Test with a skewer which will come out clean when cooked. Cool on a wire tray.

Herb rolls

These are ideal for picnics and barbecues. Mix and knead the dough as above. Pinch off pieces weighing 75 g/3 oz each and roll into balls. Place on a warmed, floured baking sheet leaving room between for expansion. Flatten the tops, brush with milk and cover with poppy or sesame seeds. Bake near the top of a preheated moderately hot oven at 200°C/400°F, Gas Mark 6 for 20 minutes, or until well risen and golden brown. Cool on a wire tray. Serve fresh, buttered and filled with watercress, lettuce and tomato, ham or cheese, or toasted and filled with sausage or crispy bacon.
MAKES 8 ROLLS

Cheese and bacon loaf

It is best to use a mature hard cheese for this loaf to give it a good taste. Do not add salt as there is usually sufficient in the bacon. Chopped cooked ham can be used instead of fried bacon.

METRIC	IMPERIAL
100 g streaky bacon or pieces	4 oz streaky bacon or pieces
100 g plain flour	4 oz plain flour
100 g wholemeal flour	4 oz wholemeal flour
1 teaspoon bicarbonate of soda	1 teaspoon bicarbonate of soda
½ teaspoon cream of tartar	½ teaspoon cream of tartar
½-1 teaspoon dry mustard	½-1 teaspoon dry mustard
50 g butter or margarine	2 oz butter or margarine
75-100 g grated mature cheese	3-4 oz grated mature cheese
1 egg, beaten	1 egg, beaten
150 ml milk	¼ pint milk
TO FINISH:	TO FINISH:
milk	milk
grated cheese	grated cheese
MAKES 1 LOAF	

Remove rind and gristle from the bacon. Put the bacon in a cold frying pan and cook slowly until very crisp, then chop.
Sift the flours, bicarbonate of soda, cream of tartar and mustard into a mixing bowl. Cut the fat into the flour and rub in to a breadcrumb consistency. Mix in the grated cheese and chopped bacon thoroughly. Stir in the egg and milk and mix to a very soft dough.
Turn on to a floured board and knead lightly and quickly into a smooth dough. Shape into a large round bun and place on a greased baking sheet. Brush with milk and cover with grated cheese. With a sharp knife slash the top across into four and then into eight equal triangles.
Bake in the centre of a preheated moderately hot oven at 200°C/400°F, Gas Mark 6 for 35 to 40 minutes until well risen and golden brown. Test with a skewer which will come out clean when the loaf is cooked.
Serve hot with a hearty soup or one-pot meal. Alternatively, cool on a wire tray and serve spread with butter or cream cheese.

Cheese and bacon buns

Mix and knead the dough as above. Divide and shape into buns and bake as for Herb Rolls.
MAKES 8 TO 12 BUNS

Bran loaf; Cheese and bacon buns; Cheese and bacon loaf; Herb rolls; Herb soda bread

Bran loaf

Chopped nuts can be added if liked.

METRIC	IMPERIAL
100 g wholemeal or plain flour	4 oz wholemeal or plain flour
1 teaspoon cream of tartar	1 teaspoon cream of tartar
½ teaspoon baking powder	½ teaspoon baking powder
1 tablespoon caster sugar	1 tablespoon caster sugar
½ teaspoon salt	½ teaspoon salt
100 g bran	4 oz bran
50 g butter or margarine	2 oz butter or margarine
150 ml buttermilk or 150 ml milk soured with 2 teaspoons lemon juice	¼ pint buttermilk or ¼ pint milk soured with 2 teaspoons lemon juice

MAKES 1 LARGE OR 2 SMALL LOAVES

Sift the flour, cream of tartar, baking powder, sugar and salt into a mixing bowl. Mix in the bran. Cut the fat into the flour and rub in to a breadcrumb consistency. Stir in the buttermilk and mix thoroughly. Turn into a prepared 23 x 13 cm/9 x 5 inch loaf tin and smooth the top. Alternatively, divide between 2 small tins. Bake in the centre of a preheated moderately hot oven at 190°C/375°F, Gas Mark 5 for about 1 hour (less for small loaves) or until a skewer inserted comes out clean. Allow to shrink slightly, remove from the tin and cool on a wire tray. Slice thickly and serve with butter.

Scones

Scones are made with the same type of dough as scone loaves, but are cut into individual rounds or triangles and baked quickly in a hot oven or on a griddle (p.44).

Plain oven scones

METRIC	IMPERIAL
225 g plain white or wheatmeal flour	*8 oz plain white or wheatmeal flour*
½ teaspoon salt	*½ teaspoon salt*
4 teaspoons baking powder	*4 teaspoons baking powder*
25-50 g butter or margarine	*1-2 oz butter or margarine*
150 ml milk	*¼ pint milk*
little water	*little water*
milk or flour to finish	*milk or flour to finish*
MAKES ABOUT 12	

Heat the oven to 230°C/450°F, Gas Mark 8, and warm a baking sheet. Sift the flour, salt and baking powder into a mixing bowl. Cut the fat into the flour and rub in to a breadcrumb consistency. Make a well in the centre, pour in the milk and mix into a soft spongy dough, adding a little water if necessary.

Turn the dough out on to a well floured board, knead quickly and lightly. Roll out the dough with a floured rolling pin or flatten with floured hands until 1.5 cm/¾ inch thick. Cut into rounds with a 6 cm/2½ inch floured pastry cutter or tumbler. Place on the baking sheet.

Shape the remaining dough into a ball and flatten into a circle, cut into quarters and place on the baking sheet. Brush the scones with milk for a glazed finish or rub with flour for a soft crust. Bake near the top of the hot oven for 7 to 10 minutes until well risen and golden on top.

Cheese scones

METRIC	IMPERIAL
225 g plain flour	*8 oz plain flour*
½ teaspoon salt	*½ teaspoon salt*
1 teaspoon dry mustard	*1 teaspoon dry mustard*
4 teaspoons baking powder	*4 teaspoons baking powder*
50 g butter or margarine	*2 oz butter or margarine*
75-100 g mature Cheddar cheese, grated	*3-4 oz mature Cheddar cheese, grated*
1 egg, beaten	*1 egg, beaten*
150 ml milk or water	*¼ pint milk or water*
TO FINISH:	*TO FINISH:*
milk	*milk*
grated cheese	*grated cheese*
MAKES ABOUT 12	

Sift the flour, salt, mustard and baking powder into a mixing bowl. Cut the fat into the flour and rub in to a breadcrumb consistency. Mix in the grated cheese. Beat the egg with half the liquid and stir into the dry ingredients. Work into a soft dough adding more liquid as necessary.

Turn on to a well floured board and roll out lightly until 1.5 cm/¾ inch thick. Cut out rounds with a 6.5 cm/2½ inch cutter. Work the remaining dough into a round and cut into triangles as for Plain Oven Scones. Place on a warmed baking sheet. Brush with milk and sprinkle with grated cheese.

Bake in a preheated hot oven at 220°C/425°F, Gas Mark 7 for 10 to 15 minutes until well risen and golden. Cool on wire tray. Serve with butter, cream cheese or salad filling.

Cheese scones; Plain oven scones

Afternoon tea scones

These are usually made with dried fruit which can be sultanas, seedless raisins, or candied peel or a mixture. If no buttermilk is available, sour 150 ml/¼ pint fresh milk with 2 teaspoons lemon juice.

METRIC	IMPERIAL
225 g plain flour	8 oz plain flour
pinch of salt	pinch of salt
½ teaspoon cream of tartar	½ teaspoon cream of tartar
½ teaspoon bicarbonate of soda	½ teaspoon bicarbonate of soda
40 g butter or margarine	1½ oz butter or margarine
25 g caster sugar	1 oz caster sugar
50 g sultanas	2 oz sultanas
approx. 150 ml buttermilk or soured milk	approx. ¼ pint buttermilk or soured milk
milk for glazing	milk for glazing

MAKES ABOUT 14

Sift the flour, salt, cream of tartar and bicarbonate of soda into a mixing bowl. Cut the fat into the flour and rub in to a breadcrumb consistency. Mix in the sugar and sultanas. Stir in sufficient liquid to give a soft manageable dough. Knead lightly on a floured board until smooth. Roll out lightly until about 1.5 cm/½ inch thick and cut into rounds with a 5 cm/2 inch cutter. Work the trimmings into a small round, flatten and cut across into 4 triangles. Place the scones on a warmed floured baking sheet. Brush the tops with milk. Bake near the top of a preheated hot oven at 230°C/450°F, Gas Mark 8 for about 10 minutes until well risen and golden. Cool on a wire tray. Serve split and buttered.

Any scones left until the next day are excellent split, toasted and buttered, and served hot.

Spiced treacle scones

METRIC	IMPERIAL
225 g plain flour	8 oz plain flour
½ teaspoon salt	½ teaspoon salt
½ teaspoon bicarbonate of soda	½ teaspoon bicarbonate of soda
1 teaspoon cream of tartar	1 teaspoon cream of tartar
½ teaspoon ground cinnamon	½ teaspoon ground cinnamon
½ teaspoon ground ginger or mixed spice	½ teaspoon ground ginger or mixed spice
25 g butter or margarine	1 oz butter or margarine
25 g caster sugar	1 oz caster sugar
1 rounded tablespoon treacle	1 rounded tablespoon treacle
120 ml milk	4 fl oz milk
milk for glazing	milk for glazing

MAKES ABOUT 14

Sift the flour, salt, bicarbonate of soda, cream of tartar, cinnamon and ginger or mixed spice into a mixing bowl. Cut the fat into the flour and rub in to a breadcrumb consistency. Mix in the sugar.

Dissolve the treacle in the milk over very gentle heat, cool slightly and stir into the flour to make a soft dough. Turn on to a floured board, knead lightly until smooth. Roll out to a good 1.5 cm/½ inch thick piece and cut into rounds with a 5 cm/2 inch cutter. Work up the trimmings, roll out into a round and cut across into 4 triangles. Place the scones on a warmed and greased baking sheet and brush with milk. Bake near the top of a preheated hot oven at 230°C/450°F, Gas Mark 8 for 12 to 15 minutes. Cool on a wire tray. Serve split and spread with butter or cream cheese. Delicious with ginger marmalade.

Spiced treacle scones; Afternoon tea scones

Girdle scones

Scones can be cooked very successfully on a girdle or griddle instead of in the oven. It is economical with fuel and is very popular in Scotland (where it is called a girdle) and Ireland, and also in Wales, where it is called a bakestone.

The traditional griddle is thick cast iron with a hoop handle which folds down for storage. Some modern griddles made of aluminium have a side handle which can get too hot for safety. The griddle should be heated slowly and evenly. The hot plate on an Aga or Raeburn cooker is ideal. Gas or electric burners tend to concentrate the heat in the centre of the griddle so the scones must be watched and moved around so they brown evenly. The heat should be kept moderate or the scones will brown outside before they are cooked through.

Test the heat of a griddle by sprinkling it with flour which should take a few minutes to turn biscuit colour. A frying pan can be used instead of a griddle if it has a really thick heavy base. A well-seasoned griddle which has frequent use will not need greasing for scone doughs, except for drop scones and similar batter mixtures.

Plain girdle scones

Follow the recipe for Plain Oven Scones (p.42) making a soft but not sticky dough. Divide it in two and knead lightly until smooth. Roll out each half into a round 1 cm/½ inch thick and cut across into four or six equal triangles. Cook on the heated griddle for about 5 minutes until nicely browned underneath. Turn and cook the other side until golden and the scones are cooked through. Wrap in a cloth if to be served hot, or cool on a wire tray. Griddle scones left overnight can be split, toasted, and buttered and served hot. Split and fried in bacon fat they are delicious for breakfast or high tea with fried eggs or sausages.

Potato cakes

These are great favourites in Ireland and Scotland for tea or for high tea with bacon and sausages. It is easiest to make them with hot freshly cooked potatoes. If using cold potatoes, melt the butter before adding it. Choose a floury type of potato and cook in well-salted water.

METRIC	IMPERIAL
500 g cooked floury potatoes	*1 lb cooked floury potatoes*
1 teaspoon salt	*1 teaspoon salt*
50 g butter, softened	*2 oz butter, softened*
approx. 4 tablespoons self-raising flour	*approx. 4 tablespoons self-raising flour*
butter for filling	*butter for filling*
MAKES 8 TO 10	

Drain the cooked potatoes well and cover with a teacloth until dry and floury. Sieve into a mixing bowl with the salt. Beat in the butter. Work in sufficient flour to make a soft dough which is easy to handle. Turn on to a floured board and roll or pat out to 2 cm/¾ inch thick. Cut into rounds with a 7.5 cm/3 inch scone cutter. Place on the hot greased griddle and cook over moderate heat until golden brown underneath. Turn and cook other side.
Remove from the griddle, split, butter generously and close together. Keep warm while cooking the next batch. Serve hot.

Drop scones

These are sometimes called Scots pancakes as they are made with a batter, not a dough. There are a variety of recipes but the following is excellent for tea-time, being quick and easy to make.

METRIC	IMPERIAL
100 g self-raising flour	*4 oz self-raising flour*
2 tablespoons caster sugar	*2 tablespoons caster sugar*
1 egg, beaten	*1 egg, beaten*
approx. 150 ml milk	*approx. ¼ pint milk*
MAKES ABOUT 18	

Sift the flour into a mixing bowl and mix in the sugar. Make a well in the centre and drop in the egg. Stir in the milk gradually and mix to a creamy batter. The thicker the batter, the thicker the pancake will be. Heat the griddle and grease it lightly. Using a large spoon drop the batter off the point in round 'puddles' on to the griddle, leaving space for spreading. Cook over a moderate heat until the top surface is covered with bubbles, and when the underneath is golden, turn over with a palette knife and cook the other side. When golden, lift off the griddle and wrap in a cloth. Serve as soon as possible with butter, honey or preserves.
If any are left until the next day, they can be crisped under the grill before serving.

Fruited girdle scones

Follow the recipe for Afternoon Tea Scones (p.43). Shape and bake as for Plain Girdle Scones. Cool on a wire tray and serve with butter or clotted cream.

Above: Plain girdle scones; Fruited girdle scones
Far left: Potato cakes
Left: Drop scones

Cakes & biscuits

Cake making is enjoyed by many home cooks, and with today's modern ovens and mixers the hazards and hard work of our grandmothers' days have virtually disappeared. There are various methods of making cakes and they can be divided into four main groups: plain cakes and buns, rich cakes, whisked sponge cakes and melted mixtures.

Cake ingredients

Flour

Ordinary plain or self-raising flour is used for cake making, strong flour is not required. It should always be sifted to aerate it.

Raising agents

Baking powder, bicarbonate of soda and cream of tartar are used according to the type of mixture. They should be carefully measured by level teaspoons and sifted with the flour so they are evenly dispersed. Extra baking powder is sometimes needed when using self-raising flour. Very rich cakes with a high proportion of eggs do not need any other raising agent at all.

Fat

Butter gives the best flavour, but margarine can be used. Soft (tub) margarine is very satisfactory for all-in-one cakes. Lard can be used if the mixture is well spiced or strongly flavoured. If using hydrogenated fats such as Trex or Spry from which most of the water content has been removed, the quantity should be reduced by one fifth e.g. 90 g/3½ oz instead of 100 g/4 oz.

Sugar

Caster sugar is preferable to granulated sugar for most cakes as it creams smoothly and melts easily during baking. Soft brown sugar is used in dark coloured cakes and melted mixtures. Demerara or crushed loaf sugar is sometimes used for toppings on cakes or buns.
Liquid sweeteners and how to measure them: golden syrup, treacle and honey can also be used as sweeteners in conjunction with sugar. As they are sticky, it is easier to weigh them.
Allow about 25 g (1 oz) for each tablespoon. Place the required weights in a mug or saucer on the balance scales and the treacle in an identical mug or saucer, dusted with flour, in the scoop on the other side and balance carefully. If using spring-weight scales, weigh the floured mug or saucer before adding the sweetener, place on the scales, and deduct its weight from the total sum.

Fruit

Dried fruit is now sold already cleaned, but if it is necessary to wash it, it must be well dried before use or it will affect the consistency of the cake. Glacé cherries are very heavy and tend to sink unless halved or quartered. Crystallized angelica is used mainly for decoration, but the trimmings can be chopped and used with or instead of candied peel. Stem ginger is preserved in syrup and can be chopped and used in the cake mixture.

Spices and seeds

Ground cinnamon, nutmeg and ginger can be bought individually or already mixed (i.e. mixed spices). Buy in very small quantities and keep tightly closed. Caraway and coriander seeds can be bought already ground, or buy them whole and crush as required.

Shelled nuts

Almonds are sometimes used with the skins on, but frequently blanched and skinned. They can be bought either way. To blanch almonds, put them in a saucepan of water and bring to the boil. Remove the almonds and drop into cold water. Drain, then rub in a soft cloth or pinch off the skins. Split the almonds in half or shred long ways as required. For chopped almonds it is cheaper to buy almond nibs. Hazel nuts and walnuts are used unblanched. Walnut halves are best for decorating, for chopping it is cheaper to buy broken walnuts.

Pointers to successful baking

1. Assemble all necessary ingredients and utensils before starting to mix the cake.

2. Arrange the oven shelves as required and preheat the oven to the correct temperature. Usually small cakes are placed near the top of the oven, larger cakes in the centre and rich fruit cakes on a lower shelf so the top of the cake is in the centre of the oven.

3. Light cake mixtures need a fairly hot oven, the richer the mixture the cooler the temperature. If the recipe requires the temperature to be lowered during baking, remember that in an electric oven it drops more slowly than in a gas one.

4. Do not open the oven door and let in cold air before the cake has time to set. When testing for readiness do it quickly and never slam the oven door.

5. To test if a cake is ready, insert a warm skewer which will come out clean if the cake is cooked. For light sponges, press the surface and when cooked it will be springy to the touch. If finger dents remain, the cake is not ready.

6. Leave the cake to shrink slightly before turning it out of the tin. Cool on a wire tray which allows air to circulate underneath or the cake will have a damp base.

7. Leave until quite cold before storing in an airtight tin or plastic container, or condensation will spoil the cake.

Some common faults in cake making

A damp heavy cake, sometimes called a 'sad cake'
a) Too high a proportion of liquid or sugar in the mixture.
b) Too cool an oven or cake placed too low in oven.
c) Cake not cooled properly before storing in tin.

Fruit sunk to bottom of cake
a) Too much baking powder so cake rose too fast.
b) Mixture too wet and rose so slowly that fruit sank.
c) Use of wet fruit.
d) Oven not hot enough.

Cake collapsed in the middle
a) Cake rose too fast because oven too hot. Alternatively, too much baking powder.
b) Cold draught caused by opening oven door before cake was set or slamming the door shut.

Cake tins

How to choose

To get the best results select a tin close to the size given in the recipe. If the tin is larger, the cake mixture will be spread thinner and cook quicker, if smaller the depth of the mixture will be increased and take longer cooking.

A square tin holds approximately the same quantity of mixture as a round tin which measures 2.5 cm/1 inch larger in diameter than the side of the square tin if they are the same depth. That is, an 18 cm/7 inch square tin equals a 20 cm/8 inch round tin.

The most convenient tins to use have a non-stick lining and a detachable base. When the cake is cooked, allow it to shrink slightly, then place it on an inverted jar or tin taller than the depth of the tin. Gently push down the sides, leaving the cake on the jar. Lift it off, remove the base, and place the cake on a wire tray to cool.

Back row: Swiss roll tin; square shallow baking tin; round sandwich tin; large loaf tin; large and small patty (bun) tins; wooden spoons; angel cake tin
Front row: Round cake tin with detachable base; square deep baking tin; round non-stick baking tin; flan ring; small loaf tin; kitchen spoon; individual sponge finger tins and sponge finger tray (behind)

How to line round and square tins

Plain cakes which cook fairly quickly can be put into an unlined tin which has a non-stick surface. In an ordinary tin it is advisable to line the base. Rich mixtures need a completely lined tin to protect them during the long slow baking.

Baking parchment is silicon treated which gives it a non-stick surface. Greaseproof paper needs to be lightly greased. To prevent the lining slipping in the tin, grease the tin before putting in the lining.

1. Cut a round or square of baking parchment or greaseproof paper to fit neatly the bottom of the tin. Cut double thickness for rich cakes.

2. Plain cakes do not need a side lining. For rich cakes measure the circumference of the tin and cut a strip of double thickness 5 cm/2 inches deeper than the side of the tin and long enough to overlap.

3. Fold up 2.5 cm/1 inch along the bottom of the strip. For round tins snip the fold at 1 cm/½ inch intervals up to the crease. For square tins the strip only needs to be snipped at each corner so it can be mitred.

4. Place the strip round the inside of the tin with the snipped edge on the bottom of the tin. Fit in the bottom circle. If using greaseproof paper, not baking parchment, grease the lining.

Sandwich tins

For rich mixtures grease the tins and line the base as above. For light sponges, grease the tin lightly. Put in a teaspoon of flour mixed with a teaspoon of caster sugar and shake it round the tin. Tip out any excess.

Swiss roll tins

Cut a sheet of parchment or greaseproof paper large enough to cover the base and rise at least 2.5 cm/1 inch above the sides. Grease the tin lightly, press in the lining and slit the corners down to the base, so the corners can be mitred. Grease the lining if it is greaseproof paper.

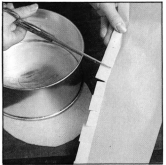

Snip folded edge of greaseproof paper

Line tin with paper and put in cut out disc

Fit in the bottom disc of paper securely

Mitring the lining of a Swiss roll tin

Plain cakes

Plain cakes contain not more than 50 per cent fat which is rubbed into the flour, and one to two eggs to 225 g/8 oz plain flour.

Lunch fruit cake

This light fruit cake is delicious eaten the day it is baked. Candied peel or currants can be substituted for the glacé cherries if preferred.

METRIC	IMPERIAL
225 g plain flour	8 oz plain flour
1 teaspoon baking powder	1 teaspoon baking powder
½ teaspoon grated nutmeg	½ teaspoon grated nutmeg
½ teaspoon ground ginger	½ teaspoon ground ginger
100 g butter or margarine	4 oz butter or margarine
100 g sugar	4 oz sugar
2 teaspoons grated orange or lemon rind	2 teaspoons grated orange or lemon rind
50 g sultanas	2 oz sultanas
50 g seedless raisins	2 oz seedless raisins
50 g glacé cherries, chopped	2 oz glacé cherries, chopped
2 eggs, beaten	2 eggs, beaten
little water to mix	little water to mix
TO FINISH:	TO FINISH:
4 glacé cherries, halved	4 glacé cherries, halved
granulated sugar	granulated sugar

MAKES ONE 15CM/6 INCH CAKE

Sift the flour, baking powder and spices into a mixing bowl. Cut the fat into the flour and rub in to a breadcrumb consistency. Mix in the sugar, grated rind and fruit. Stir in the beaten eggs and sufficient water to give a soft dropping consistency. Turn into a greased 15 cm/6 inch round cake tin.
Arrange the halved cherries on top of the cake and dredge with granulated sugar. Bake in the centre of a preheated moderately hot oven at 190°C/375°F, Gas Mark 5 for 15 minutes, then reduce to 180°C/350°F, Gas Mark 4 for a further 1 hour and test with a skewer. Allow to shrink slightly, remove from the tin and cool on a wire tray.

Honey and ginger cake

In this recipe honey is used as part of the sugar content and this will keep the cake moist longer than the average plain cake.

METRIC	IMPERIAL
225 g plain flour	8 oz plain flour
1 teaspoon ground ginger	1 teaspoon ground ginger
100 g butter or margarine	4 oz butter or margarine
50 g caster sugar	2 oz caster sugar
100 g stem ginger, chopped	4 oz stem ginger, chopped
1 teaspoon bicarbonate of soda	1 teaspoon bicarbonate of soda
150 ml milk	¼ pint milk
50 g clear honey	2 oz clear honey
1 egg, beaten	1 egg, beaten

MAKES ONE 15CM/6 INCH CAKE

Line the base of a 15 cm/6 inch cake tin (p.49). Sift the flour and ground ginger into a mixing bowl. Cut the fat into the flour and rub in to a breadcrumb consistency. Mix in the sugar and stem ginger.
Dissolve the bicarbonate of soda in half the milk and stir into the honey. Make a well in the dry ingredients and stir in the milk mixture and beaten egg. Mix to a soft dropping consistency adding more milk as required.
Turn into the prepared tin and level the top. Bake in the centre of a preheated moderate oven at 170°C/325°F, Gas Mark 3 for about 1 hour, until set and golden. Allow to shrink slightly, remove from the tin and cool on a wire tray.

Lunch fruit cake; Honey and ginger cake

Plain buns

The plain cake method of rubbing the fat into the flour makes excellent buns. The mixture is made a little stiffer than for large cakes and can be varied in many ways with dried fruit, spices or jam. You can leave them plain or top with glacé icing. Self-raising flour can be used instead of plain flour and baking powder.

Basic bun mixture

METRIC	IMPERIAL
225 g plain flour	8 oz plain flour
pinch of salt	pinch of salt
1 ½ teaspoons baking powder	1 ½ teaspoons baking powder
75 g butter or margarine	3 oz butter or margarine
50-75 g sugar	2-3 oz sugar
1 egg, beaten	1 egg, beaten
approx. 75 ml milk or water	approx. 3 fl oz milk or water

MAKES 12 TO 16

Sift the flour, salt and baking powder into a mixing bowl. Cut the fat into the flour and rub in to a breadcrumb consistency. Mix in the sugar thoroughly.
Using a fork, stir in the egg and sufficient milk or water to give a stiff consistency — the fork should stand up in the dough. If it is too slack, the mixture will spread too much during baking. Flavour to taste (see below) and put in little heaps or small balls on a greased baking sheet, or in bun tins. Bake near the top of a preheated hot oven at 220-230°C/425-450°F, Gas Mark 7-8 for 10 to 15 minutes. Cool on a wire tray.

Flavourings and toppings

The Basic Bun Mixture can be flavoured in a variety of ways.

Chocolate buns

Add 25 g/1 oz cocoa to the flour before sifting and ½ teaspoon vanilla essence with the milk. Put into greased bun tins to bake.
For parties: when cold, spread a little Chocolate Glacé Icing (p.150) on top and sprinkle with chocolate strands.

Rock buns

Add 50-75 g/2-3 oz mixed dried fruit and 25 g/1 oz chopped mixed peel when mixing in the sugar. Bake in little rocky heaps on a greased baking tray.

Cherry buns

Add 100 g/4 oz chopped glacé cherries tossed in flour, and mix in with the sugar. Bake in greased bun tins.
For parties: when cold coat with Lemon Glacé Icing (p.150) and decorate with halved cherries.

Coconut buns

Mix in 50 g/2 oz desiccated coconut with the sugar before adding it. Bake in little heaps on a greased baking tray.
For parties: when cold, spread a little Vanilla Glacé Icing (p.150) on top and sprinkle with shredded coconut.

Row, one, from the top: Plain bun; Rock bun; Raspberry bun; Raspberry bun; Plain bun. Row two, from the top: Chocolate bun; Cherry bun; Coconut bun; Ginger bun; Orange bun. Row three, from the top: Chocolate bun; Cherry bun; Coconut bun; Ginger bun; Lemon bun

Ginger buns

Add 1 teaspoon ground ginger to the flour before sifting. Use soft brown sugar instead of white and add 50 g/2 oz chopped stem ginger to the dry ingredients. Bake in little heaps on a greased baking sheet.
For parties: when cold, spread a little Lemon Glacé Icing (p.150) on top and decorate with crystallized ginger.

Lemon or orange buns

Add 2 teaspoons grated lemon rind or the grated rind of 1 orange to the dry ingredients. Use the juice of ½ lemon or 1 orange with water for mixing. Bake in greased bun tins.
For parties: when cold spread with a little Lemon or Orange Glacé Icing (p.150) on top, and decorate with triangles of crystallized lemon or orange slices.

Raspberry buns

Divide the basic mixture into 12 equal pieces and with floured fingers roll into little balls. Make a hole in each bun and put in a teaspoon of raspberry jam. Squeeze the opening together and invert the buns on to a greased baking tray. Brush with milk and sprinkle with crushed cube sugar before baking.

Coffee walnut buns

METRIC	IMPERIAL
100 g plain flour	*4 oz plain flour*
100 g wholemeal flour	*4 oz wholemeal flour*
pinch of salt	*pinch of salt*
2 teaspoons baking powder	*2 teaspoons baking powder*
100 g butter or margarine	*4 oz butter or margarine*
75 g soft brown sugar	*3 oz soft brown sugar*
50 g walnuts, chopped	*2 oz walnuts, chopped*
1 egg	*1 egg*
2 tablespoons coffee essence	*2 tablespoons coffee essence*
milk to mix	*milk to mix*
TOPPING:	*TOPPING:*
Coffee Glacé Icing(p.150)	*Coffee Glacé Icing (p.150)*
halved walnuts	*halved walnuts*

MAKES 12 TO 16

Sift the flour, salt and baking powder into a mixing bowl. Cut the fat into the flour and rub in to a breadcrumb consistency. Mix in the sugar and chopped nuts. Beat the egg and coffee essence together, then stir into the mixture adding sufficient milk to give a stiff dough.
Using 2 forks heap the mixture in rocky mounds on a greased baking sheet. Bake near the top of a preheated moderately hot oven at 200°C/400°F, Gas Mark 6 for 15 to 20 minutes. Remove from the tins and cool on a wire tray. When cold spread with Coffee Glacé Icing and top each one with a half walnut.

Almond buns

These little buns have a rich centre of almond paste, and are topped with flaked almonds.

METRIC	IMPERIAL
175 g plain flour	*6 oz plain flour*
½ teaspoon baking powder	*½ teaspoon baking powder*
pinch of salt	*pinch of salt*
75 g butter or margarine	*3 oz butter or margarine*
50 g caster sugar	*2 oz caster sugar*
1 egg, beaten	*1 egg, beaten*
ALMOND PASTE:	*ALMOND PASTE:*
50 g ground almonds	*2 oz ground almonds*
25 g caster sugar	*1 oz caster sugar*
25 g icing sugar	*1 oz icing sugar*
1 egg yolk	*1 egg yolk*
squeeze of lemon juice	*squeeze of lemon juice*
TOPPING:	*TOPPING:*
1 egg white, beaten	*1 egg white, beaten*
flaked almonds	*flaked almonds*

MAKES 16

Sift the flour, baking powder and salt into a mixing bowl. Cut the fat into the flour and rub in to a breadcrumb consistency. Stir in the sugar and bind into a stiff dough with the beaten egg, adding a spoonful of water if necessary.
To make the almond paste, mix together the ground almonds and sugars. Bind with the egg yolk into a stiff paste, and flavour to taste with the lemon juice. Roll into 16 marbles using sugared fingers.
Roll the dough into a sausage shape and divide into 16 equal portions. Shape into balls on a floured board and flatten slightly. Place a marble of almond paste in the

centre of each bun and gather the edges together over it. Turn upside down and place on a greased baking sheet. Brush the buns with the beaten egg white and sprinkle with flaked almonds. Bake in a preheated hot oven at 220°C/425°F, Gas Mark 7 for 15 minutes or until well risen and golden brown. Cool on a wire tray.

Above: Almond buns; Coffee walnut buns

Quick cakes

These contain the same proportions of fat, eggs and flour as plain cakes, but the method is different.

Boiled fruit cake

This unusual method of making fruit cake comes from Ireland and is very labour saving.

METRIC	IMPERIAL
75 g golden syrup	3 oz golden syrup
100 g sugar	4 oz sugar
100 g butter or margarine	4 oz butter or margarine
150 ml water	¼ pint water
100 g currants	4 oz currants
100 g sultanas	4 oz sultanas
225 g plain flour	8 oz plain flour
1 teaspoon bicarbonate of soda	1 teaspoon bicarbonate of soda
1 teaspoon mixed spices	1 teaspoon mixed spices
1 teaspoon ground ginger	1 teaspoon ground ginger
1 egg, beaten	1 egg, beaten

MAKES ONE 15 CM/6 INCH CAKE

Dissolve the syrup, sugar and fat in the water in a saucepan over moderate heat. Add the dried fruit and boil gently for 9 to 10 minutes. Pour into a mixing bowl to cool. Meanwhile grease well a round 15 cm/6 inch cake tin and line the base with greased greaseproof paper (p.49).
Sift the flour with the bicarbonate of soda and spices. Stir it into the cooled boiled mixture and beat in the egg. Turn into the prepared tin and bake in the centre of a preheated moderate oven at 180°C/350°F, Gas Mark 4 for about 1½ hours or until a skewer inserted comes out clean. Allow the cake to shrink slightly. Turn out on to a wire tray, remove the lining paper and leave to cool.

Mixer fruit cake

This is a one-stage cake made with soft (tub) margarine which does not need to be rubbed into the flour before adding the other ingredients. It is ideal for the electric mixer, but be careful not to overbeat the mixture. If no mixer is available use a wooden spoon.

METRIC	IMPERIAL
225 g self-raising flour	8 oz self-raising flour
2 teaspoons mixed spice	2 teaspoons mixed spice
1 teaspoon baking powder	1 teaspoon baking powder
100 g soft brown sugar	4 oz soft brown sugar
175 g mixed dried fruit	6 oz mixed dried fruit
100 g soft margarine	4 oz soft margarine
2 eggs	2 eggs
2 tablespoons water	2 tablespoons water

MAKES ONE 15CM/6 INCH CAKE

Grease a 15 cm/6 inch round cake tin and line the base (p.49). Sift the flour, mixed spice and baking powder into the mixing bowl, mix in the sugar and dried fruit lightly with the fingers. Add the margarine, eggs and water and beat with a wooden spoon or in the electric mixer until well combined. Turn into the prepared tin and smooth the top. Bake in the centre of a preheated moderate oven at 170°C/325°F, Gas Mark 3 for about 1¾ hours or until a skewer inserted comes out clean. Allow the cake to shrink slightly. Turn out on to a wire tray, remove the lining paper and leave to cool.

Yorkshire jam cake

This is similar in texture to strawberry shortcake, but is filled with jam instead of fruit. It is delicious when made with home-made jam, and served with clotted cream.

METRIC	IMPERIAL
350 g plain flour	12 oz plain flour
pinch of salt	pinch of salt
3 teaspoons baking powder	3 teaspoons baking powder
175 g butter or margarine	6 oz butter or margarine
175 g caster sugar	6 oz caster sugar
1 large or 2 small eggs, lightly beaten	1 large or 2 small eggs, lightly beaten
a little water	a little water
50 g jam, warmed	2 oz jam, warmed
TO GLAZE:	TO GLAZE:
milk	milk
caster sugar	caster sugar

Sift the flour, salt and baking powder into a mixing bowl. Cut the fat into the flour and rub in to a breadcrumb consistency. Mix in the sugar thoroughly. Stir in the eggs with a palette knife. Mix to a soft but not sticky dough, adding a little water if necessary. Shape into a ball and cut in half. On a floured board, roll each half out into a circle 1.5 cm/½ inch thick. Place one on a greased baking sheet, prick it all over and spread with the warm jam, leaving a narrow margin round the edge. Cover with the remaining half of the dough, and pinch the edges firmly together. Brush the top with milk and sprinkle with sugar. Bake in the centre of a preheated moderately hot oven at 190°C/375°F, Gas Mark 5 for 30 to 35 minutes, until well risen and golden brown. Cool on a wire tray.

Left: Yorkshire jam cake; Boiled fruit cake mixture and finished cake; Mixer fruit cake mixture

Rich cakes

Creaming butter and sugar until light and fluffy

Gradually beating in the eggs

Folding in the sifted flour

These contain a high proportion of both fat and sugar which are creamed together, and three to four eggs to every 225 g/8 oz flour.

Creaming butter and sugar

Success with rich cakes depends largely on creaming the butter and sugar thoroughly until light and fluffy like whipped cream, and pale in colour. Use butter which has softened at room temperature. Do not be tempted to heat the butter as if it melts, it will make the cake heavy. Old-fashioned cooks put the mixing bowl on their knees and beat with the spread hand; the natural warmth speeds up the creaming, compared with using a wooden spoon. Modern cooks can use the electric mixer, which is very quick and efficient. Cut up the fat before putting it in the bowl with the sugar and run the mixer at low speed. Do not overbeat or the mixture will turn from a cream into an oily emulsion and make the cake heavy.

Adding eggs

Whisk the eggs, add a little at a time and beat until fully incorporated before adding the next spoonful. If the mixture starts to curdle, add 2 tablespoons of the measured flour before adding more eggs.

Folding in flour

Sift the flour with any spices and raising agent and fold it into the creamed mixture using a concave spatula or large metal spoon, not a wooden one. If the flour is beaten in by hand or in the mixer instead of folded, it will produce a much closer texture.

Maturing and storage of cakes

Rich cakes made by the creaming method remain moist much longer than the plain cakes and improve with keeping. They are apt to crumble if cut when freshly made. When completely cold, store in an airtight tin or plastic container.

Family fruit cake

Dried fruit can be bought already mixed or you can vary the mixture of sultanas, seedless raisins, currants and chopped candied peel to your own taste. This type of cake is best left overnight before cutting, and it keeps well in an airtight tin or plastic container.

METRIC	IMPERIAL
175 g butter or margarine	6 oz butter or margarine
175 g caster sugar	6 oz caster sugar
2 teaspoons grated lemon rind	2 teaspoons grated lemon rind
3 eggs, whisked	3 eggs, whisked
225 g plain flour	8 oz plain flour
pinch of salt	pinch of salt
1½ teaspoons baking powder	1½ teaspoons baking powder
175-225 g mixed dried fruit	6-8 oz mixed dried fruit
water to mix	water to mix

MAKES ONE 18 CM/7 INCH CAKE

Line the sides and base of a round 18 cm/7 inch cake tin (p.49). Cream the fat and sugar with the lemon rind until light and fluffy. Beat in the eggs a tablespoonful at a time, beating well between each addition. If the mixture starts to curdle, add a spoonful of the measured flour.
Sift the flour, salt and baking powder and fold it into the mixture. Scatter the fruit over the mixture and fold it in carefully. Add a little water to make a soft dropping consistency. The mixture should drop off the spoon in 5 seconds.
Turn the mixture into the prepared tin. Smooth it out and with the back of the spoon make a slight hollow in the centre so it will not rise to a peak in the oven.
Bake in the centre of a preheated moderate oven at 180°C/350°F, Gas Mark 4 for 1¼ to 1½ hours until well risen and golden brown. Test with a skewer (p.48). Allow to shrink slightly. Turn out on to a wire tray, remove the lining paper and leave to cool.

Cherry cake

Use 100 g/4 oz glacé cherries instead of the dried fruit. Chop into halves or quarters, toss in a little flour and fold into the cake mixture carefully so they are evenly distributed. Add a little water as required and turn the mixture into the prepared cake tin. Smooth the top and decorate with some halved glacé cherries. Sprinkle with sugar and bake as for Family Fruit Cake.

Orange madeira cake

Omit the dried fruit and add the grated rind of 1 orange to the beaten eggs. Mix with orange juice instead of water. When the cake has been in the oven about 30 minutes and begun to set, place 2 slices of candied citron peel on top in the centre and continue cooking as for Family Fruit Cake. This cake is traditionally expected to rise in the centre and 'smile', that is, break open slightly.

Scots seed cake

In earlier days the top of this cake was decorated with the old-fashioned caraway comfits, which were reputed to aid digestion. They are nowadays replaced with caraway seeds. These can be sprinkled on top of the cake, or ¼ teaspoon of ground caraway seeds mixed in with the flour if preferred. The following recipe makes a small cake, for double the ingredients use a 18 cm/7 inch tin. Bake for a little longer.

METRIC	IMPERIAL
100 g butter or margarine	4 oz butter or margarine
100 g caster sugar	4 oz caster sugar
2 large eggs, separated	2 large eggs, separated
1 tablespoon whisky or brandy	1 tablespoon whisky or brandy
100 g plain flour	4 oz plain flour
¼ teaspoon baking powder	¼ teaspoon baking powder
¼ teaspoon grated nutmeg	¼ teaspoon grated nutmeg
50 g blanched almonds, shredded	2 oz blanched almonds, shredded
50 g candied orange peel, chopped	2 oz candied orange peel, chopped
25 g candied citron peel, chopped	1 oz candied citron peel, chopped
TO FINISH:	TO FINISH:
caraway seeds	caraway seeds
granulated sugar	granulated sugar

MAKES ONE 15 CM/6 INCH CAKE

Line the sides and base of a round 15 cm/6 inch cake tin (p.49). Cream the fat and sugar until light and fluffy. Gradually beat in the egg yolks. Whisk the egg whites until stiff but not brittle, and fold in alternately with the flour, sifted with the baking powder and nutmeg. Fold in the almonds, candied peel and whisky or brandy. Turn into the prepared tin. Sprinkle with caraway seeds and granulated sugar.
Bake in the centre of a preheated moderate oven at 160°C/325°F, Gas Mark 3, for 1½ hours or until set and golden. Test with a skewer (p.48). Allow the cake to shrink slightly. Turn out on to a wire tray, remove the lining paper and leave to cool.

Scots seed cake; Family fruit cake

Sandwich cakes

These rich cakes are sometimes called butter sponges, because they have a spongy texture, but they are richer than whisked sponges, being made by the creaming method (p.54). The cake mixture is baked in two shallow tins and sandwiched together with a variety of fillings and topped with sifted sugar, butter cream, glacé icing etc. The basic mixture makes the popular Victoria Sandwich, named after the good Queen. In those days the cook put the eggs she was using on the scales, instead of weights, and put an equal weight of flour and sugar in the scoop.

Victoria sandwich cake

This basic mixture may be flavoured in a variety of ways (see below).

METRIC	IMPERIAL
175 g butter or margarine	*6 oz butter or margarine*
175 g caster sugar	*6 oz caster sugar*
3 eggs, beaten	*3 eggs, beaten*
¼ teaspoon vanilla essence	*¼ teaspoon vanilla essence*
175 g plain flour	*6 oz plain flour*
1½ teaspoons baking powder	*1½ teaspoons baking powder*
1-2 tablespoons water	*1-2 tablespoons water*
TO FINISH:	*TO FINISH:*
strawberry jam to fill	*strawberry jam to fill*
caster sugar for dredging	*caster sugar for dredging*

MAKES ONE 18 CM/7 INCH CAKE

Grease two 18 cm/7 inch sandwich tins (p.49). Cream the fat and sugar together until light and fluffy. Add the eggs, beaten with the vanilla essence, a little at a time, beating well between each addition, with a wooden spoon. If the mixture starts to curdle, add a little of the flour.
Sift the flour and baking powder together and fold, a little at a time, quickly and lightly into the creamed mixture. Use a concave spatula or large metal spoon.
Make sure the flour is completely incorporated into the mixture, but do not over-fold or the cake will not rise so well. Mix to a soft dropping consistency. Add a tablespoon or two of warm water if necessary. Divide the mixture evenly between the two tins and smooth it over.
Bake in the top third of a preheated moderately hot oven at 190°C/375°F, Gas Mark 5, for 20 to 25 minutes until set and golden. Test by pressing gently with the fingers. If the surface springs back, the cakes are ready; if the dents remain, cook a little longer.
Remove from the oven, allow to cool and shrink slightly before turning out to cool on a wire tray. When cold, spread one cake with jam and place the other on top. Dredge with sugar.

Raspberry rose sandwich

Add cochineal to the basic mixture a few drops at a time to colour it a delicate pink.
Filling and topping: spread the bottom layer with one third Raspberry Butter Cream (p.151). Place the other cake on top, spread with remaining butter cream and ruffle with a knife. Decorate with crystallized rose petals and mint leaves or angelica leaves.

Mocha and walnut sandwich

Flavour the basic mixture with 2 teaspoons coffee essence or 2 teaspoons instant coffee, dissolved in 1 tablespoon water.

Filling and topping: spread the bottom layer with one third Mocha Butter Cream (p.151) and sprinkle with 2 tablespoons chopped walnuts. Press the other cake on top and cover with the remaining butter cream. Mark with the tines of a fork into a chequer board pattern and decorate with 9 half walnuts.

Lemon mimosa sandwich

Add 2 teaspoons grated lemon rind to the basic mixture instead of vanilla and colour a delicate yellow with a few drops of yellow colouring.

Filling and topping: spread the bottom layer with one third of Lemon Butter Cream (p.151). Press the other cake on top and swirl on the remaining butter cream. Decorate with crystallized mimosa balls and angelica leaves.

Orange sandwich

Add 2 to 3 teaspoons grated orange rind to the basic mixture instead of vanilla and tint with a few drops of orange colouring.

Filling and topping: spread the bottom layer with one third of Orange Butter Cream (p.151). Press the other cake on top and cover with the remaining butter cream. Mark with swirls from the edge to the centre of the cake, using a palette knife. Decorate with crystallized orange slices.

Chocolate and almond sandwich

Flavour the basic mixture with ¼ teaspoon almond or ratafia essence instead of vanilla.

Filling and topping: toast 50 g/2 oz flaked almonds under the grill until golden coloured. Spread the bottom layer with one third of Chocolate Butter Cream (p.151) and cover with 2 tablespoons chopped browned almonds. Press the other cake on top and ruffle on the remaining butter cream. Decorate the edge with a ring of flaked almonds and arrange the remainder in the centre.

Little rich cakes

Similar proportions of ingredients and the same method are used here as for Sandwich Cakes.

Lemon curd and caraway cakes

These delightful cakes are quick and easy to make and bake, either by hand or with the mixer. They are delicious plain but can be topped with Lemon Curd Glacé Icing.

METRIC	IMPERIAL
150 g soft margarine	*6 oz soft margarine*
100 g caster sugar	*4 oz caster sugar*
150 g lemon curd	*6 oz lemon curd*
225 g self-raising flour	*8 oz self-raising flour*
pinch of salt	*pinch of salt*
1 teaspoon caraway seeds	*1 teaspoon caraway seeds*
3 eggs, beaten	*3 eggs, beaten*

MAKES ABOUT 30

Cream the margarine and sugar together until light and fluffy. Beat in the lemon curd. Sift the flour and salt and mix in the caraway seeds. Beat the eggs into the creamed mixture, one at a time, with 2 tablespoons flour each time. Fold in the remaining flour. Spoon the mixture into greased patty pans until three quarters full. Bake in a preheated moderate oven at 180°C/350°F, Gas Mark 4, for 20 minutes until golden and firm to the touch. Allow the cakes to shrink slightly, then remove from tins and cool on a wire tray.
For parties: top with Lemon Curd Glacé Icing (p.150). Mix 75 g/3 oz sifted icing sugar with 3 teaspoons lemon curd into a spreading consistency. Swirl over the tops of the cakes and decorate each one with 3 mimosa balls or a tiny crystallized lemon slice.

Glacé fancies

These little iced cakes may also be made with the Genoese Sponge mixture (p.62).

METRIC	IMPERIAL
basic Victoria Sandwich Cake mixture (p.56)	*basic Victoria Sandwich Cake mixture (p.56)*
500 g apricot jam	*1 lb apricot jam*
1 tablespoon water	*1 tablespoon water*
GLACÉ ICING:	*GLACÉ ICING:*
500 g icing sugar	*1 lb icing sugar*
lemon juice to mix	*lemon juice to mix*
FOR DECORATION:	*FOR DECORATION:*
crystallized flowers, angelica etc.	*crystallized flowers, angelica etc.*

MAKES 44

Line a Swiss roll tin 30 × 20 cm/12 × 8 inches (p.49). Make up the mixture for Victoria Sandwich and pour it into the tin, spreading it evenly into the corners. Bake in a preheated moderately hot oven at 190°C/375°F, Gas Mark 5 for about 20 minutes until golden and springy to the touch. Allow to cool slightly, then turn out upside down on to a wire tray. Carefully peel off the lining paper and

leave the cake until completely cold before cutting. With a sharp knife trim the edges and divide the cake lengthwise into 4 equal strips. Cut the first strip across into 6 squares. Cut the next strip into 8 squares, then each square diagonally into 2 triangles. Cut the third strip into 8 squares, and each square in half to make 2 rectangles. With a 4 cm/1½ inch pastry cutter, cut the next strip into 6 rounds.

Make the trimmings into crumbs. Gently warm the apricot jam with the water. Use a little to bind the cake crumbs together stiffly, then mould into marble sized balls. Brush the remaining jam thinly over the sides of the cakes. Press a ball in the centre of some of the cakes.

Sift the icing sugar and make into glacé icing (p.150) with the lemon juice. Divide the icing into 3 bowls; leave one white, colour one pink and one pale green. The icing should be of a pouring consistency but thick enough to coat the back of a wooden spoon. Place the cakes on a wire tray over a large dish and pour over the glacé icing. Neaten with a knife dipped in hot water.

Decorate to taste with crystallized flowers, angelica leaves, silver balls, glacé cherries etc. When the icing has set, put the cakes into paper cases.

Carleton cakes

METRIC	IMPERIAL
100 g plain flour	4 oz plain flour
25 g ground rice	1 oz ground rice
1 teaspoon baking powder	1 teaspoon baking powder
75 g butter or margarine	3 oz butter or margarine
50 g caster sugar	2 oz caster sugar
2 eggs, separated	2 eggs, separated
25 g candied citron peel, chopped	2 oz candied citron peel, chopped
25 g blanched flaked almonds, shredded	1 oz blanched flaked almonds, shredded
3 tablespoons water	3 tablespoons water
1 thin slice candied citron peel to decorate	1 thin slice candied citron peel to decorate

MAKES 12

Sift the flour, rice and baking powder together. Cream the fat with the sugar until light and fluffy. Stir in the egg yolks and beat well. Mix in the flour, then the citron peel and almonds. Stir in the water and beat until smooth. Beat the egg whites until stiff but not brittle. Fold them into the mixture. Spoon into well greased patty pans. Cut the citron peel slice into small wedges and place one in the centre of each cake. Bake in a preheated moderately hot oven at 200°C/400°F, Gas Mark 6 for about 15 minutes. Remove from the tins and cool on a wire tray. Best when freshly baked.

Left: Glacé fancies

Whisked sponge cakes

These are the true sponge cakes in which the eggs and sugar are whisked together until almost white, and thick enough to show the trail of the whisk. It is thorough whisking which produces a feather-light texture, no raising agent is needed. The sifted flour is folded in very quickly and lightly and, for a richer cake, some melted butter is added. Fatless sponges should be eaten fresh as they dry out quickly if stored. If well sealed they can be frozen successfully.

Basic whisked sponge

METRIC	IMPERIAL
75 g caster sugar	3 oz caster sugar
3 eggs	3 eggs
75 g flour	3 oz flour
½ teaspoon vanilla essence or 2 teaspoons grated lemon rind	½ teaspoon vanilla essence or 2 teaspoons grated lemon rind

MAKES ONE 18 CM/7 INCH CAKE

Making the sponge: whisk the sugar and eggs together until light and thick. The mixture is not ready until it falls off the whisk in ribbons and remains on top of the mixture in the bowl for several seconds before sinking. An electric beater will do this quickly, but a rotary whisk, although slower, is equally successful provided you beat long enough.

Sift half the flour over the mixture and fold it in quickly and lightly, using a concave spatula or large metal spoon. Then sift and fold in the remaining flour and the vanilla or lemon rind. Fold by hand as the electric mixer will beat the mixture into a much closer texture.

Make sure no little pockets of dry flour remain, but do not continue folding too long as the mixture will lose its lightness.

Baking the sponge: grease a round 18 cm/7 inch cake tin and line the base (p.49). Mix together a tablespoon each of flour and caster sugar, shake it around in the tin to form a thin coating and tip out any surplus.

Pour in the sponge mixture and level the top. Bake in the top third of a preheated moderately hot oven at 190°C/375°F, Gas Mark 5, for about 25 minutes until well risen and golden brown and the top is springy to the touch. Do not open the oven while the cake is rising, nor bang the oven door as a cold draught can sink the cake. Allow the sponge to shrink slightly. Turn out on to a wire tray, remove the lining paper and leave to cool.

Filling and topping: when the sponge is quite cold, split it carefully with a sharp knife. Spread the bottom half with a preserve or fresh fruit and whipped cream. Replace the top and dredge with caster or sieved icing sugar. Any of the fillings and toppings given on page 56 for Victoria Sandwich Cake are also suitable.

The whisked egg and sugar falling off the beaters in ribbons

Sponge sandwich

Prepare two 18 cm/7 inch sandwich tins as for previous recipe. Make up the Basic Whisked Sponge mixture and divide it equally between the two tins. Level it off and bang the base of each tin on the table to settle the mixture. Bake near the top of a preheated moderate oven at 180°C/350°F, Gas Mark 4, for 20 minutes until golden and springy to the touch. Allow to shrink slightly before turning out to cool on a wire tray. Fill and decorate as for Victoria Sandwich Cake (p.56).

Swiss roll

Line a Swiss roll tin 30 × 20 cm/12 × 8 inches (p.49).
Make up the Basic Whisked Sponge mixture and pour it
into the prepared tin, tilting it backwards and forwards so
it covers the tin evenly. Smooth it into the corners with a
palette knife. Bake near the top of a preheated hot oven at
220°C/425°F, Gas Mark 7, for 8 to 9 minutes until golden
and the top is springy to the touch. Do not overcook, or it
will crack when rolled up.
Meanwhile, wring out a teacloth in hot water and lay it on
the table. Place a sheet of greaseproof paper on top and
dredge it with caster sugar. When cooked, turn the sponge

Rolling up a Swiss roll with sugared paper

out upside down on the paper. Peel off the lining. Quickly
cut off the crisp edges with a large, sharp knife.
Cut a slit across the near narrow end of the sponge about
1.5 cm/½ inch from the edge. Spread the sponge with
warm jam. Roll up, using the paper, tucking in the first
edge neatly and roll up evenly into a good shape. Remove
paper and cool on a wire tray. Sprinkle with caster sugar.

Swiss roll; Sponge fingers; Sponge drops

Variations

Instead of spreading the sponge with jam, lay a sheet of
greaseproof paper over it and roll it up. When cold, unroll
carefully and spread with a Chocolate or other Butter
Cream (p.151) or with jam and whipped cream, fresh
raspberries or sliced strawberries. Re-roll carefully and
dredge with sifted icing sugar, or decorate with piped
whipped cream.

Sponge fingers

METRIC/IMPERIAL
3 tablespoons caster sugar
1 large egg
4 level tablespoons strong flour, sifted
MAKES 10 TO 12

Brush a sponge finger tray with oil or melted lard and dust
with flour and sugar. Whisk the sugar and egg in an
electric mixer as in the Basic Whisked Sponge recipe. If
using a rotary beater, whisk in a bowl over a saucepan of
simmering water until white and thick. Remove from the
heat and continue whisking until cool. Fold in the flour.
Using a plain meringue nozzle (1.5 cm/1¾ inch) pipe the
mixture into the hollows in the tray, or fill with a spoon.
Bake near the top of a preheated moderately hot oven at
200°C/400°F, Gas Mark 6, for 8 to 10 minutes until
golden. Remove from the oven, carefully lift out the
sponge fingers and cool on a wire tray.
For parties: dip the ends of the fingers in Glacé Icing (p.150)
or melted chocolate and then in chocolate or coloured
sugar strands, or hundreds and thousands or chopped nuts.

Sponge drops

Line a baking tray with parchment or greased greaseproof
paper. Pipe the mixture in small rounds, or use a teaspoon,
leaving room for it to spread. Bake as above for about 8
minutes until golden. Remove and leave to cool.
Sandwich in pairs with jam or lemon curd or whipped
cream. Dust with sifted icing sugar.
Makes approximately 12 pairs.
For parties: dip one half of each sponge drop into melted
chocolate.

Genoese sponge

This is a basic recipe for a whisked sponge mixture enriched with butter which has been melted and cooled. It needs a lot of whisking and entails rather hard work if you do not have an electric mixer. It is richer than a fatless sponge so keeps better, and it is lighter than a Victoria Sandwich Cake.

Basic Genoese sponge

METRIC	IMPERIAL
40 g unsalted butter	1½ oz unsalted butter
3 large eggs	3 large eggs
75 g caster sugar	3 oz caster sugar
75 g plain flour	3 oz plain flour

MAKES ONE 18 CM/7 INCH CAKE

Prepare two 18 cm/7 inch sandwich tins or a Swiss roll tin 30 × 20 cm/12 × 8 inches. Heat the butter gently until liquid, then leave for any sediment to settle.
Put the eggs and sugar in a mixing bowl. Whisk with an electric beater, or by hand with a rotary whisk over a bowl of simmering water until the mixture is thick enough to show the trail of the whisk (see p.60). Take care the water does not touch the bottom of the bowl. If overheated the sponge will be tough.
Sift the flour and fold in half of it carefully. Pour half the melted butter round the edge of the mixture and fold it in. Fold in the remaining flour alternately with the rest of the butter, taking care not to use any sediment. Work quickly and lightly or the butter will sink to the bottom.

Pour into the two sandwich tins or Swiss roll tin and bake in the preheated oven at 190°C/375°F Gas Mark 5 for 20 to 25 minutes, until golden and springy to the touch. Allow the cake(s) to shrink slightly, then turn on to a wire tray to cool.
When cold, fill and ice the sandwich cake as for Victoria Sandwich Cake (p.56) or cut up the slab cake and ice as for Glacé Fancies (p.58).

Almond and chocolate layer cake

METRIC	IMPERIAL
50 g unsalted butter	2 oz unsalted butter
4 large eggs	4 large eggs
100 g caster sugar	4 oz caster sugar
100 g plain flour	4 oz plain flour
25 g nibbed almonds	1 oz nibbed almonds
¼ teaspoon almond essence	¼ teaspoon almond essence
Chocolate Joy Icing (see opposite)	Chocolate Joy Icing (see opposite)
2-3 tablespoons flaked almonds, toasted	2-3 tablespoons flaked almonds, toasted

MAKES ONE 18 CM/7 INCH CAKE

Line the base of a round 18 cm/7 inch cake tin (p.49). Grease and dust with a flour and caster sugar mixture. Follow carefully the method for the basic recipe for Genoese Sponge: melt the butter and set aside to cool and for the sediment to sink. Whisk the eggs and sugar until white and thick. Fold in the flour, almond nibs, butter and almond essence.

Angel cake

This is a whisked sponge made without butter and using only the whites of the eggs.

METRIC	IMPERIAL
100 g plain flour	4 oz plain flour
175 g caster sugar	6 oz caster sugar
5-6 (175 ml) egg whites	5-6 (6 fl oz) egg whites
½ teaspoon cream of tartar	½ teaspoon cream of tartar
½ teaspoon vanilla or almond essence	½ teaspoon vanilla or almond essence

MAKES ONE 18 CM/7 INCH CAKE

Sift the flour and sugar together 3 to 4 times. Beat the egg whites until foaming; add the cream of tartar and whisk until stiff but not dry. Sift the flour and sugar on to the whisked egg whites carefully, about 2 tablespoonfuls at a time, then fold in the flavouring essence. Turn the mixture into an ungreased 18 cm/7 inch angel cake tin. Bake in a preheated moderate oven at 160°C/325°F, Gas Mark 3, for 1 hour or until a skewer inserted comes out clean. Remove from the oven and invert on to a wire tray. Leave until quite cold before turning out of the tin.

This is a sweet cake and it is best to choose a sharp filling for contrast. Slice the cake across in three, or down into 8. Spread the slices with lemon curd and re-assemble the cake. Decorate with piped Lemon Butter Cream (p.151) and crystallized lemon slices, or spread with Lemon Glacé Icing (p.150).

Right: Angel cake

Pour into the prepared tin and bake in the centre of a preheated moderately hot oven at 190°C/375°F, Gas Mark 5, for about 1 hour until well risen and springy to the touch. Test with a skewer which will come out clean when the cake is cooked. Allow to shrink slightly and turn on to a wire tray to cool.

When quite cold, cut across into 3 layers. Spread the two bottom layers with Chocolate Joy and re-assemble the cake. Swirl the rest of the Chocolate Joy over the top and sides of the cake. Arrange a ring of almonds round the top of the cake and put the remainder in the centre.

Chocolate joy icing

METRIC	IMPERIAL
225 g icing sugar	8 oz icing sugar
50 g cocoa	2 oz cocoa
50 g unsalted butter	2 oz unsalted butter
1 egg yolk	1 egg yolk
¼ teaspoon vanilla essence	¼ teaspoon vanilla essence
3-4 tablespoons warm water	3-4 tablespoons warm water

Sift the icing sugar and cocoa together. Cream the butter until light and fluffy and beat in the icing sugar and cocoa. Flavour the egg yolk with the vanilla, add 2 to 3 tablespoons warm water and beat into the butter cream. Add a little more water if necessary to make a spreading consistency.

Melted mixtures

This method of making cakes is frequently used for gingerbread. The fat is melted with the sweetener — sugar, honey, golden syrup or treacle — then mixed into the dry ingredients. It must not be too hot or the flour will lump. Bicarbonate of soda is the usual raising agent, with eggs for the richer mixtures.

Gingerbread loaf

METRIC	IMPERIAL
100 g butter or margarine	4 oz butter or margarine
25 g sugar	1 oz sugar
100 g treacle or golden syrup	4 oz treacle or golden syrup
225 g plain flour	8 oz plain flour
1 teaspoon bicarbonate of soda	1 teaspoon bicarbonate of soda
1 teaspoon ground ginger	1 teaspoon ground ginger
1 teaspoon mixed spice	1 teaspoon mixed spice
2 eggs, beaten	2 eggs, beaten

Grease and line a small loaf tin. Melt the fat, sugar and treacle or syrup over gentle heat. Sift the flour with the soda and spices, into a mixing bowl. Stir in the cooled liquid and then the beaten eggs. Mix thoroughly and beat well until a smooth batter. Pour into the prepared tin and bake in a preheated moderate oven at 180°C/350°F, Gas Mark 4, for ¾ to 1 hour. Test with a skewer. Allow to cool in the tin before turning out on to a wire tray. Gingerbread improves with keeping.

Rich fruited gingerbread

This is really a rich cake rather than a 'bread.' For festive occasions it can be frosted and decorated with ginger.

METRIC	IMPERIAL
100 g butter or margarine	4 oz butter or margarine
50 g golden syrup	2 oz golden syrup
175 g black treacle	6 oz black treacle
150 ml milk	¼ pint milk
2 eggs, beaten	2 eggs, beaten
200 g plain flour	7 oz plain flour
25 g ground almonds	1 oz ground almonds
2 teaspoons ground ginger	2 teaspoons ground ginger
1 teaspoon ground cinnamon	1 teaspoon ground cinnamon
½ teaspoon ground nutmeg	½ teaspoon ground nutmeg
¼ teaspoon ground cloves	¼ teaspoon ground cloves
1 teaspoon bicarbonate of soda	1 teaspoon bicarbonate of soda
50 g stem ginger, chopped	2 oz stem ginger, chopped
50 g sultanas	2 oz sultanas
25 g chopped candied peel or 25 g shredded blanched almonds	1 oz chopped candied peel or 1 oz shredded blanched almonds
FROSTING:	FROSTING:
225 g icing sugar	8 oz icing sugar
lemon juice to mix	lemon juice to mix
50 g crystallized ginger	2 oz crystallized ginger

MAKES ONE 18-20 CM/7-8 INCH CAKE

Grease and line the base of a round 18-20 cm/7-8 inch cake tin or a square 15-18 cm/6-7 inch tin (p.49). Heat the fat, syrup and treacle gently until melted, then stir in the milk. Cool slightly and mix in the eggs.
Sift the flour, almonds, ground ginger, cinnamon, nutmeg, cloves and soda into a mixing bowl. Make a well in the centre and mix in the liquids. Beat with a wooden spoon into a smooth batter. Scatter over half the remaining ingredients and fold in. Repeat with the rest. Pour into the prepared tin and bake in the centre of a preheated cool oven at 150°C/300°F, Gas Mark 2, for 1¾ to 2 hours, until a skewer inserted comes out clean. Allow to shrink before turning out on to a wire tray to cool. When cold, mix the unsifted icing sugar with just enough lemon juice to make a spreading consistency. Spread it over the top of the cake. It should be fairly thick and lumpy, like snow.
Decorate with some pieces of crystallized ginger.

Quick chocolate sandwich cake

This eggless cake is inexpensive of both time and money, but tastes quite rich. Vegetable oil can be used instead of cooking fat if preferred. This is a very suitable recipe for the electric mixer.

METRIC	IMPERIAL
50 g cooking fat	2 oz cooking fat
50 g golden syrup	2 oz golden syrup
250 ml milk	8 fl oz milk
175 g plain flour	6 oz plain flour
25 g cocoa	1 oz cocoa
50 g sugar	2 oz sugar
1 teaspoon bicarbonate of soda	1 teaspoon bicarbonate of soda
3 teaspoons baking powder	3 teaspoons baking powder
1 tablespoon wine vinegar	1 tablespoon wine vinegar
1 tablespoon water	1 tablespoon water
¼ teaspoon vanilla essence	¼ teaspoon vanilla essence
TO FINISH:	TO FINISH:
raspberry jam	raspberry jam
icing sugar	icing sugar

MAKES ONE 18 CM/7 INCH CAKE

Grease two 18 cm/7 inch sandwich tins. Melt the fat and syrup in the milk in a saucepan over moderate heat. Mix well and cool.

Sift the dry ingredients into a mixing bowl. Pour in the cooled liquid and beat well. Add the vinegar, water and vanilla, then beat again. Pour the mixture into the sandwich tins. Spread out evenly and cook in the centre of a preheated hot oven at 220°C/425°F, Gas Mark 7 for 15 to 20 minutes. Remove from the oven and cool on a wire tray. Sandwich together with raspberry jam and dredge the top with icing sugar sifted through a paper doyley.

Gingerbread loaf; Quick chocolate sandwich cake;
Rich fruited gingerbread

Biscuits

Biscuits and cookies are made by similar methods to cakes. The fat is either rubbed in (see page 50), creamed (see page 54) or melted (see page 64).

Oat biscuits

METRIC	IMPERIAL
100 g flour	*4 oz flour*
½ teaspoon salt	*½ teaspoon salt*
100 g rolled oats	*4 oz rolled oats*
50 g caster sugar	*2 oz caster sugar*
65 g lard or margarine	*2½ oz lard or margarine*
1 egg, beaten	*1 egg, beaten*
2-3 tablespoons milk	*2-3 tablespoons milk*

MAKES ABOUT 24

Sift the flour and salt into a mixing bowl. Mix in the rolled oats and sugar. Cut the fat into the mixture then rub in with the fingertips to a breadcrumb consistency. Bind with the beaten egg, adding a little milk as necessary to make a stiff dough. Roll out on a floured board thinly. With a plain cutter, cut out 7 cm/2½ inch rounds. Place on a greased baking sheet. Work up, roll and cut out the scraps. Bake in a preheated moderate oven at 180°C/350°F, Gas Mark 4 for 15 minutes or until crisp and golden. Cool on a wire tray.

Variation

Coat one side of the biscuits with Chocolate Glacé Icing (p.150) or melted chocolate.

Wheatmeal biscuits

These biscuits are slightly sweetened and are very good served with cream cheese. They can be made with soft brown sugar instead of white, if preferred.

METRIC	IMPERIAL
225 g wholemeal flour	*8 oz wholemeal flour*
pinch of salt	*pinch of salt*
25 g sugar	*1 oz sugar*
150 g butter or margarine	*5 oz butter or margarine*
1 egg, beaten	*1 egg, beaten*

MAKES ABOUT 24

Mix the flour, salt and sugar together. Cut the fat into the flour and rub in to a breadcrumb consistency. Stir in the beaten egg and knead into a stiff dough. (If the egg is small you may need a teaspoon of water.)
Roll out thinly on a board sprinkled with wheatmeal flour and cut into round biscuits with a plain cutter. Place on a greased baking sheet. Work up, roll and cut out the trimmings. Bake in a preheated moderate oven at 180°C/350°F, Gas Mark 4 until crisp and golden. Cool on a wire tray and store in an airtight container.

Top shelf: Coconut crisps
Bottom shelf: Sugared walnut biscuits; Oat biscuits;
Wheatmeal biscuits

Coconut crisps

These crisp little biscuits are delicate in texture and make a nice change to serve with ice cream instead of the usual wafer biscuits.

METRIC	IMPERIAL
175 g self-raising flour	6 oz self-raising flour
50 g desiccated coconut	2 oz desiccated coconut
75 g caster sugar	3 oz caster sugar
150 g butter or margarine	5 oz butter or margarine
2 eggs, separated	2 eggs, separated
50 g shredded coconut	2 oz shredded coconut
MAKES 16	

Mix together the flour, desiccated coconut and sugar. Cut the fat into the mixture and rub in to a breadcrumb consistency. Beat the egg yolks and stir into the mixture. Knead thoroughly into a stiff smooth dough. Relax in a cool place for 30 minutes. Roll out thinly on a floured board. Prick all over and cut into 5 cm/2 inch rounds. Place a little apart on a greased baking sheet. Work up, roll and cut out the trimmings. Brush the biscuits with beaten egg white and cover with shredded coconut.
Bake in a preheated moderate oven at 180°C/350°F, Gas Mark 4 for 15 minutes until set and golden. Cool on a wire tray and store in an airtight tin.

Almond crisps

Follow the recipe for Coconut Crisps and substitute 50 g/2 oz ground almonds for the desiccated coconut and top with flaked or nibbed almonds instead of the shredded coconut.

Sugared walnut biscuits

These are excellent biscuits to serve with coffee, port, or a sweet white wine.

METRIC	IMPERIAL
150 g plain flour	6 oz plain flour
120 g butter	4 ½ oz butter
75 g walnuts, ground	3 oz walnuts, ground
50 g caster sugar	2 oz caster sugar
2 teaspoons grated lemon rind	2 teaspoons grated lemon rind
1 egg, separated	1 egg, separated
1 tablespoon sherry or rum	1 tablespoon sherry or rum
approx. 1-2 teaspoons lemon juice	approx. 1-2 teaspoons lemon juice
cube sugar, crushed, for topping	cube sugar, crushed, for topping
MAKES 24 TO 36	

Sift the flour into a mixing bowl. Cut the fat into the flour and rub into a breadcrumb consistency. Mix in the nuts, caster sugar and lemon rind. Beat the egg yolk and sherry or rum together and mix in. Add enough lemon juice to make a fairly stiff dough. Knead until smooth, then chill for 30 minutes. Roll out to 1.5 cm/½ inch thick, cut into rounds with a fluted 5 cm/2 inch cutter and place on a greased baking tray. Beat the egg white until liquid then brush it over the biscuits and sprinkle with coarsely crushed loaf sugar. Bake in a preheated moderate oven at 175°/350°F, Gas Mark 4 for 15 to 20 minutes until golden. Cool on a wire tray and store in a tin or airtight container.

Sweet biscuit dough

This basic biscuit dough can be cut into a variety of shapes and left plain or coated with an icing and decorated to taste.

METRIC	IMPERIAL
125 g butter	*5 oz butter*
2-3 teaspoons grated lemon rind or ¼ teaspoon vanilla essence	*2-3 teaspoons grated lemon rind or ¼ teaspoon vanilla essence*
100 g caster sugar	*4 oz caster sugar*
2 egg yolks	*2 egg yolks*
225 g plain flour, sifted	*8 oz plain flour, sifted*

MAKES 24 TO 36 ACCORDING TO SIZE

Cream the butter with the sugar and lemon rind or vanilla essence until light and smooth. Gradually beat in the egg yolks, then the flour and knead lightly. Chill for 30 minutes or until stiff. Roll out the dough thinly on a floured board, using a floured rolling pin. Brush off any flour on top of the dough and cut into shapes in one of the following ways:

1. Using a 5 cm/2 inch cutter, cut into round biscuits.
2. Cut into rounds, then using the same cutter, in half so you have a crescent on the left and an oval on the right. Separate the shapes.
3. Cut larger rounds using a 7.5 cm/3 inch cutter. Stamp out the centre of each round with a 2.5 cm/1 inch cutter. Separate the rings. Either lightly knead the centres together and roll out to make more rings, or bake the rounds then sandwich together in pairs with jam or Butter Cream (p.151).

To bake: chill the biscuits until stiff to stop them spreading during baking. Place on a greased baking sheet and bake in a preheated moderate oven at 175°C/350°F, Gas Mark 4 about 10 minutes or until set and golden. Cool on a wire tray and serve plain or decorated to taste.

To decorate: spread with Glacé Icing (p.150) and top with whole or chopped nuts, glacé cherries, angelica, or little cake decorations (see Glacé Fancies p.58).

Dutch moppen

These crisp butter cookies are ideal to serve with ices or after-dinner coffee. Walnut halves can be used instead of almonds.

METRIC	IMPERIAL
100 g butter	*4 oz butter*
75 g caster sugar	*3 oz caster sugar*
125 g self-raising flour, sifted	*5 oz self-raising flour, sifted*
6 blanched almonds	*6 blanched almonds*
1 egg, beaten	*1 egg beaten*

MAKES 12

Cream the butter and sugar together until smooth. Work in the flour. Knead on a floured board into a large ball, working in a little more flour if it is too greasy. Scoop off small pieces with a teaspoon and roll into walnut-size balls. Place on a greased baking sheet at least 5 cm/2 inches apart to allow for spreading. Flatten the balls slightly. Split the almonds into two and press a half in the centre of each cookie. Brush the tops over with beaten egg. Bake in the centre of a preheated moderately hot oven at 190°C/375°F, Gas Mark 5 for about 10 minutes or until golden. Lift the biscuits off the baking sheet with a palette knife and cool on a wire tray. Store in an airtight tin or plastic container.

Sweet biscuit dough, plain and decorated; Dutch moppen; Cherry and nut crinkles; French honey and fruit biscuits

Cherry and nut crinkles

These are thin and crunchy. They can be made with coarsely chopped walnuts instead of almonds if preferred, and with candied orange peel instead of cherries.

METRIC	IMPERIAL
50 g butter	2 oz butter
50 g caster sugar	2 oz caster sugar
40 g plain flour, sifted	1½ oz plain flour, sifted
50 g glacé cherries, coarsely chopped	2 oz glacé cherries, coarsely chopped
50 g flaked almonds	2 oz flaked almonds

MAKES 10 TO 12

Beat the butter and sugar together until creamy. Work in the flour and cherries and then the flaked almonds. Put teaspoonfuls of the mixture on a greased baking sheet about 7.5 cm/3 inches apart to allow for spreading. Bake in a preheated moderately hot oven at 190°C/375°F, Gas Mark 5 for 7 to 8 minutes until brown. Allow to cool slightly, then remove from the baking sheet with a palette knife and cool on a wire tray. Store in an airtight tin or plastic container.

French honey and fruit biscuits

These are one of the many varieties of petit fours and are a marvellous way to use trimmings of French Flan Pastry or Almond Pastry. Any mixture of glacé or crystallized fruit can be used. Apricot jam or ginger marmalade can be used to sandwich them together instead of honey.

METRIC	IMPERIAL
75 g glacé or crystallized fruit, finely chopped	3 oz glacé or crystallized fruit, finely chopped
1 tablespoon rum	1 tablespoon rum
100 g French Flan Pastry trimmings (p.84) or Almond Pastry (p.85)	4 oz French Flan Pastry trimmings (p.84) or Almond Pastry (p.85)
3-4 tablespoons thick honey icing sugar for dusting	3-4 tablespoons thick honey icing sugar for dusting

MAKES ABOUT 9

Soak the fruit in the rum for at least 30 minutes. Roll out the pastry, sprinkle with the fruit, fold it up and knead lightly until the fruit is well mixed into the dough. Roll out fairly thinly and cut into 5 cm/2 inch rounds. Place on a greased baking sheet and bake in a preheated moderately hot oven at 190°C/375°F, Gas Mark 5 for 10 to 12 minutes until set and golden. Cool on a wire tray and sandwich together in pairs with honey. Dust lightly with sieved icing sugar.

Butterscotch nut brownies

These American cookies are made by the melting method and taste like delicious baked fudge. They keep well provided they are well hidden. Blanched almonds and cashew nuts can be used instead of walnuts and hazelnuts.

METRIC	IMPERIAL
50 g butter or margarine	2 oz butter or margarine
225 g soft brown sugar	8 oz soft brown sugar
1 egg, beaten	1 egg, beaten
¼ teaspoon vanilla essence	¼ teaspoon vanilla essence
50 g plain flour	2 oz plain flour
1 teaspoon baking powder	1 teaspoon baking powder
½ teaspoon salt	½ teaspoon salt
100 g hazelnuts and walnuts, coarsely chopped	4 oz hazelnuts and walnuts, coarsely chopped

MAKES 16

Grease and line the base of a shallow 20 cm/8 inch square tin (p.49). Melt the fat in a saucepan over gentle heat, then mix in the sugar and stir until dissolved. Cool slightly and beat in the egg and vanilla essence. Sift the flour together with baking powder and salt and mix in thoroughly. Stir in the nuts and pour into the prepared tin. Bake in a preheated moderately hot oven at 190°C/375°F, Gas Mark 5 for about 30 minutes or until set, but not hard.
Cut into 16 squares while still hot, then allow to cool in the tin. When cold, lift out carefully and store in an airtight tin or plastic container.

Coconut brownies

Follow the recipe for Butterscotch Nut Brownies and substitute 50 g/2 oz grated or desiccated coconut for the chopped nuts.

Butterscotch nut brownies; Date and lemon crunchies

Date and lemon crunchies

These are good biscuits to include in a packed lunch for hikers and outdoor workers as they are very sustaining.

METRIC	IMPERIAL
100 g butter or margarine	4 oz butter or margarine
100 g soft brown sugar	4 oz soft brown sugar
3 tablespoons golden syrup	3 tablespoons golden syrup
2 teaspoons grated lemon rind	2 teaspoons grated lemon rind
175 g rolled oats	6 oz rolled oats
50 g wholemeal flour	2 oz wholemeal flour
1 teaspoon baking powder	1 teaspoon baking powder
100 g stoned dates, chopped	4 oz stoned dates, chopped
1 tablespoon lemon juice	1 tablespoon lemon juice

MAKES 16

Melt the fat with the sugar, golden syrup, sugar and grated lemon rind in a saucepan over gentle heat. Stir well and do not allow to boil. Set aside to cool. Mix together the rolled oats, flour and baking powder. Stir in the cooled liquid ingredients and mix very thoroughly.
Turn half the mixture into a greased 18 cm/7 inch square tin, spread out evenly and press down with a wooden spoon. Mix the chopped dates with the lemon juice and spread over the oat mixture. Cover with the remaining mixture and press down firmly.
Bake in a preheated moderate oven at 180°C/350°F, Gas Mark 4 for 20 to 30 minutes until firm and golden. Remove from the oven and cut into 16 equal portions. Allow to cool then remove from the tin and cool on a wire tray. When cold store in an airtight container.

Date and apple crunchies

Follow the recipe for Date and Lemon Crunchies but omit the lemon rind and juice and add to the chopped stoned dates 225 g/8 oz apples peeled, cored and finely chopped or coarsely grated.

Savoury biscuits

These are delicious served with aperitifs or after dinner coffee.

Cheese and almond sablés

METRIC	IMPERIAL
75 g plain flour	3 oz plain flour
½ teaspoon paprika	½ teaspoon paprika
salt	salt
freshly ground black pepper	freshly ground black pepper
50 g butter or lard	2 oz butter or lard
25 g ground almonds	1 oz ground almonds
40 g hard cheese, grated	1½ oz hard cheese, grated
1 egg yolk	1 egg yolk
TO GLAZE:	TO GLAZE:
1 egg, beaten	1 egg, beaten
3-4 tablespoons grated cheese	3-4 tablespoons grated cheese

MAKES 24

Sift the flour, paprika, salt and pepper into a mixing bowl. Cut the fat into the flour and rub in to a breadcrumb consistency. Mix in the almonds and grated cheese. Stir in the egg yolk and mix into a soft dough. Roll out to 5 mm/¼ inch thick. Cut out 5 cm/2 inch rounds and place on a greased baking sheet. Brush with beaten egg and sprinkle thickly with grated cheese. Bake in a preheated moderate oven at 175°C/350°F, Gas Mark 4 for 10 minutes or until set and golden brown. Remove from the oven and cool slightly before removing from the baking tray. Serve warm or cold.

Parmesan biscuits

These are very rich, crunchy biscuits, like a cheese shortbread, ideal to serve with drinks.

METRIC	IMPERIAL
50 g salted butter	2 oz salted butter
50 g plain flour	2 oz plain flour
pinch of cayenne pepper	pinch of cayenne pepper
freshly ground black pepper	freshly ground black pepper
50 g grated Parmesan cheese	2 oz grated Parmesan cheese

MAKES 18 TO 24

Cream the butter. Season the flour with cayenne and black pepper and gradually work into the butter with the cheese. Knead until smooth and refrigerate for about 30 minutes or until stiffened. Roll out on a floured board to 5 mm/¼ inch thick. Cut into small rounds or squares and using a palette knife place on a greased baking tray. Work up the trimmings, pinch off little pieces and roll into balls. Place on the baking tray and flatten into biscuits. Prick well with a fork. Bake in a preheated moderate oven at 175°C/350°F, Gas Mark 4 for about 10 minutes until set and golden. Cool on a wire tray and store in an airtight container.

Parmesan biscuits; Cheese and almond sablés

Pastries

Pastry making is much enjoyed by many home bakers and like any other manual craft, perfection comes by practice, and by remembering certain important rules.

Pointers to successful pastry making

1. Keep everything cool; ingredients, equipment and your hands and work in a cool place if possible.
2. Always sift the flour when rubbing in fat. Use only the tips of the fingers, lifting your hands well above the bowl to aerate the flour. If you squeeze the mixture in the palms of your hands, the warmth will soften the fat and make the dough sticky and heavy.
3. Use freshly drawn water or iced water, and a knife with a rounded blade for mixing.
4. Add the water cautiously. If you add too much and have to work in extra flour to make the dough manageable, it will alter the proportion of flour to fat and bake into a hard crust. If the dough is too wet, it will shrink during cooking.
5. Allow the dough to rest in the refrigerator or cool place for a short time after mixing, especially in hot weather.
6. Roll out the pastry with quick short strokes, lifting up the rolling pin between each stroke. If you 'steam-roller' it across from side to side you will press out all the air bubbles from the pastry. Always roll away from yourself, never towards you, and sideways only when you are shaping the pastry.
7. Move the pastry about the board from time to time to make sure it is not sticking underneath. Keep the rolling pin floured and clean; do not allow any bits of dough to stick to it. Always roll one side only, never turn the pastry upside down.
8. Use the rolled side of the pastry for the upper side of a pie crust, and remove any surplus flour with a pastry brush.
9. Be careful not to stretch the pastry when putting it over a pie or lining a tin; ease it in, or it will shrink during baking and lose its shape.
10. Always cook in a preheated oven so the pastry rises quickly as the air bubbles expand and the fat globules mingle with the swelling starch grains to make the pastry light and crisp. If the temperature is too low, the fat will melt and run out leaving the pastry heavy and probably tough. Shortcrust pastry is baked at 200°C/400°F, Gas Mark 6 to 220°C/425°F, Gas Mark 7 and richer, flaky pastries at 230°C/450°F, Gas Mark 8.

To glaze pastries

Savoury pastries are brushed with beaten egg, or egg yolk diluted with a little milk. Sweet pastries can be brushed lightly with water and dredged with sugar, or for a sparkly glaze, brushed with beaten egg white and sprinkled with caster sugar.

To store pastry

Uncooked dough will keep for several days in the refrigerator. It must be well covered, preferably in a polythene bag to keep out the air. If well sealed it also freezes very successfully.

Cooked pastries can be kept for two or three days in an airtight tin or plastic container unless they contain a perishable filling. They usually freeze and reheat successfully. Flan cases should be stored empty and filled on the day required, as the filling will make the bottom crust soggy.

Weighing pastry dough

The quantity of pastry given in a recipe is measured by the weight of flour used in it; that is, 225 g/8 oz plain shortcrust means pastry made with 225 g/8 oz flour and 100 g/4 oz fat (finished weight is 350 g/12 oz). If you buy ready-made pastry dough, it is measured by the finished weight, that is 225 g/8 oz shortcrust dough would contain only 150 g/5 oz flour and 65 g/2½ oz fat, so it would not be sufficient for a recipe requiring 225 g/8 oz pastry.

Shortcrust pastry

Plain shortcrust pastry

This pastry contains half as much fat as flour. The fat can be butter, lard, margarine or vegetable shortening, or a blend of any two. The combination of butter and lard is particularly good, because the butter gives flavour and the lard a crisp, short texture. The fat is rubbed into the flour, which can be plain or self-raising.

METRIC	IMPERIAL
225 g flour	8 oz flour
pinch of salt	pinch of salt
50 g butter	2 oz butter
50 g lard	2 oz lard
cold water to mix	cold water to mix

MAKES 225 G/8 OZ PASTRY

Sift the flour and salt into a mixing bowl. Cut the fat into the flour, toss until well coated, then rub it in with the fingertips to a breadcrumb consistency.
Gradually stir in cold water until beginning to bind. Gather together with the fingers, add a little more water if too crumbly. Work into a soft, not sticky, ball of dough leaving the bowl clean.
The pastry is now ready to use, or to be relaxed in a cool place.

English fruit pie

The traditional English fruit pie is made in a deep oval or round pie dish with a lip.
Any fresh fruit in season is prepared and piled into the dish with sugar, sometimes spiced, and covered with pastry, usually shortcrust.

Plum pie

METRIC	IMPERIAL
900 g plums	2 lb plums
50-75 g sugar	2-3 oz sugar
approx. 2 tablespoons water	approx. 2 tablespoons water
225 g Plain Shortcrust Pastry	8 oz Plain Shortcrust Pastry
caster sugar for dredging	caster sugar for dredging

Filling the pie: wash the plums. Cut round the natural crease of each plum with a small sharp knife. Twist the two halves against each other and remove the stone. Place the plums, cut side down in a 1.2 litre/2 pint pie dish and sprinkle each layer with sugar. Pile up the fruit in the centre of the dish so the pastry will be domed. Add about two tablespoons water. Reduce the water according to any increase in the quantity of sugar, as the fruit produces a lot of juice during cooking which will boil up through the crust if there is too much.

Covering the pie: roll out the pastry to about 5 mm/¼ inch thick. Cut off a strip the same width as the lip of the pie dish. Damp the dish lip with a pastry brush and press on the strip of pastry. Damp the pastry strip. Roll the remaining pastry round the rolling pin from the far side towards you. Unroll it from the near end, back over the pie and press the lid firmly on to the strip. This will prevent the lid from shrinking off the lip of the dish when it is baked. Trim the edges off neatly with a sharp knife; slice it off, do not saw it.

Rolling pastry over the pie

Knocking back the pastry edge

Knocking back: with the forefinger of your left hand (if right-handed) press the lid down and outwards. With a knife held horizontally in the other hand, the back of it towards the pastry, knock back the pastry, flaking the edge. Mark in ridges with the tines of a fork held vertically.

Baking: place the pie on a baking sheet and cook in a preheated hot oven at 220°C/425°F, Gas Mark 7 for 15 minutes to raise the pastry, then lower the heat to 190°C/375°F, Gas Mark 5 for 20 to 25 minutes to cook the fruit. When crisp and golden, remove the pie and dredge with caster sugar. It is best served hot, with cream or custard.

Greengage or apricot pie: make as Plum Pie.

Apple pie: peel, core and slice cooking apples. Sweeten with white or brown sugar and spice with a few whole cloves.

Blackberry and apple pie: make as apple pie, replacing some of the sliced apple with cleaned blackberries and omitting the cloves.

Cherry pie: stalk and stone the cherries. Add a pinch of cinnamon to the sugar.

Gooseberry pie: top, tail and wash the gooseberries. Sweeten well and omit the water.

Rhubarb pie: trim off the leaves and the white base of the stalks and cut into 2.5 cm/1 inch lengths. Add the grated rind of an orange to the sugar. Using orange juice instead of water will give a delightful flavour.

Plum pie, before and after baking

Double crust pie

This is baked in a shallow round pie dish with a lip, and has a pastry base as well as lid. The filling can be savoury or sweet. In Lancashire and Yorkshire they like to serve cheese with their apple pies, and an old country saying is 'apple pie without the cheese is like a kiss without a squeeze'. In the following recipe, the cheese is cooked inside the pie with the apples and it makes a happy marriage.

Cheese and apple pie

METRIC	IMPERIAL
750 g cooking apples, peeled, cored and sliced	1½ lb cooking apples, peeled, cored and sliced
2 tablespoons sugar	2 tablespoons sugar
100 g Lancashire or Cheddar cheese, coarsely grated	4 oz Lancashire or Cheddar cheese, coarsely grated
225 g Plain Shortcrust Pastry (p.74)	8 oz Plain Shortcrust Pastry (p.74)
TO GLAZE:	TO GLAZE:
1 egg beaten with 1 tablespoon water	1 egg beaten with 1 tablespoon water

Grease an 18 cm/7 inch shallow round pie dish and damp the lip. Shape the pastry into a ball and divide it in half. Roll out one half thinly into a round and line the pie dish, pressing the pastry on to the lip. Fill with the apples, sprinkling each layer with sugar and grated cheese, reserving some of the cheese for glazing. Roll out the remaining pastry into a round about 5 mm/¼ inch thick and slightly larger than the top of the pie. Damp the edge of the lining pastry, roll the lid over the rolling pin, unroll it over the pie and press the two edges of the pastry firmly together. Trim off the edges and knock back as for English Fruit Pie (p.75), and ridge the edge (p.75).

Brush the top with the beaten egg and water and sprinkle with grated cheese. Place on a baking sheet and bake in a preheated oven at 220°C/425°F, Gas Mark 7 for 20 minutes or until well risen and golden. Reduce the heat to 190°C/375°F, Gas Mark 5 for a further 20 to 25 minutes to cook the apples. Serve hot. A popular choice for high tea.

Cheese and apple pie; Mincemeat and apple tart

Rich shortcrust pastry

This pastry is made with a higher proportion of fat than plain shortcrust, and is also enriched with egg yolk. It needs careful handling and must be rested before rolling out or it will crack. It is used for savoury and sweet pies, flans and open tarts, called plate pies.

METRIC	IMPERIAL
225 g plain flour	8 oz plain flour
pinch of salt	pinch of salt
75 g butter or margarine	3 oz butter or margarine
50 g lard	2 oz lard
1 egg yolk	1 egg yolk
3-4 tablespoons water	3-4 tablespoons water

MAKES 225 G/8 OZ PASTRY

Sift the flour and salt into a mixing bowl. Cut the fat into the flour and rub in to a breadcrumb consistency. Beat the egg yolk with 2 tablespoons water and stir in to bind to a fairly firm dough, adding a little more water as necessary. Knead lightly until smooth but do not overwork it. Leave to rest in the refrigerator or cool place for at least 30 minutes before rolling out.

Mincemeat and apple tart

This is an open tart or plate pie filled with apple and mincemeat. If preferred the apple can be omitted and 2 to 3 tablespoons mincemeat used instead.

METRIC	IMPERIAL
225 g Rich Shortcrust Pastry	8 oz Rich Shortcrust Pastry
1 medium cooking apple, peeled and thinly sliced	1 medium cooking apple, peeled and thinly sliced
1-2 tablespoons sugar	1-2 tablespoons sugar
150 g mincemeat	6 oz mincemeat

Grease the base and damp the lip of a 20 cm/8 inch ovenproof plate or shallow pie dish. Roll out the pastry into a round 5 mm/¼ inch thick and slightly larger than the plate. Cut off a narrow strip from the outer edge and press it on to the damp edge of the plate. Damp the strip with a pastry brush.

Roll the remaining pastry over the rolling pin and unroll it over the plate. Press the pastry edges firmly together and trim off the surplus. Knock back the edge (p.75). Prick the base firmly all over with a fork to stop the pastry blistering during baking. Cover with the apple slices and sprinkle with sugar. Cover with mincemeat. Cut the pastry trimmings into 4 narrow strips. Damp one end of each strip and press it on one side of the pastry edge. Twist it across the pie and secure it on the other side. Cut out 8 small circles or fancy shapes, damp the ends of the pastry strips and cover with the shapes.

Bake in the centre of a preheated moderately hot oven at 190°C/375°F, Gas Mark 5 for 30 to 35 minutes or until crisp and golden. Serve hot with cream or custard.

Flans

These are open tarts shaped and baked in a flan ring instead of a pie plate. In order to get a really crisp base, the pastry case is baked blind (empty) and then filled. If the filling, which can be savoury or sweet, requires baking, it is put into the crisp case and the flan returned to the oven to finish cooking.

Shortcrust Pastry, plain or rich, is used to line the ring. Sweet Shortcrust is usually used for sweet fillings and cheese pastry adds extra flavour to savoury flans.

How much pastry to use: an 18 cm/7 inch flan ring needs 100 g/4 oz pastry. A 20 cm/8 inch flan ring needs 150 g/6 oz pastry. A 22 cm/10 inch flan ring needs 225 g/8 oz pastry.

Apricot flan

Lining a flan ring

1. Chose a flan ring with a fluted edge for a sweet flan, and plain if you prefer, for a savoury flan.

Place it, ungreased, on a greased baking sheet. Roll out the pastry about 5 mm/¼ inch thick, into a round which will extend at least 4 cm/1½ inches beyond the ring all round.

2. Lift the pastry about 2.5 cm/1 inch off the board and let it fall back gently so that it will shrink before it is put into the ring or it may shrink during baking. Fold the pastry edges from the outside into the centre, into a five-side shape, small enough to fit inside the ring.

3. Lift the pastry into the ring, open it out, easing it carefully into the angle at the base of the ring, taking care not to stretch it. Press the pastry into the flutes with a floured finger.

4. Roll the rolling pin firmly across the top of the flan ring

which has a sharp edge which will cut off the surplus pastry. Remove the trimmings and prick the base all over with a fork.

Baking blind

1. Line the flan case with greaseproof paper and cover with a layer of dried beans to prevent the base blistering.
2. Bake in a preheated oven at 200°C/400°F, Gas Mark 6 for 15 to 20 minutes until the sides of the flan are set and golden. Remove from the oven, lift out the lining paper and beans, which can be used repeatedly. Return the flan to the oven for about 5 minutes or until the base is crisp.
3. Remove from the oven, allow the pastry to shrink slightly, then carefully lift off the flan ring. Use a fish slice under the flan when moving it, do not lift it by the sides as they are thin and brittle.

Sweet shortcrust pastry

This sweetened rich shortcrust is used for French fruit flans, tarts and little fancy cakes.

METRIC	IMPERIAL
225 g plain flour	8 oz plain flour
pinch of salt	pinch of salt
50 g butter	2 oz butter
50 g lard or vegetable	2 oz lard or vegetable
shortening	shortening
25 g caster sugar	1 oz caster sugar
1 egg yolk	1 egg yolk
a little water	a little water

MAKES 225 G/8 OZ PASTRY

Follow the recipe for Rich Shortcrust Pastry (p.77) mixing in the sugar after rubbing in the fat. Mix to a firm dough with the egg and water. Knead lightly until smooth and rest well before rolling it out.

Fruit flan

Sweet Shortcrust is the best pastry for this flan case, and ripe fresh fruit or firm, well drained canned fruit for the filling. Fresh strawberries and raspberries are excellent, but not when canned or frozen as they are then too soft and juicy and will soak into the pastry case. You can use all one fruit or two of contrasting colour which can be arranged in an attractive pattern of circles or wedges. Coat red fruits with Red Currant Glaze (p.152) and light coloured or mixed fruits with Apricot Glaze.

Apricot flan

The pastry case can be made in advance and stored in a tin or frozen, but should be filled on the day it is required. Serve with a jug of pouring cream or a bowl of clotted cream.

METRIC	IMPERIAL
1 × 18 cm Sweet Shortcrust	1 × 7 inch Sweet Shortcrust
flan case, baked blind	flan case, baked blind
450 g ripe apricots or 450 g	1 lb ripe apricots or 1 lb
canned apricot halves	canned apricot halves
25 g blanched almonds	1 oz blanched almonds
100 g Apricot Glaze	4 oz Apricot Glaze

Place the baked flan case on the serving plate as it is better to avoid lifting it after filling. Wash and stalk the fresh apricots and remove the stones as for plums (p.74). If using canned fruit, drain thoroughly in a large sieve and use some of the syrup instead of water in the glaze. Arrange the apricots, cut side uppermost, neatly in concentric circles. Place a blanched almond in the centre of each half.
Make the apricot glaze (p.152) and as soon as it is ready strain it over the fruit, coating it evenly and completely. Brush a little remaining glaze round the top edge of the flan case to finish. Serve the same day.

Variations

1. Ripe fresh greengages or Victoria plums with Apricot Glaze.
2. Ripe fresh strawberries, raspberries or loganberries with Red Currant Glaze.

Sweet tartlets

Sweet Shortcrust Pastry is best for tartlets with a sweet filling and small deep patty pans (5 cm/2 inches × 1.5 cm/½ inch deep) are preferable to the larger shallow type. For some recipes the pastry cases are baked blind and for others the filling is baked with the pastry.

Balmoral tarts

These rich tea-time treats are reputed to have been favourites with Queen Victoria and her household.

METRIC	IMPERIAL
100 g Sweet Shortcrust Pastry (p.79)	*4 oz Sweet Shortcrust Pastry (p.79)*
50 g butter	*2 oz butter*
50 g caster sugar	*2 oz caster sugar*
1 egg, separated	*1 egg, separated*
25 g cake crumbs	*1 oz cake crumbs*
15 g glacé cherries, chopped	*½ oz glacé cherries, chopped*
15 g mixed chopped peel	*½ oz mixed chopped peel*
½ teaspoon cornflour	*½ teaspoon cornflour*
1 teaspoon brandy, optional	*1 teaspoon brandy, optional*
sieved icing sugar to finish	*sieved icing sugar to finish*

MAKES ABOUT 8

Roll out the pastry thinly, just under 5 mm/¼ inch thick. Cut out rounds about 2.5 cm/1 inch larger than the top of the patty pans, using a fluted cutter. Grease the pans, then line with the pastry and prick the base with a fork. Place them on a baking sheet.
Soften the butter, beat in the sugar and when creamy beat in the egg yolk. Stir in the crumbs, chopped cherries and peel and the cornflour and mix well with the brandy if used. Whisk the egg white until stiff but still moist, and fold into the mixture. Fill the pastry cases with the mixture and bake in a preheated moderately hot oven at 190°C/375°F, Gas Mark 5 for 20 minutes or until set and golden. Allow the tarts to shrink slightly before lifting out on to a wire tray to cool. When cold, sift icing sugar over the tops.

Custard tarts

A rich egg custard flavoured with vanilla and sprinkled with spice makes a delightfully smooth filling for these crisp pastry tarts.

METRIC	IMPERIAL
175 g Sweet Shortcrust Pastry (p.79)	*6 oz Sweet Shortcrust Pastry (p.79)*
450 ml milk	*¾ pint milk*
2 eggs	*2 eggs*
2-3 teaspoons sugar	*2-3 teaspoons sugar*
¼ teaspoon vanilla essence	*¼ teaspoon vanilla essence*
grated nutmeg to finish	*grated nutmeg to finish*

MAKES 8

Roll out the pastry thinly and line greased patty pans as for Balmoral Tarts. Bake blind (see barquettes on page 83) in a preheated moderately hot oven at 200°C/400°F, Gas Mark 6 for 12 to 15 minutes until set but not brown, then remove from the oven. Lower the heat to 170°C/325°F,

Gas Mark 3. Warm the milk over a low heat and meanwhile beat the eggs and sugar together. Stir the warm milk into the beaten eggs and flavour with vanilla. Strain the custard into the partially baked cases. Sprinkle the tops with grated nutmeg and return the tarts to the centre of the oven for 15 to 20 minutes until the custard is set. Serve cold.

Balmoral tarts; Individual fruit tarts; Custard tarts

Individual fruit tarts

These can be served for tea or as dessert at a buffet lunch. In summer fresh strawberries, raspberries, loganberries and stoned cherries are popular. In winter you can use grapes, sliced banana, canned mandarins, pineapple wedges, sliced apricots and stoned cherries. 225 g/8 oz Sweet Shortcrust Pastry makes approximately 12 tarts. Choose shallow patty pans approximately 5 cm/3 inches in diameter and grease them; and a fluted cutter a size larger.

Roll out the pastry very thinly, less than 5 mm/¼ inch thick. Cut out the pastry circles, line the tins with them and prick the base. Place them on a baking sheet and bake blind (p.79) in a preheated moderately hot oven at 200°C/400°F, Gas Mark 6 for about 15 minutes or until crisp and golden. Remove from the oven and lift out the paper and beans.

When cold, fill the tarts with the fresh or canned fruit, arranged in an attractive pattern. Glaze thinly with Red Currant Glaze for red fruit, or Apricot Glaze (p.152) for yellow and light coloured or mixed fruits.

Serve individual tarts the day they are filled. The tartlet cases can be baked in advance and stored in an airtight container and filled as required.

Cheese shortcrust pastry

This pastry is used for savoury flans, tartlets and barquettes (little boat shapes), biscuits, canapés and hors d'oeuvres.

METRIC	IMPERIAL
175 g plain flour	6 oz plain flour
¼ teaspoon salt	¼ teaspoon salt
¼ teaspoon dry mustard	¼ teaspoon dry mustard
50 g lard	2 oz lard
25 g butter	1 oz butter
75 g dry Cheddar cheese, grated	3 oz dry Cheddar cheese, grated
1 egg yolk	1 egg yolk
cold water to mix	cold water to mix

MAKES 175 G/6 OZ PASTRY

Sift the flour, salt and mustard into a mixing bowl. Cut the fat into the flour and rub in to a breadcrumb consistency. Mix in the grated cheese and bind with the egg yolk and a little water as for rich shortcrust, into a soft but not sticky dough. Rest the pastry in the refrigerator or cool place for 30 minutes before rolling out.

Tarte ricotta

This savoury Italian flan is excellent made with a mixture of cream and curd cheese when ricotta is not available. You can buy smoked salmon trimmings or frozen 'cocktail pieces' inexpensively and Westphalian smoked ham instead of Parma prosciutto (ham).

METRIC	IMPERIAL
175 g Cheese Shortcrust Pastry	6 oz Cheese Shortcrust Pastry
225 g ricotta cheese or 100 g cream cheese and 100 g curd cheese	8 oz ricotta cheese or 4 oz cream cheese and 4 oz curd cheese
salt	salt
freshly ground black pepper	freshly ground black pepper
2 eggs, beaten	2 eggs, beaten
50 g smoked salmon trimmings, or Parma or Westphalian ham	2 oz smoked salmon trimmings, or Parma or Westphalian ham
50 g gruyère cheese	2 oz gruyère cheese

Roll out the pastry into a round 5 mm/¼ inch thick and line a 20-23 cm/8-9 inch flan ring (p.78) and bake blind (p.79) in a preheated moderately hot oven at 200°C/400°F or Gas Mark 6. Sieve the ricotta or cream and curd cheeses into a mixing bowl through a wire sieve, using a wooden spoon, and season with salt and pepper to taste. Gradually stir in the beaten eggs. Do not beat vigorously or the mixture may curdle. Cut the smoked salmon or ham into shreds and mix it with the cheese.
Turn the mixture into the pastry case and level the top. Slice the gruyère cheese very thinly into triangles or strips about 3 cm/1 inch wide. Arrange the pieces, overlapping slightly in a pattern on top of the filling.
Bake in the preheated oven for 30 minutes or until the filling is well risen and golden brown. Serve hot with a tossed green salad garnished with stoned black olives as a first course for 6 or for lunch or supper as a main dish for 4. Remaining pastry can be made into barquettes.

Ricotta barquettes

Place 12 or more greased boat-shaped patty tins, according to size, on a baking sheet in rows touching each other. Roll out the remaining pastry 5 mm/¼ inch thick into a rectangle which will extend a little beyond the outside of the tins. Lay the pastry over the tins loosely and ease it into the hollows. Roll the rolling pin firmly over the tins so cutting the pastry off at the edges. Lift off the trimmings. Pinch off a small piece of dough and roll it into a small ball. Use it to press the pastry lining down into the tins. Prick the base of the barquettes. Line with scraps of greaseproof paper and put in dried beans.

Chill the pastries for 20 minutes, then bake blind in a preheated moderately hot oven at 200°C/400°F, Gas Mark 6 for about 15 minutes or until set. Remove from the oven, lift out the beans and fill with half quantity of the ricotta mixture, two-thirds full. Top with thin slivers of gruyère cheese and return to the oven for 15 minutes or until the filling is well risen and golden. Serve hot as hors d'oeuvres or cocktail snacks.

Tarte ricotta; French onion tarts

French onion tarts

These individual savoury tarts make an excellent first course for dinner, or for a buffet lunch.

METRIC	IMPERIAL
175 g Cheese Shortcrust Pastry (p.82)	6 oz Cheese Shortcrust Pastry (p.82)
25 g butter	1 oz butter
1 tablespoon oil	1 tablespoon oil
500 g onions, peeled and finely sliced	1 lb onions, peeled and finely sliced
75 ml double cream	3 fl oz double cream
75 ml single cream	3 fl oz single cream
2 egg yolks	2 egg yolks
salt	salt
freshly ground black pepper	freshly ground black pepper
pinch of grated nutmeg	pinch of grated nutmeg
TO GARNISH:	TO GARNISH:
black olives, stoned	black olives, stoned
sprigs of parsley	sprigs of parsley
MAKES 6	

Roll out the pastry very thinly. Line 6 tartlet tins measuring 7.5 cm/3 inches at base and 10 cm/4 inches across the top. Prick the base, then bake blind (p.79) in a preheated moderately hot oven at 200°C/400°F, Gas Mark 6 for 15 minutes or until set and slightly coloured. Lower the heat to 180°C/350°F, Gas Mark 4.

To make the filling, heat the butter and oil in a pan, add the onions and cook, covered, for about 20 to 30 minutes until softened but not browned. Stir occasionally.

Beat the egg yolks together with the cream in a bowl and stir in the cooked onion. Season with salt and freshly ground black pepper and a pinch of nutmeg. Remove the pastry cases from the tins and spoon in the filling. Return them to the oven and bake for a further 20 minutes or until the filling is set and golden brown on top.

Serve hot, each tart garnished with a stoned black olive and fresh parsley.

French flan pastry
(Pâte sucrée)

This rich sweet pastry is very short and crunchy and is made with unsalted butter, caster sugar and egg yolks. No water is used, and the ingredients are worked together with the fingers of one hand on a marble top or pastry board. The dough must be made in advance so that it can be well chilled before using. If removed from a very cold refrigerator, allow the pastry to rest at kitchen temperature for 15 minutes before rolling out. This pastry is used for flan cases and tartlets and the trimmings make excellent biscuits (see French Honey and Fruit Biscuits, page 69).

Basic pâte sucrée

METRIC	IMPERIAL
100 g plain flour	*4 oz plain flour*
pinch of salt	*pinch of salt*
50 g unsalted butter, cut into small pieces	*2 oz unsalted butter, cut into small pieces*
50 g caster sugar	*2 oz caster sugar*
few drops of vanilla essence	*few drops of vanilla essence*
2 egg yolks, beaten	*2 egg yolks, beaten*

Sift the flour and salt on to a marble slab or pastry board. Make a well in the centre of the flour and put in the butter and sugar. Add the vanilla to the egg yolks and drop into the well.
With the fingers of one hand pinch and work the butter, sugar and egg yolks together. Gradually draw in the flour, using a palette knife in the other hand to keep the flour from spreading over the board.
When all the ingredients are amalgamated, knead the dough until smooth. Be careful not to over work the dough as it will become sticky. Put into a plastic bag and leave to relax in a cool place for 2 hours or until required.

Normandy apple flan

METRIC	IMPERIAL
350 g cooking apples, peeled, cored and sliced	*12 oz cooking apples, peeled, cored and sliced*
15 g butter	*½ oz butter*
100 g sugar	*4 oz sugar*
100 g Pâte Sucrée	*4 oz Pâte Sucrée*
3-4 small dessert apples	*3-4 small dessert apples*
juice of 1 lemon	*juice of 1 lemon*
TO GLAZE:	*TO GLAZE:*
75 g butter, melted	*3 oz butter, melted*
50 g caster sugar	*2 oz caster sugar*

Cook the apples with the butter over gentle heat into a thick purée. Sweeten to taste with the sugar. Mash thoroughly or sieve. Leave to cool.
Roll out the pastry thinly and line a 20 cm/8 inch flan ring with it and bake blind (p.79) in a preheated moderately hot oven at 200°C/400°F, Gas Mark 6 for 15 minutes until set. Remove from oven, lift off the ring and the paper or foil lining the flan. Peel, quarter and core the dessert apples. Slice carefully into thin crescents and drop at once into the lemon juice.

Normandy apple flan

Spread the apple purée over the base of the flan case. Arrange on top the apple slices, overlapping in a circle round the outer edge. When the circle is completed, lift the first slice slightly and tuck the edge of the last slice underneath it. Make a smaller circle in the centre, running in the opposite direction. Brush the apples liberally with melted butter and sprinkle with caster sugar.
Return the flan to the oven and bake for a further 15 minutes until the apple slices are softened and golden. Serve with Chantilly Cream (p.152) or clotted cream.

Pâte sucrée ingredients

Pinching together

Aurora tartlets

These tartlets are called Aurora because the filling of peaches coated in red currant glaze is crimson like the sun at dawn. Poached fresh peaches can be used in season, instead of canned.

METRIC	IMPERIAL
175 g Almond Pastry	6 oz Almond Pastry
12 tablespoons Pastry Cream (p.152)	12 tablespoons Pastry Cream (p.152)
12 canned peach halves	12 canned peach halves
Red Currant Glaze (p.152)	Red Currant Glaze (p.152)

Roll out the chilled pastry very thinly and line 12 tartlet tins (p.81). Place on a baking sheet, prick well and line each one with a small piece of kitchen foil. Bake in a preheated moderately hot oven at 200°C/400°F, Gas Mark 6 for 10 minutes. Remove the foil and return the pastry to the oven for a further 5 minutes until crisp and golden. Lift out of the tin and cool on a wire tray.
Put a spoonful of Pastry Cream in each tartlet and place a peach half on top, rounded side uppermost. Warm the red currant glaze and spoon or brush evenly over the peaches. Serve cold.

Below: Aurora tartlets

Almond pastry (Pâte Frolle)

This pastry is made in a similar way to French Flan Pastry and is used for tartlets and petit fours. The trimmings make delicious fancy biscuits.

METRIC	IMPERIAL
175 g plain flour	6 oz plain flour
pinch of salt	pinch of salt
100 g ground almonds	4 oz ground almonds
75 g caster sugar	3 oz caster sugar
100 g butter, softened	4 oz butter, softened
1 egg, beaten	1 egg, beaten
1 teaspoon grated lemon rind	1 teaspoon grated lemon rind

Sift the flour and salt on to a pastry board. Mix in the ground almonds and sugar. Make a well in the centre and add the butter, egg and grated lemon rind. Work together with the fingers of one hand, gradually drawing in the dry ingredients and using a knife in the other hand to gather them together. Knead into a smooth dough. Put into a polythene bag and leave in a cool place to relax for at least one hour before rolling out.

Rough puff pastry

This is a rich pastry with a high proportion of fat which is rolled, instead of rubbed into the dough to give it a flaky texture. It is the quickest of the flaky pastries to make but it is not as light as true flaky or puff pastry. It is best when served hot and reheats very successfully. It also freezes very well.

Rough puff pastry

METRIC	IMPERIAL
225 g plain flour	8 oz plain flour
pinch of salt	pinch of salt
75 g butter	3 oz butter
75 g lard	3 oz lard
1 teaspoon lemon juice	1 teaspoon lemon juice
approx. 250 ml cold water	approx. 8 fl oz cold water

MAKES 225 G/8 OZ PASTRY

Sift the flour and salt into a mixing bowl. Cut the fat into cubes of walnut size and toss them in the flour until well coated. Add the lemon juice to 150 ml/5 fl oz of the cold water and stir it into the flour, leaving the lumps of fat whole. Mix into a dough adding a little more water if necessary to make it bind. With floured fingers, gather the dough into a ball and place it on a floured board. Shape it into a rectangular brick and turn it lengthwise. With a floured pin, roll the dough out with short jerky rolls into a rectangle about 1 cm/½ inch thick. Keep the sides straight and the corners square. Mark the dough across in 3 equal sections.
Fold up the bottom third, keeping the fingers inside and thumbs on top of the dough. Seal the edges to enclose the air in a little 'tent'. Fold down and seal the top third in the same way. Seal all the edges with the rolling pin and give the dough a quarter turn to left or right. Roll out again into a rectangle, still using short jerky movements and lifting the pin frequently so the air is not rolled out of the pastry. Repeat the rolling, folding and turning 3 or 4 times until there are no streaks of fat in the dough. Be careful to keep the rolling pin floured and free from fat. Chill the pastry until quite cold and stiff before using.
Cheese d'artois

Cheese d'artois

These cheese savouries should be served hot and can be made with either Rough Puff or Flaky Pastry.

METRIC	IMPERIAL
50 g butter	2 oz butter
2 eggs	2 eggs
100 g Cheddar cheese, grated	4 oz Cheddar cheese, grated
1 teaspoon paprika	1 teaspoon paprika
salt	salt
freshly ground black pepper	freshly ground black pepper
225 g Rough Puff Pastry	8 oz Rough Puff Pastry
100 g sliced continental smoked sausage, skinned and diced	4 oz sliced continental smoked sausage, skinned and diced
TO GLAZE:	TO GLAZE:
1 egg yolk beaten with 1 tablespoon water	1 egg yolk beaten with 1 tablespoon water

MAKES 12

Melt the butter and leave to cool, but not harden. Beat the eggs in a bowl with a fork and mix in the butter, grated cheese and paprika. Add salt and pepper.
Divide the pastry dough in half and roll out each half thinly (less than 5 mm/¼ inch) into a rectangle 15 x 20 cm/6 x 8 inches. Place one half on the baking sheet and mark it lightly into 5 cm/2 inch squares. Put some smoked sausage in each square and cover with the cheese mixture. Brush the edges of the pastry round the fillings with water, cover with the remaining sheet of pastry and mark the top into corresponding squares. Press the damp edges firmly together.
Brush all over with the beaten egg yolk and water. Cut 2 or 3 slits in the top of each square to let the steam escape. Bake in a preheated hot oven at 230°C/450°F, Gas Mark 8 for 20 minutes or until well risen and golden brown. Remove from the oven and cut into squares.
Serve hot as hors d'oeuvres or a dinner savoury, garnished with watercress.
For cocktail savouries, line small patty pans, prick the base and three-quarters fill with cheese mixture. Bake as above for 15 minutes or until well risen and golden.

Beef and sausage loaf en croûte

Beef and sausage loaf en croûte

This is a tasty and satisfying dish which is not expensive.

METRIC	IMPERIAL
225 g minced steak	8 oz minced steak
100 g pork sausagemeat	4 oz pork sausagemeat
50 g fresh brown breadcrumbs	2 oz fresh brown breadcrumbs
75 g peeled and chopped Bramley apples	3 oz peeled and chopped Bramley apples
50 g peeled and finely chopped onions	2 oz peeled and finely chopped onions
1 tablespoon chopped fresh parsley	1 tablespoon chopped fresh parsley
¼ teaspoon dried savory	¼ teaspoon dried savory
1 teaspoon salt	1 teaspoon salt
freshly ground black pepper	freshly ground black pepper
4 tablespoons beef stock or bouillon	4 tablespoons beef stock or bouillon
1 egg, beaten	1 egg, beaten
225 g Rough Puff Pastry	8 oz Rough Puff Pastry
sprigs of parsley or watercress to garnish	sprigs of parsley or watercress to garnish
TO GLAZE:	TO GLAZE:
1 egg yolk beaten with 1 tablespoon water	1 egg yolk beaten with 1 tablespoon water

Line the base of a small (500 g/1 lb) loaf tin with greaseproof paper and grease (p.49). Mix the minced meat, sausagemeat, breadcrumbs, apples and onion together. Mix in the parsley, savory, salt, and black pepper to taste, mixing thoroughly. Combine the stock with the beaten egg and stir into the meat mixture.

Turn into the prepared tin and level the top. Bake in the centre of a preheated moderate oven at 180°C/350°F, Gas Mark 4 for 40 minutes or until set and the juice runs amber coloured. Remove from the oven and allow to cool in the tin.

When the meat loaf is quite cold, roll out the pastry on a floured board into a rectangle 5 mm/¼ inch thick. Cut off a rectangle approximately 28 x 30 cm/11 x 12 inches. Place the meat loaf in the centre. Brush the edges lightly with water and fold the pastry round the meat loaf like a neat parcel, sealing the joins well. Place on a baking sheet with the join underneath. Glaze with the beaten egg yolk and water. Cut two slits across the top for steam to escape. Cut a strip 2.5 cm/1 inch wide off the remaining pastry and cut across diagonally to make 4 pastry leaves. Mark 'veins' on the leaves with a knife, brush with egg glaze and arrange on each corner of the loaf.

With a fluted cutter cut some small rounds from the remaining pastry, glaze and arrange them in the centre of the loaf. Place in the centre of a preheated hot oven at 220°C/425°F, Gas Mark 7 for 30 minutes or until well risen and golden brown. Reduce the heat to 190°C/375°F, Gas Mark 5 and continue cooking for 10 minutes. Place on a hot serving dish and garnish with parsley or watercress sprigs.

Serve with onion sauce, apple sauce or gravy.

Served cold, this is excellent for picnics, but it is advisable to use Flaky Pastry (p.88) instead of Rough Puff Pastry.

Flaky pastry

This has a lighter, more flaky texture than rough puff pastry due to the way the fat is incorporated. It is similar to puff pastry, but is quicker and easier to make so is popular with home cooks.

Flaky pastry

METRIC	IMPERIAL
225 g plain flour	8 oz plain flour
pinch of salt	pinch of salt
75 g butter or margarine	3 oz butter or margarine
75 g lard	3 oz lard
1 teaspoon lemon juice	1 teaspoon lemon juice
approx. 250 ml cold water	approx. 8 fl oz cold water

MAKES 225 G/8 OZ PASTRY

Sift the flour and salt into a mixing bowl. Cream the fats together on a plate, shape into a round and divide into four. Rub one quarter of the fat into the flour as for shortcrust (p.74). Add the lemon juice to 150 ml/5 fl oz of the water. The acid helps to crisp the pastry. Add sufficient liquid to the flour and fat to bind it into a soft but not sticky dough. Gather the dough into a ball, knead it lightly and shape it into a 'brick'.

Step 1: roll it out on a floured board into a neat rectangle about 1.5 cm/½ inch thick, mark it across into 3 equal sections.

Step 2: with a rounded knife, flake the second quarter of fat evenly over the top two-thirds of the dough, leaving a narrow border round the edge.

Step 3: fold the bottom third of the dough up, seal in the air as for rough puff pastry (p.86). Fold down and seal the top section. Give the dough a quarter turn to right or left. Repeat steps 1, 2 and 3 twice more, flaking in the third and then the last quarter of fat. Roll out and fold the dough once

Rolling out dough

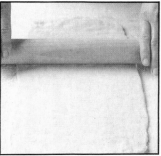

Flaking on fat

Folding up dough

Sealing the edges

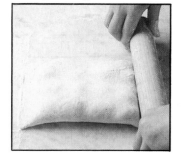

Mille feuilles

or twice more until there are no fatty streaks to be seen. In hot weather if the dough becomes sticky, it may be advisable to refrigerate it for a short time during making. Make sure the dough does not stick to the board or the rolling pin.

Put the finished dough into a plastic bag and chill in the refrigerator for 2 hours or overnight if preferred.

If freezing, allow 6 hours for the dough to defrost in the refrigerator before using.

Mille feuilles

METRIC	IMPERIAL
100 g Flaky Pastry	4 oz Flaky Pastry
75 g white Lemon Glacé Icing (p.150)	3 oz white Lemon Glacé Icing (p.150)
75 g Chocolate Glacé Icing (p.150)	3 oz Chocolate Glacé Icing (p.150)
6-8 tablespoons raspberry or strawberry jam	6-8 tablespoons raspberry or strawberry jam
150 ml double or whipping cream, whipped	¼ pint double or whipping cream, whipped

MAKES 6

Roll out the pastry thinly into a rectangle 20 x 25 cm/8 x 10 inches. Cut the pastry lengthwise into 2 strips each 10 cm/4 inches wide. Cut each strip into 5 rectangles each 5 cm/2 inches wide. Lay the pieces on an ungreased baking tray, prick all over and chill for 30 minutes. Bake in a preheated hot oven at 230°C/450°F, Gas Mark 8 for 8 minutes or until well risen and golden. Remove from the oven and allow to cool. Slit each biscuit in half laterally. Arrange the biscuits in groups of 3, selecting the best from each group for the top. The tops may be iced simply, or given a feather icing effect.

For feather icing, put the chocolate icing in a piping bag with a writing nozzle (no. 2 size). Spread a top biscuit with white icing and immediately pipe lines of chocolate icing about 1.5 cm/½ inch apart across it. Using a wet skewer pull it across the lines at 2.5 cm/1 inch intervals. Turn the biscuit round and pull the lines down in the opposite direction. This will produce a feather effect. If all the lines are pulled down in the same direction it produces a marbled effect. Leave to set and trim the edges.

If preferred, the tops can be spread with plain glacé icing and decorated with finely chopped nuts.

Sandwich each biscuit together with jam and whipped cream with the iced one on top.

Bake the vol-au-vents near the top of a preheated hot oven at 230°C/450°F, Gas Mark 8 and the lids on the shelf below. After 10 minutes, when the pastry is well risen and golden brown, remove the lids from the oven.

Lower the heat to 220°C/425°F, Gas Mark 7 and bake the vol-au-vents for a further 10 minutes or until cooked. Take out of the oven, and remove any soft dough from inside the cases and off the bottom of the lids.

Fill and serve at once. Alternatively, cool the pastries on a wire tray and store in an airtight container.

When required heat in a preheated moderately hot oven at 190°C/375°F, Gas Mark 3 for about 15 minutes. Heat the filling separately, then fill the cases and top with the lids. Garnish with sprigs of fresh watercress or parsley.

Vol-au-vents

These deep pastry cases can be filled with a variety of savoury fillings, such as chicken, ham or prawns with mushroom bound with a well flavoured white sauce, or kidneys or sweetbreads in a rich brown sauce.

METRIC
225 g Flaky Pastry
1 egg, beaten
Chicken and Ham filling

IMPERIAL
8 oz Flaky Pastry
1 egg, beaten
Chicken and Ham filling

MAKES ABOUT 8

Roll out the pastry to 1 cm/½ inch thick. With a floured cutter, 6 cm/2½ inches wide, cut out rounds and place half of them on the damp baking sheet. Prick through with a fork and damp the edges. With a 4 cm/1½ inch cutter cut the centre out of the remaining rounds. Lift the rings and place them on top of the rounds on the baking sheet and press together.

Put the small rounds on a separate baking sheet as they will cook quicker. Brush the rings and the small rounds, which will be used as lids, with beaten egg. Make a criss cross pattern on the top of the rings with a knife. Chill the pastries for 30 minutes.

Chicken and ham filling

METRIC
50 g mushrooms, sliced
1 tablespoon finely chopped onion
40 g butter
40 g flour
300 ml chicken stock
50 g cooked chicken, diced
50 g cooked ham, diced
salt
freshly ground black pepper
lemon juice to taste
1 tablespoon chopped parsley

IMPERIAL
2 oz mushrooms, sliced
1 tablespoon finely chopped onion
1½ oz butter
1½ oz flour
½ pint chicken stock
2 oz cooked chicken, diced
2 oz cooked ham, diced
salt
freshly ground black pepper
lemon juice to taste
1 tablespoon chopped parsley

Fry the mushroom and onion in the butter until softened. Remove from the heat and stir in the flour. Gradually stir in the stock, bring to boil and simmer over a low heat for 5 minutes. Add the chicken, ham and salt, pepper and lemon juice to taste. Mix in the chopped parsley.

Vol-au-vents

Pâtisseries made with pastry trimmings

From left: Turnovers; Fleurons; Cream cornets (sweet and savoury); Sacristains; Palmiers

Many attractive pâtisseries can be made with the trimmings of flaky and puff pastry. To keep the flaky texture of the pastry, do not knead the scraps together, but lay them on top of each other and then roll out.

Turnovers

Roll out the pastry thinly into a rectangle which will cut into 2 or more squares. Mark each square across into 2 triangles. Brush the edges with water. Put some sliced and sweetened apples on one triangle, or spread with jam. Fold the other half over the filling and press the edges together. Knock them back and mark with the tines of a fork as for pie edging (p.75). Place on a greased baking tray, brush with milk or egg white and dredge with caster sugar. Bake in a preheated hot oven at 220°C/425°F, Gas Mark 7 for 20 minutes or until well risen and golden. Serve hot or cold.

Fleurons

These are little fancy shapes of flaky or puff pastry trimmings which are used to garnish fish, chicken or beef dishes made with a cream sauce. They can also be substituted for fried bread croûtons on meat or poultry dishes made with a brown roux or wine sauce.
Roll out the pastry ½ cm/¼ inch thick. Cut into crescents or diamonds with a small cutter. Place on an ungreased baking tray and brush with beaten egg. Bake in a preheated hot oven at 220°C/425°F, Gas Mark 7 for 5 minutes or until crisp and golden. Cool on a wire tray and store in an airtight container. Reheat in a moderate oven for 10 minutes before serving.

Cream cornets

225 g/8 oz pastry (finished weight) makes 8 cornets. Roll out the pastry very thinly into a rectangle 60 cm/24 inches long. Cut it into strips 2.5 cm/1 inch wide. Brush with water. Starting at the pointed end of the horn tin, wrap the strip evenly round the tin so that the strip overlaps by 1.5 cm/½ inch on each turn, finishing neatly at the open end. Brush with beaten egg white and dip into caster sugar. Place on an ungreased baking tray and chill for 30 minutes. Bake in a preheated hot oven at 220°C/425°F, Gas Mark 7 for 15 minutes or until crisp and golden. Remove from the oven, allow to cool slightly, then remove the tin carefully from the pastry by giving it a gentle twist.
When cold, put a teaspoon of cherry jam in the bottom of each pastry cornet. Using a rose meringue nozzle, pipe in whipped cream finishing at the top with a rosette. Decorate with a glacé cherry or cherry jam.

Savoury cornets

Roll out the pastry as above and cut into strips 30 cm/12 inches long and wind them half way up the tins. Brush with Egg Wash (p.16) and bake as for Cream Cornets. When cold fill with cream cheese flavoured with herbs or anchovy essence. Serve as cocktail snacks.

Sacristains

These twists of flaky or puff pastry are a handy way to use trimmings and they can be served for tea or coffee or with ice creams instead of wafers.

METRIC	IMPERIAL
100 g Flaky Pastry trimmings (p.88) (finished weight)	*4 oz Flaky Pastry trimmings (p.88) (finished weight)*
3-4 tablespoons granulated sugar	*3-4 tablespoons granulated sugar*
1 egg, beaten	*1 egg, beaten*
1 teaspoon milk	*1 teaspoon milk*
approx. 2 tablespoons flaked almonds	*approx. 2 tablespoons flaked almonds*

MAKES 12 TO 18

Roll out the pastry very thinly into a strip 10 cm/4 inches wide on a board sprinkled with granulated sugar instead of flour. Trim the edges. Beat the egg with the milk and brush over the pastry.
Sprinkle generously with flaked almonds and more sugar. Cut into strips 2½ cm/1 inch wide. Twist each strip into a spiral. Place it on an ungreased baking sheet and press down the ends so the spiral will not unwind during baking. Chill them thoroughly in the refrigerator.
Bake in a preheated moderately hot oven at 200°C/400°F, Gas Mark 6 for 8 to 10 minutes or until crisp and golden. Cool on a wire tray.

Palmiers

225 g/8 oz pastry (*finished* weight) makes 8 pairs.
Roll out the pastry under 5 mm/¼ inch thick into a strip 45 cm/18 inches long. Brush the surface with water and sprinkle generously with caster sugar. Fold each end of the pastry into 3, then fold over making 8 equal layers altogether. The pastry should now be about 6 cm/2½ inches wide and 1½ cm/½ inch thick. Cut the strip into slices 1 cm/½ inch thick and lay with the folds showing, about 8 cm/3 inches apart, on a well greased baking sheet. Chill for at least 30 minutes.
Bake in a preheated hot oven at 230°C/450°F, Gas Mark 8 until set and just beginning to colour. Remove from the oven and turn over with a palette knife. Return to the oven and bake until crisp and golden and the glaze has caramelized. Cool on a wire tray. Sandwich together in pairs with jam and whipped cream or serve plain.

Preparing pastry trimmings from left: Turnovers; Fleurons; Cream cornets; Sacristains; Palmiers

Choux pastry

This is a French pastry which is made with hot instead of cold water. It is used for éclairs, cream puffs, and some savoury pastries.

Choux pastry

METRIC	IMPERIAL
75 g plain flour	3 oz plain flour
40 g butter or margarine	1½ oz butter or margarine
150 ml water	¼ pint water
2 eggs, beaten	2 eggs, beaten

MAKES 75 G/3 OZ PASTRY

Sift the flour on to a piece of kitchen or greaseproof paper. Melt the fat in the water over gentle heat. It must not boil before the fat is melted or it will evaporate and reduce the quantity.
When melted, bring to the boil, remove the pan from the heat and tip in all the flour. Beat with a wooden spoon until smooth, then return to moderate heat and beat until the dough forms a ball and leaves the sides of the pan clean. Do not overheat or the dough will turn oily.
Cool the mixture slightly and add the beaten eggs a spoonful at a time, beating well between each addition. If added too quickly the dough will turn too liquid to pipe.
The dough can be stored in the refrigerator, well wrapped, and used the next day. The baked pastry should be served the day it is made.

Paris brest

Serve this on the day it is made.

METRIC	IMPERIAL
75 g Choux Pastry	3 oz Choux Pastry
2 tablespoons flaked almonds	2 tablespoons flaked almonds
225 g strawberry conserve or sliced fresh strawberries	8 oz strawberry conserve or sliced fresh strawberries
300 ml double or whipping cream	½ pint double or whipping cream
1-2 tablespoons kirsch or other liqueur	1-2 tablespoons kirsch or other liqueur
1-2 tablespoons icing sugar	1-2 tablespoons icing sugar
sieved icing sugar for dusting	sieved icing sugar for dusting

Flour a baking sheet and draw an 18 cm/7 inch circle in the flour with the handle of a wooden spoon. Put the choux dough in a forcing bag with a plain 2.5 cm/1 inch nozzle. Pipe a round on the circle and neaten the join with a palette knife. Sprinkle with flaked almonds. Cover with a large roasting tin 25 x 30 cm/10 x 12 inches. Bake just above the centre of a preheated hot oven at 220°C/425°F, Gas Mark 7 for 40 minutes. Do not be tempted to lift the tin before then as the pastry will collapse. Lift off the tin and continue baking for 10 to 15 minutes or until crisp and golden brown. Remove from the oven, slice the ring across horizontally and remove the top.
Whip the cream and flavour with kirsch or other liqueur and sweeten with icing sugar. When cold spread the bottom of the ring with strawberry conserve or sliced fresh strawberries and spoon the cream on top. Replace the pastry top and dust with sieved icing sugar.

Paris brest; Cream puffs

Carolines

Cream puffs

These are an easy alternative to the Paris Brest gâteau. Pipe the choux pastry on a floured baking sheet in little round buns, or use a wet teaspoon to shape them. Place them 5 cm/2 inches apart to leave room for expansion. Cover with the large roasting tin and bake as for Paris Brest for 30 minutes. Remove the tin and continue baking until crisp and golden. Remove from the oven and slit the sides to allow steam to escape. When cold, put in a little lemon curd and fill with sweetened whipped cream. Coat with Lemon or Chocolate Glacé Icing (p.150).

Carolines

These savoury choux pastries are an attractive addition to the buffet table or to serve at a cocktail party.
Pipe the choux pastry, using a small nozzle ½ cm/¼ inch wide into 5 cm/2 inch lengths on the baking sheet leaving room for expansion. Bake in a preheated hot oven at 220°C/425°F, Gas Mark 7 for 15 to 20 minutes or until crisp and hollow. Slit the sides for the steam to escape, and cool.
When cold fill with a savoury mixture, such as:-
1. Cream cheese with chopped ham or smoked salmon.
2. Cream cheese and chopped parsley with chopped salted nuts or chopped stuffed olives.
3. Flaked cooked salmon or shrimps in tartare sauce.
4. Chopped cooked tongue with horseradish cream.
Garnish with chopped fresh parsley or sliced stuffed olives or sprinkle with paprika. Arrange a selection on a plate and garnish with sprigs of fresh watercress or parsley to indicate they are savoury and not sweet.

Baking for festivals

Baking for festivals has always been a busy and often happy time for the home cook, whether it is making Hot Cross Buns for Good Friday or a feast for Christmas day. To make sure that cooking for a festival feast is a happy time and not a round of unremitting toil, the secret is to plan ahead and, where possible, cook ahead.

The refrigerator and freezer can be used to full advantage, but a word of warning about the latter. Some people have become so freezer-happy that they freeze mincemeat, plum pudding and Christmas cake instead of allowing them to mature, well-wrapped and stored, over the weeks preceding Christmas. Rich cakes like the Simnel Cake should be kept for at least a month after they are baked and before they are cut, or they will be crumbly and lack flavour. Wrap them closely in kitchen foil or store in an airtight container. Icing and decorating can be done a week or two before they are required.

Mince pies will keep perfectly in an airtight tin over the twelve days of Christmas.

Rich shortbreads and fancy biscuits made in advance, keep excellently in a good tin.

Yeasted loaves, fancy rolls and buns like Hot Cross Buns, allowed to cool after baking, then closely wrapped and put in the freezer, will regain their fresh spongy texture after defrosting.

Butter sponge cakes like the childrens' Treasure Chest Birthday Cake can also be made in advance and frozen, but alternatively will keep fresh for several days in an airtight tin in the larder.

Baking for Easter

Hot cross buns

These spiced yeast buns are traditionally served hot on Good Friday. Nowadays they can be made well in advance, closely wrapped and frozen and when required, defrosted and heated in a hot oven. Alternatively you can make the dough on the previous day, put it in an oiled polythene bag and refrigerate overnight. Next day when it has doubled in bulk, knock it back and make the buns.

METRIC	IMPERIAL
450 g strong white flour	1 lb strong white flour
150 ml milk	¼ pint milk
4 tablespoons water	4 tablespoons water
25 g fresh yeast	1 oz fresh yeast
or	or
15 g dried yeast	½ oz dried yeast
1 teaspoon caster sugar	1 teaspoon caster sugar
1 teaspoon salt	1 teaspoon salt
½ teaspoon mixed spice	½ teaspoon mixed spice
½ teaspoon ground cinnamon	½ teaspoon ground cinnamon
½ teaspoon grated nutmeg	½ teaspoon grated nutmeg
50 g caster sugar	2 oz caster sugar
50 g butter or margarine	2 oz butter or margarine
1 egg, beaten	1 egg, beaten
100 g currants	4 oz currants
40 g chopped mixed peel	1½ oz chopped mixed peel
50 g Plain Shortcrust Pastry (p.74)	2 oz Plain Shortcrust Pastry (p.74)
TO GLAZE:	TO GLAZE:
3 tablespoons caster sugar	3 tablespoons caster sugar
4 tablespoons milk and water mixed	4 tablespoons milk and water mixed
MAKES 12	

Put 100 g/4 oz of the flour into a small bowl. Warm the milk and water, then blend in the yeast and the teaspoon of sugar. Mix this into the flour and leave in a warm place to froth (see Method 2 p.14), for about 15 minutes for fresh yeast, about 20 minutes for dried.

Meanwhile, sift the remaining flour, salt, mixed spice, cinnamon, nutmeg and sugar into a mixing bowl. Melt and cool the butter, but do not allow to harden, then add it to the frothy yeast mixture with the beaten egg. Stir this into the flour and mix well with a wooden spoon. Scatter in the currants and mixed peel and mix into a fairly soft dough. Add a spoonful of water if necessary.

Turn the dough on to a floured board and knead well (p.14). Put into an oiled polythene bag and leave to rise until doubled in bulk, (1 to 1½ hours at room temperature). Turn on to a floured board and knock back the dough (p.15). Divide into 12 pieces and shape into small round buns. Press down briefly on each bun with the palm of the hand, then place the buns well apart on a floured baking sheet. Cover and put in a warm place to rise until doubled in size (20 to 30 minutes). Meanwhile, roll out the pastry thinly and cut into 24 thin strips about 9 cm/3½ inches long.

When the buns have risen, damp the pastry strips and lay 2 strips across each bun to make a cross. Bake the buns in a preheated moderately hot oven at 190°C/375°F, Gas Mark 5 for 20 minutes or until golden brown and firm to the touch.

Meanwhile, make the glaze by dissolving the sugar in the milk and water over a low heat. When the buns are ready brush them twice with the glaze. Serve the buns hot, split and buttered.

Left: Hot cross buns

Simnel cake

This is the traditional fruit cake for the Easter festival. It should be made at least a fortnight in advance to allow it to mature. A special feature is the layer of marzipan baked in the middle of the cake and also covering the top. The marzipan balls surmounting it represent the eleven faithful apostles. The centre can be decorated with a nest of Easter eggs.

METRIC	IMPERIAL
175 g butter or margarine	6 oz butter or margarine
175 g caster sugar	6 oz caster sugar
3 large eggs	3 large eggs
225 g plain flour	8 oz plain flour
1 teaspoon ground cinnamon	1 teaspoon ground cinnamon
1 teaspoon ground nutmeg	1 teaspoon ground nutmeg
300 g currants	12 oz currants
100 g sultanas	4 oz sultanas
75 g chopped mixed peel	3 oz chopped mixed peel
1-2 tablespoons milk	1-2 tablespoons milk
500 g Marzipan (p.98)	1 lb Marzipan (p.98)
3-4 tablespoons apricot jam	3-4 tablespoons apricot jam
1 egg, beaten, for glazing	1 egg, beaten, for glazing

Line an 18 cm/7 inch round cake tin (p.49). Cream the butter and sugar together and beat in the eggs gradually, following the method for rich cakes (p.54). Sift the flour with the spices and fold it in, then the fruit. Mix to a soft dropping consistency with a little milk. Put half the mixture into the tin and level it off.

Divide the marzipan into 3 and roll out one-third on a sugared board into a round slightly smaller than the tin. Pinch the edges to prevent the paste cracking. Lay the marzipan round on top of the cake mixture then cover with the rest of the mixture and level it off. Tie a band of brown paper round the outside of the tin and 5 cm/2 inches above it to protect the top of the cake during baking.

Place it in a preheated moderate oven so that the top of the cake is in the centre of the oven and bake at 170°C/325°F, Gas Mark 3 for 1 hour. Reduce the heat to 150°C/300°F, Gas Mark 2 for a further 2 hours or until the cake is firm to the touch.

Allow to cool in the tin before turning out on to a wire rack to cool. Leave on the lining paper, wrap the cake in foil and store for at least 2 weeks.

When required, unwrap the cake. Heat the jam and sieve it if lumpy. Roll out one of the reserved pieces of marzipan into a round to put on the top of the cake. Brush the apricot glaze over the top of the cake and press on the marzipan round. With the forefinger of one hand and the finger and thumb of the other, pinch the edge of the marzipan into flutes. Flatten the remaining ball of marzipan and divide it into 12 equal parts. Roll 11 pieces into small balls. Brush the top and sides of the marzipan on the cake with beaten egg. Press on the balls in a ring round the edge of the cake and glaze them with beaten egg. Place on a baking sheet and bake near the top of a preheated hot oven at 230°C/450°F, Gas Mark 8 for 5 minutes or until nicely coloured. Alternatively brown under a hot grill. Cool the cake.

To make the nest, roll the remaining piece of marzipan into a thin sausage and shape it into a ring. Brush with beaten egg and dip into chocolate strands. Place in the centre of the cake. Fill it with sugar Easter eggs.

Making Simnel cake (left) and the finished cake (below)

Baking for Christmas

Christmas cake

This cake can be made just a week or two before Christmas as it does not need so long to mature as the dark spicy variety. Glacé fruit is used instead of currants and the fresh orange and lemon flavour and lighter texture appeal to young children as well as adults. The decoration is gay and festive and is easy for the busy home cook to do very successfully.

METRIC	IMPERIAL
225 g butter	8 oz butter
225 g caster sugar	8 oz caster sugar
grated rind and juice of 1 orange	grated rind and juice of 1 orange
grated rind and juice of 1 lemon	grated rind and juice of 1 lemon
4 eggs, beaten	4 eggs, beaten
250 g plain flour	9 oz plain flour
175 g sultanas	6 oz sultanas
100 g glacé cherries, chopped	4 oz glacé cherries, chopped
75 g glacé pineapple, chopped	3 oz glacé pineapple, chopped
50 g candied orange and lemon peel, chopped	2 oz candied orange and lemon peel, chopped
25 g candied citron peel or angelica, chopped	1 oz candied citron peel or angelica, chopped
100 g crystallized ginger, chopped	4 oz crystallized ginger, chopped
50 g walnuts, chopped	2 oz walnuts, chopped
50 g blanched almonds, shredded	2 oz blanched almonds, shredded
3 tablespoons sherry	3 tablespoons sherry

Line a 20 cm/8 inch round cake tin (p.49). Cream the butter and sugar with the orange and lemon rind until light and fluffy. Beat in the eggs a tablespoonful at a time, beating well between each addition. Add a spoonful of the flour at any sign of curdling.

Fold in the flour alternately with the fruit, candied peel and nuts. When thoroughly mixed, stir in the orange and lemon juice and sherry. Turn into the prepared cake tin and make a deep hollow in the centre. Tie a band of brown paper round the outside of the tin and 5 cm/2 inches above it to protect the top of the cake.

Place in a preheated moderate oven so that the top of the cake is in the centre and bake at 350°F/180°C, Gas Mark 4 for 20 minutes. When the cake starts to brown, put a sheet of greaseproof paper over the top (resting on the collar) to prevent it over-browning. Reduce the heat to 300°F/150°C, Gas Mark 1 for a further 2 hours and 40 minutes. A skewer inserted will come out clean when the cake is cooked. Remove from the tin and, leaving on the lining paper, cool on a wire tray. When cold put in an airtight tin until coating with marzipan.

To coat in marzipan: shape the marzipan into a fat sausage and divide into 3 equal portions. Sprinkle the pastry board with icing sugar and roll out one portion of the marzipan into a round to fit on top of the cake, using the base of the cake tin as a guide. Brush the top of the cake with beaten egg white, press on the marzipan round and mould the edges to fit neatly. Roll the sugared rolling pin across it to flatten it evenly.

Measure round the cake with a piece of string and cut it in half. Roll the remaining 2 portions of marzipan out on the sugared board to the same length as the string, with the width matching the height of the cake. Brush the sides of the cake with beaten egg white. Press one strip of marzipan round half the cake, then repeat with the other half. Knead all the joins neatly together. Stand a jam jar against the cake and roll it round the cake, pressing on the paste firmly and evenly, smoothing out the joins and sharpening the angle round the top edge.

Leave the cake, covered with a clean cloth, in a warm, dry place overnight for the marzipan to dry out and firm up before coating with icing.

Marzipan

METRIC	IMPERIAL
275 g ground almonds	10 oz ground almonds
275 g caster sugar	10 oz caster sugar
2 egg yolks	2 egg yolks
2 tablespoons lemon or orange juice	2 tablespoons lemon or orange juice
1 egg white, beaten, for brushing	1 egg white, beaten, for brushing

Sift the almonds and sugar into a mixing bowl. Beat the egg yolks with the fruit juice and stir into the dry ingredients. Work into a stiff paste and knead until smooth. The warmth of the hands brings out the oil in the almonds. If this makes the paste sticky, work in a little more sugar. If dry and crumbly, add a little more juice.

Right: Christmas cake
Above: stages of preparation

Royal icing

METRIC	IMPERIAL
3 egg whites	3 egg whites
750 g icing sugar, sifted	1½ lb icing sugar, sifted
1 teaspoon glycerine	1 teaspoon glycerine
approx. 3 tablespoons	approx. 3 tablespoons
lemon juice	lemon juice

Beat the egg whites in a large bowl and gradually stir in the icing sugar and glycerine. Add sufficient lemon juice to make a thick spreading consistency. Beat until smooth and glossy.

DECORATIONS:
1 box of miniature Christmas crackers
6 red cake candles with red holders
12 miniature Christmas tree baubles or miniature sprigs
*   of holly leaves with berries, or 6 of each*
Miniature Christmas tree(s), Father Christmas with
*   reindeer, etc.*

To decorate: spread a little icing in the centre of the cake board and place the cake on top. This will prevent it slipping. Fill in any gaps in the icing between the bottom edge of the cake and the board. Put a little ruffled icing in

To ice: place the cake on a large upturned plate. Reserving a little for decoration, put a mound of Royal Icing in the centre of the top. With a palette knife, spread it out evenly to the edges, covering the top completely. Now coat the sides, making sure the icing meets round the top edge of the cake. Clean the knife with hot water, shake off any drops and, holding it horizontally, at an angle, draw it across the top of the cake, ending at the edge with an upwards movement and leaving the icing smooth. Clean the knife, and with the rounded end, draw up the icing into peaks all round the sides of the cake and round the edge of the top to give a rough snow effect.

the centre of the cake and arrange the Christmas figures and trees on the icing to make an attractive snow scene. Put a dab of icing on the side of each miniature cracker and press them round the sides of the cake in a zig-zag pattern. Put a miniature Christmas tree bauble on a tiny sprig of artificial holly in each V between the crackers. Finally, insert the red candle holders with their candles, in the top of the cake round the edge.

Rich Scots shortbread; Shortbread fingers; Mince pies

Rich Scots shortbread

Carved wooden shortbread moulds are becoming rather
rare and expensive, but the mixture can be pressed into a
fluted flan ring which will prevent it spreading and losing
shape during baking.
Decorated with Lemon Glacé Icing (p.150) and a sprig of
heather tied up with tartan ribbon, shortbread makes an
attractive Christmas gift.

METRIC	IMPERIAL
225 g plain flour	8 oz plain flour
100 g rice flour or ground rice	4 oz rice flour or ground rice
100 g caster sugar	4 oz caster sugar
pinch of salt	pinch of salt
225 g unsalted butter	8 oz unsalted butter

Sift the two flours (or flour and rice), sugar and salt, into a
mixing bowl. Soften the butter slightly, cut it up and rub it
into the dry ingredients with your fingers. When it starts to
bind, gather it together with one hand into a ball. Knead it
on a lightly floured board until it is a soft, smooth and
pliable dough.
Place a 20 cm/8 inch flan ring on a greased baking tray and
put in the dough. Press it out evenly with your knuckles to
fit the ring. With the back of a knife, mark it into 6 or 8
triangles. Prick right through to the baking sheet with a
fork in a neat pattern. Chill for at least 1 hour before
baking to firm it up.
Bake in the centre of a preheated cool oven at
150°C/300°F, Gas Mark 2 for 45 minutes to 1 hour or until
it is a pale biscuit colour but still soft. Remove from the
oven and leave to cool and shrink before removing the
ring, then dust lightly with caster sugar. When cold store
in an airtight tin.

Shortbread fingers

Press the shortbread mixture into a greased 20 cm/8 inch
square tin. With a sharp knife, cut it across right down to
the base, into strips 2.5 cm/1 inch wide and then across
into fingers of equal length. Prick through neatly to the
base with a fork. Chill and bake as for Rich Scots
Shortbread. When ready, remove from the oven, cut
through again in the same slits, but leave to cool before
loosening the edge and turning out upside down on a
sugared, greaseproof paper. Separate the fingers, turn
right side up and store when cold.

Mince pies

If using bought mincemeat, it will be improved with a dash of brandy or rum, or a little lemon juice.

METRIC	IMPERIAL
175 g Sweet Shortcrust Pastry (p.79)	6 oz Sweet Shortcrust Pastry (p.79)
225 g (about 12 tablespoons) mincemeat	8 oz (about 12 tablespoons) mincemeat
icing sugar for dusting	icing sugar for dusting

MAKES 12

Roll out the pastry very thinly, 2.5 mm/⅛ inch thick. Cut out 12 rounds with a plain or fluted cutter and line pastry pans (p.81). Prick the bottom of each pie and put a teaspoon of mincemeat in each one. Damp the edges. Cut out 12 more rounds with a smaller cutter, cover the filling in each tart. Press down with the blunt end of the smaller cutter so the lids are secure. Cut a small cross in the centre of each lid to allow steam to escape.

Place the tarts on a baking sheet and bake in a preheated hot oven at 220°C/425°F, Gas Mark 7 for 12 to 15 minutes or until well risen and golden. Dust generously with icing sugar and serve hot. When cold the tarts can be stored in an airtight container, or frozen.

Variations

Cut a slightly larger cross in the pie lids. Brush with water. Prise open the centre points of the cross and press them back on the lid to show the mincemeat. Dust with caster sugar before baking.

If you prefer pies with less pastry and more mincemeat, do not put lids on the pies. Instead, cut out little pastry stars and put one on the filling in each pie.

Flaky or puff pastry pies

Roll out 175 g/6 oz Flaky (p.88) or Rough Puff Pastry (p.86) very thinly and cut one half into rounds with a 7 cm/2¾ inch plain cutter. Put the rounds on a clean baking sheet. Damp the edges and put a teaspoon of mincemeat in the centre. Cut out the other rounds with an 8 cm/3 inch cutter and cover the filling. Press down the edges with the blunt end of a 5 cm/2 inch cutter to seal in the filling. Cut a small cross in the top of each lid. Brush with milk and dust with caster sugar. Chill for 30 minutes and bake in a preheated hot oven at 230°C/450°F, Gas Mark 8 for about 15 minutes or until well risen and golden. Serve hot.

Children's birthday party

Treasure chest birthday cake

The Treasure Chest can be a Pirate's Chest with golden doubloons cascading out of it on to the 'beach' or a Candy Box overflowing with an exciting assortment of colourful candies.

METRIC
225 g butter or margarine
225 g caster sugar
4 eggs, beaten
¼ teaspoon vanilla essence
225 g self-raising flour
1-2 tablespoons warm
    water
Chocolate Joy Icing (p.63)
DECORATIONS:
350 g coloured sugar drops
350 g chocolate 'money' in
    gold foil or 350 g
    assorted candies
8 large plastic cocktail
    sticks
birthday candles with
    novelty holders
small pebbles for Pirate's
    Chest or silver paper
    doyley for Candy Box

IMPERIAL
8 oz butter or margarine
8 oz caster sugar
4 eggs, beaten
¼ teaspoon vanilla essence
8 oz self-raising flour
1-2 tablespoons warm
    water
Chocolate Joy Icing (p.63)
DECORATIONS:
12 oz coloured sugar drops
12 oz chocolate 'money' in
    gold foil or 12 oz
    assorted candies
8 large plastic cocktail
    sticks
birthday candles with
    novelty holders
small pebbles for Pirate's
    Chest or silver paper
    doyley for Candy Box

Line the base and grease a large tin measuring approximately 35 x 23 cm/14 x 9 inches. A shallow tin is preferable, but a roasting tin will do.
Cream the fat and sugar together until light and fluffy. Gradually blend in the eggs and vanilla, following the method for Victoria Sandwich Cake (p.56) and fold in the flour. Add a little water to give a soft dropping consistency. Spread the mixture evenly in the prepared tin and bake in a preheated moderately hot oven at 190°C/375°F, Gas Mark 5 for about 20 minutes or until set and golden. Allow to shrink before turning out on to a wire tray to cool.
When cold, cut the cake across into 3 equal sized rectangles. Put one piece aside for the lid. Cut a rectangle 7.5 x 18 cm/3 x 7 inches out of the centre of another piece. Place the third piece on a 30 cm/12 inch square cake board. Spread the border with Chocolate Joy Icing and place the hollowed out piece on top to make a box. Coat the outside and edges of the box and the lid with Chocolate Joy Icing and stud it closely with coloured sugar drops. You can mix the colours or select a different colour for each row. Chill the cake until the icing is set.

The pirate's chest

When set, fill the box to overflowing with chocolate 'money' wrapped in gold foil, so some of the 'coins' cascade on to the board. Place the lid on top, tilting it open and securing it with cocktail sticks along the back edge, pushing them down into the back of the box.
Cover the cake board with small sweets to represent pebbles on a beach.
If you make a little pirate's flag, with the skull and crossbones insignia and stick it in a painted cotton reel, it will be much appreciated. Stand the birthday candles in novelty holders round the cake or use novelty candles.

The candy box

Cover the cake board with a lace paper doyley and place the cake on top. Line the box with a silver paper doyley and fill to overflowing with an assortment of chocolates and candies. Stand the birthday candles in novelty holders round the cake or use novelty candles.

Treasure chest birthday cakes: The candy box;
The pirate's chest. Above: assembling a cake

Crocodile rolls

Children enjoy helping to make these fun rolls. It is best to draw a crocodile shape, without feet, on thick paper and use this as a pattern. Size is a matter of choice — for a birthday lunch, 18 cm/7 inches is suitable, a little smaller for tea parties.

METRIC	IMPERIAL
450 g white or brown Quick Bread Dough (p.24)	*1 lb white or brown Quick Bread Dough (p.24)*
1 egg, beaten	*1 egg, beaten*
20 currants for eyes	*20 currants for eyes*
peeled tomato skin for tongues	*peeled tomato skin for tongues*
almonds, split and shredded for teeth	*almonds, split and shredded for teeth*
MAKES 10	

Cut out a crocodile paper shape without feet, measuring 18 cm/7 inches from head to tail. Roll out the dough thinly to about ½ cm/¼ inch thick. Lay the pattern on the dough and cut round it. Move the pastry shapes to the baking sheet, leaving space between them for the feet to be added. Curve the tails in different directions.

Use the trimmings for the feet. Cut 40 strips of dough 1.5 cm/½ inch wide and 2.5 cm/1 inch long. Brush with beaten egg and insert one end of the strip under each crocodile's body. Slit the other end into 3 'toes' and separate well. Using the paper pattern cut an extra 'head' for each crocodile and insert it, unglazed, under the head of the one on the baking tray. With the points of sharp scissors, snip the dough into points from the head to tail, to make scales. Push 2 currants into each head for eyes. Leave the crocodiles in a warm place for the dough to rise (about 40 minutes) or until twice as thick. Bake in a preheated hot oven at 220°C/425°F, Gas Mark 7 for 20 minutes or until risen and golden.

Slit each head carefully from the nose to make an open mouth. Cut the red pimento into little pointed 'tongues' and insert. Use the almonds as teeth to prop open the mouth.

Allow one crocodile for each place setting. The child's name or initials can be piped on with Parsley Butter (see below) or written on a flag and stuck into the crocodile. To make the flags, cut sticky labels into pennant shapes. Damp the wide end, fold it round the top of a cocktail stick and press it firmly together.

Parsley butter

Cream 15 g/½ oz chopped fresh parsley into 75 g/3 oz softened salted butter and flavour with a squeeze of lemon juice.

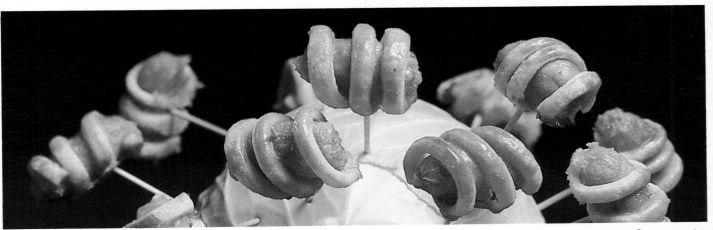

Sausage twists

Sausage twists

Nowadays savoury food is popular at children's parties as well as sweet treats. Chipolata sausages are a great favourite and, made into twists, are even more attractive.

METRIC	IMPERIAL
500 g chipolata sausages	1 lb chipolata sausages
225 g Plain Shortcrust Pastry (p.74) or Flaky Pastry (p.88) trimmings	8 oz Plain Shortcrust Pastry (p.74) or Flaky Pastry (p.88) trimmings
1 egg, beaten	1 egg, beaten
cocktail sticks	cocktail sticks
MAKES 32	

Divide each sausage in half by twisting it in the middle. Roll out the pastry very thinly into a strip 25 cm/10 inches wide. Cut into narrow strips about ½ cm/¼ inch wide. Wind a strip round each sausage leaving 1 cm/½ inch gap between each twist. Place on a greased baking sheet with the joins underneath. Brush with beaten egg and bake in a preheated hot oven at 220°C/425°F, Gas Mark 7 for 15 minutes or until crisp and golden. Push a cocktail stick into the centre of each sausage and insert the other end into a firm green cabbage heart, cleaned, cut in half and placed cut side down on a decorative plate. Alternatively, stick the twists into a brown cob loaf.

Crocodile rolls

Gingerbread men

These are always popular with children at parties, either to eat on the spot or to take home. You can make an attractive table-centre by covering a large square or round cake tin with silver or gold foil; fill it with crackers standing on end and party novelties such as masks, paper hats, etc. Arrange the gingerbread men round the outside of the tin where they will be shown to good advantage. Use biscuit cutters in man shape for the football players. Younger children may prefer a teddy bear shape.

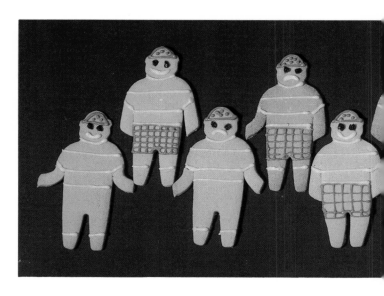

METRIC	IMPERIAL
225 g plain flour	*8 oz plain flour*
2 teaspoons baking powder	*2 teaspoons baking powder*
1-2 teaspoons ground ginger	*1-2 teaspoons ground ginger*
75 g butter or margarine	*3 oz butter or margarine*
50 g caster sugar	*2 oz caster sugar*
1 tablespoons golden syrup or treacle, warmed	*1 tablespoon golden syrup or treacle, warmed*
1-2 tablespoons milk	*1-2 tablespoons milk*
DECORATIONS:	*DECORATIONS:*
24 currants for eyes	*24 currants for eyes*
Royal Icing (p.99) or Glacé Icing (p.150) made with 175 g icing sugar	*Royal Icing (p.99) or Glacé Icing (p.150) made with 6 oz icing sugar*
colouring to choice	*colouring to choice*
MAKES 12	

Sift the flour, baking powder and ginger into a mixing bowl. Cut the fat into the flour and rub in to a breadcrumb consistency. Mix in the sugar and golden syrup or treacle. Gradually work into a dough of firm, rolling consistency, adding a little milk as necessary. If the dough is too soft, the shapes will spread in the oven and be spoiled. Knead until smooth.
Roll out thinly on a lightly floured board and cut out shapes with the shaped cutter. Work up the trimmings, roll out and cut more shapes. Put the men on a greased baking sheet and push 2 currants in each head for eyes. Gently push the arms in different directions so some of the players have one or both arms pointing upwards, some downwards, some sideways. Using your fingertips, roll the trimmings into 'footballs'. Chill for about 30 minutes until stiffened. Bake in a preheated hot oven at 200°C/400°F, Gas Mark 6 for 10 to 12 minutes or until set. Allow to cool slightly before taking off the baking sheet.
To decorate: divide the icing into 2 small bowls. Add a few drops of green or blue colouring to one bowl and mix well. The birthday child may wish to choose the colours of his or her favourite team. The icing must be of piping consistency. Put into separate icing bags with writing nozzles (no. 2) or into paper cornets. Using the white icing, draw eyebrows over the currant eyes. Then mouths, some turning up in a cheerful smile, some turning down.
Pipe a round hat on each head and fill it in with icing dots. Pipe on the football shorts and fill in with criss-cross lines. With the other colour, pipe the striped jersey and football socks. Leave to dry. If storing in an airtight container, put greaseproof paper between the layers.

Traffic light biscuits

These sweet biscuits are helpful reminders of the traffic code as well as enjoyable for the children to eat.

METRIC	IMPERIAL
Sweet Biscuit Dough (p.68)	*Sweet Biscuit Dough (p.68)*
75-100 g red jam	*3-4 oz red jam*
75-100 g yellow jam	*3-4 oz yellow jam*
75-100 g green jam	*3-4 oz green jam*
sifted icing sugar for dusting	*sifted icing sugar for dusting*
MAKES 12 TO 18	

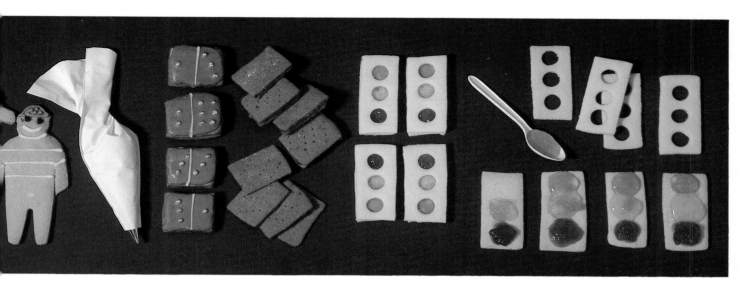

Preparing biscuits; Gingerbread men; Chocolate dominoes; Traffic light biscuits

Roll out the chilled biscuit dough very thinly, 3 mm/⅛ inch thick. Cut into rectangles 7.5 x 4 cm/3 x 1½ inches. Put half of them on a greased baking sheet and prick well. With an apple corer, cut out and remove 3 circles, 1.5 cm/½ inch wide, down the centre of the remaining biscuits at equal intervals. Work up the pastry circles, roll out and make into more biscuits. Chill the rectangles for 30 minutes, then bake in a preheated moderate oven at 175°C/350°F, Gas Mark 4 for about 10 minutes or until set and golden. When cold, spread the plain biscuits with jam; red on the top third, yellow on the centre third and green on the bottom third. Dust the other biscuits with sieved icing sugar and place on top so the colours of the jams show through the holes like traffic lights.

Chocolate dominoes

These look amusing if they are arranged on a board as if they are really dominoes.

METRIC	IMPERIAL
225 g self-raising flour	8 oz self-raising flour
pinch of salt	pinch of salt
1 tablespoon cocoa	1 tablespoon cocoa
100 g butter or margarine	4 oz butter or margarine
100 g caster sugar	4 oz caster sugar
1 egg, beaten	1 egg, beaten
1-2 tablespoons water	1-2 tablespoons water
100 g Chocolate Butter Cream (p.151)	4 oz Chocolate Butter Cream (p.151)
175 g Chocolate Glacé Icing (p.150)	6 oz Chocolate Glacé Icing (p.150)
75 g Glacé Icing (p.150)	3 oz Glacé Icing (p.150)
silver balls for dots	silver balls for dots

Sift the flour, salt and cocoa into a mixing bowl. Cut the fat into the flour and rub in to a breadcrumb consistency. Mix in the sugar. Stir in the egg and just enough water to mix to a very stiff dough. Knead until smooth and roll out very thinly to 3 mm/⅛ inch. Cut into rectangles 5 x 3 cm/2 x 1¼ inches and place on a greased baking tray. Prick all over and chill for 30 minutes. Bake in a preheated moderately hot oven at 190°C/375°F, Gas Mark 5 for 15 minutes or until set. When cold, sandwich the biscuits together with Butter Icing.

Make the Chocolate Glacé Icing to a pouring consistency and pour it over the biscuits. Mark a line across the centre of each biscuit and with tweezers push in silver balls on either side to represent the domino dots. Vary the numbers as much as possible. Leave until set and pipe a line of Glacé Icing across the centre of each biscuit.

Traffic light biscuits; Gingerbread men; Chocolate dominoes

Traditional breads & cakes of the British Isles

As you travel about the British Isles you cannot fail to notice the similarities in the choice of ingredients and baking methods between Scotland, Ireland and Wales. These regions share a common heritage of mountain and moorland where oats and potatoes will grow in the poor soil and withstand the rough weather, but wheat is difficult and white flour was long regarded as a luxury.

Because for many years peat burning on the open hearth was the main fuel, cooking was done on iron griddles or bakestones over the fire instead of in an oven and these traditions still survive. Eating habits are also similar — a preference for a robust breakfast and high tea, with dinner in the middle of the day instead of in the evening. These circumstances have produced a wide variety of tea breads, scone loaves, griddle cakes and scones with many recipes using oatmeal or potato instead of wheat flour.

From the lush valleys of the English West Country come the recipes for pastries rich in butter and featherlight egg sponges filled with clotted cream and from the fruitful orchards of the Southern Counties we have the traditional cherry, apple and plum pies.

Scotland

Oatcakes

These are as vital to a Scotsman as crusty bread to a Frenchman. They are served with honey, marmalade or jam for breakfast, or with crowdie (highland curd cheese) for high tea. They are specially good with fried herring or smoked haddock.

METRIC	IMPERIAL
100 g medium oatmeal	*4 oz medium oatmeal*
½ teaspoon salt	*½ teaspoon salt*
pinch of bicarbonate of soda	*pinch of bicarbonate of soda*
2 teaspoons melted bacon fat or dripping	*2 teaspoons melted bacon fat or dripping*
approx. 50 ml hot water	*approx. 2 fl oz hot water*

Mix the oatmeal, salt and bicarbonate of soda in a bowl. Make a well in the centre, pour in the melted fat and add enough water to make a stiff dough which can be squeezed into a ball. Sprinkle the board and your hands with oatmeal and knead the mixture until there are no cracks. Flatten the ball and roll it out into a round just under ½ cm/¼ inch thick. Invert a plate on top and trim off the ragged edges. (Work up the trimmings and roll out and add them to the next batch of dough.) Cut the round 'bannock' across into 4 triangles called farls. With a palette knife lift them on to a warmed and greased griddle (p.44) and cook over moderate heat for 20 minutes or until the farls curl at the corners. Turn and cook the other side for 5 minutes or finish under a moderate grill.

Store the oatcakes in an airtight tin and toast under a moderate grill or in the oven before serving.

If you prefer very thin oatcakes, make a slightly softer dough and roll it out as thin as possible. Trim the bannock and cut it into 6 farls. The thin oatcakes will cook quicker and require care in handling, before and after cooking.

Petticoat tails

This is reputed to have been a favourite of Mary Queen of Scots and some people say its charming name is a corruption of the French 'petites gatelles' (little cakes). However there are many Scots who maintain the origin of the name lies in the shape of the dough which, before it is cut up, resembles a petticoat.

METRIC	IMPERIAL
350 g plain flour	12 oz plain flour
pinch of salt	pinch of salt
2 teaspoons caraway seeds (optional)	2 teaspoons caraway seeds (optional)
100 g caster sugar	4 oz caster sugar
150 g butter	6 oz butter
4 tablespoons milk	4 tablespoons milk

Sift the flour with the salt into a mixing bowl. Mix in the caraway seeds, if used, and the sugar. Melt the butter in the milk, but do not overheat. Mix it into the flour and knead lightly. Roll out on a floured board into a round just over ½ cm/¼ inch thick.

Invert a dinner plate on top and cut round with a sharp knife. Using the forefinger of one hand and the forefinger and thumb of the other hand, pinch a fluted edge all round. Cut out a round in the centre of the cake with a tumbler and cut the surrounding circle into 8 wedges to make the 'petticoat tails'.

Line a baking sheet with parchment or greased greaseproof paper and place the biscuits on top. Bake in a preheated moderate oven at 180°C/350°F, Gas Mark 4 for about 20 minutes or until crisp and golden. When serving, arrange the petticoat tails round the centre biscuit.

Apple buns

These can be served hot or cold. You will need 500 g/1 lb cooking apples to make 300 ml/½ pint thick apple purée. Ground coriander seed added with the sugar will enhance the flavour.

METRIC	IMPERIAL
225 g plain flour	8 oz plain flour
1 teaspoon cream of tartar	1 teaspoon cream of tartar
½ teaspoon bicarbonate of soda	½ teaspoon bicarbonate of soda
pinch of salt	pinch of salt
100 g butter or margarine	4 oz butter or margarine
100 g caster sugar	4 oz caster sugar
1 egg	1 egg
1-2 tablespoons water	1-2 tablespoons water
approx. 300 ml thick sweetened apple purée	approx. ½ pint thick sweetened apple purée
½ teaspoon ground coriander	½ teaspoon ground coriander
caster sugar or whipped cream to finish	caster sugar or whipped cream to finish

MAKES 12 TO 18

Sift the flour, cream of tartar, bicarbonate of soda and salt into a mixing bowl. Cut the fat into the flour and rub in to a breadcrumb consistency. Mix in the sugar, stir in the beaten egg and add a little water to mix to a stiff but not sticky dough, like shortcrust pastry. Roll out to 5 mm/¼ inch thick, divide in half and cut one half into rounds and line greased bun tins. Put 1 to 2 teaspoons of apple purée in each one. Cut the remaining pastry into smaller rounds, put them on top and press the pastry edges firmly together. Work up the trimmings, roll out and make more buns. Bake near the top of a preheated hot oven at 220°C/425°F, Gas Mark 7 for 15 minutes or until well risen and golden. Serve hot dredged with caster sugar, or cool on a wire tray and serve each bun topped with a swirl of whipped cream.

Apple buns; Oatcakes; Petticoat tails

Honey and cream scones

These delicious scones can also be cooked on the griddle.

METRIC	IMPERIAL
175 g whole wheat flour	6 oz whole wheat flour
175 g plain flour	6 oz plain flour
2 teaspoons bicarbonate of soda	2 teaspoons bicarbonate of soda
1 teaspoon cream of tartar	1 teaspoon cream of tartar
25 g butter or margarine	1 oz butter or margarine
150 ml soured cream	5 fl oz soured cream
100 g clear honey	4 oz clear honey
1 egg	1 egg
milk for glazing	milk for glazing

MAKES ABOUT 12

Sift the flour, soda and cream of tartar into a mixing bowl. Cut the fat into the flour and rub in to a breadcrumb consistency. Mix the soured cream and honey together until the honey is dissolved. Beat in the egg.
Make a well in the flour, pour in the liquid and mix into a soft dough. Turn on to a floured board and knead in a little extra flour if necessary. Roll out to 1 cm/½ inch thick and cut into rounds with a 5 cm/2 inch cutter. Work up the trimmings into a round and cut into 4 triangles. Place on a warmed floured baking sheet and brush the scones with milk. Bake near the top of a preheated hot oven at 230°C/450°F, Gas Mark 8 for about 10 minutes. Serve hot, split and spread with butter and honey or cold spread with butter or clotted cream.

Orkney broonie

This oatmeal gingerbread with its Norse name is a reminder of the Islands' past history. If no buttermilk is available, you can sour fresh milk with 1 tablespoon of lemon juice.

METRIC	IMPERIAL
175 g plain flour	6 oz plain flour
2 teaspoons ground ginger	2 teaspoons ground ginger
pinch of salt	pinch of salt
1 teaspoon baking powder	1 teaspoon baking powder
175 g medium oatmeal	6 oz medium oatmeal
75 g butter	3 oz butter
2 tablespoons treacle	2 tablespoons treacle
100 g soft brown sugar	4 oz soft brown sugar
1 egg, beaten	1 egg, beaten
approx. 250 ml buttermilk or soured milk	approx. 8 fl oz buttermilk or soured milk

MAKES ONE 900 G/2 LB LOAF

Sift the flour with the ginger, salt and baking powder into a mixing bowl and mix in the oatmeal. Cut the fat into the flour and rub in to a breadcrumb consistency. Melt the treacle with the sugar, stir in half the buttermilk (or soured milk) and the beaten egg. Stir this into the dry ingredients and beat well, adding more buttermilk if needed, until the batter drops off the spoon. Pour into a large 900 g/2 lb greased loaf tin and bake in a preheated moderate oven at 180°C/350°F, Gas Mark 4 for 1¼ hours or until well risen and a skewer inserted comes out clean. Allow to cool and set. Like most gingerbreads, this is best eaten hot or left overnight. Serve sliced and buttered.

Scots cream cookies

These are similar to Devonshire splits and in no way resemble American cookies. They should be very light. The secret is to have a really soft dough and handle it lightly on a well-floured board.

METRIC	IMPERIAL
225 g strong white flour	8 oz strong white flour
¼ teaspoon salt	¼ teaspoon salt
25 g caster sugar	1 oz caster sugar
25 g butter or margarine	1 oz butter or margarine
10 g fresh yeast	¼ oz fresh yeast
approx. 150 ml warm water	approx. ¼ pint warm water
TO FINISH:	TO FINISH:
12 teaspoons raspberry jam	12 teaspoons raspberry jam
12 teaspoons whipped cream	12 teaspoons whipped cream
icing sugar for dredging	icing sugar for dredging
MAKES 10 TO 12	

Sift the flour and salt into a mixing bowl and warm it. Mix in the sugar. Cut the fat into the flour and rub in to a breadcrumb consistency. Blend the yeast with the warm water. Stir into the flour mixture and beat well with a wooden spoon into a soft dough, adding a little more warm water if necessary. This should be a very soft dough, more like a batter, and it should be beaten until it begins to leave the sides of the bowl. Turn out on to a well floured board and knead with a light touch for 5 minutes until the mixture feels silky. Put back in the warm basin, cover with a clean damp cloth and leave to rise until doubled in bulk (about 1 hour in a warm room). Knead again on a floured

board for 5 minutes. Wet a tablespoon. Scoop off pieces of dough weighing about 40 g/1½ oz. Roll each one into a smooth ball and place on a warmed greased baking tray leaving room for expansion. Cover with a clean damp cloth and leave to prove for 10 minutes until the dough is springy to the touch. Bake in the centre of a preheated hot oven at 220°C/425°F, Gas Mark 7 for 10 minutes or until golden brown and well risen. A skewer inserted in the side will come out clean when they are cooked.
Cool on a wire tray. When cold, cut a slit across the top with scissors. Squeeze the sides to open the slit. Insert a teaspoon of raspberry jam and top with a teaspoon of whipped cream. Dredge with icing sugar.

Aberdeen buttery rowies

These yeast-leavened pastry rolls are rather like croissants and reflect the French influence on Scottish cooking, which has persisted since the days of Mary Queen of Scots. The rolls should always be served hot and reheat very successfully. They are a breakfast treat with butter and honey or marmalade, or for tea with crowdie (curd cheese) or cream cheese.

METRIC	IMPERIAL
450 g strong white flour	1 lb strong white flour
¼ teaspoon salt	¼ teaspoon salt
15 g fresh yeast	½ oz fresh yeast
or	or
10 g dried yeast	¼ oz dried yeast
1 tablespoon sugar	1 tablespoon sugar
450 ml tepid water	¾ pint tepid water
225 g butter	8 oz butter
100 g lard	4 oz lard
beaten egg for glazing	beaten egg for glazing

Sift the flour and salt into a warm mixing bowl. Cream the fresh yeast with the sugar and when liquid, add 150 ml/¼ pint of the tepid water. If using dried yeast, dissolve it in the water with the sugar and leave it to froth (see yeast cookery, p.14). Stir the yeast liquid into the flour with the remaining water. Mix into a dough, cover and leave in a warm place until it has doubled in bulk.
Meanwhile, cream the butter and lard together and divide it into 3 equal portions.
When the dough has risen, knock it back (p.15), place on a floured board and roll it out into a strip about 20 cm/8 inches wide and not more than 5 mm/¼ inch thick. Mark across into 3 equal portions and flake one-third of the fat on to the top two-thirds of the pastry. Fold, turn and roll out again as for Flaky Pastry (p.88). Repeat twice more until the fat is used up. If the dough is getting sticky, chill it for 30 minutes before continuing.
Roll out the dough again and cut it into rounds 6-7.5 cm/2½-3 inches. With floured fingers, shape the rounds into oval shapes. Place them well apart on a floured baking sheet, cover and leave in a warm place for 30 minutes or until doubled in bulk. Brush with beaten egg and bake in a preheated hot oven at 220°C/425°F, Gas Mark 7 for 20 minutes or until well risen and golden.

Honey and cream scones; Orkney broonie;
Aberdeen buttery rowies; Scots cream cookies

Wales

Teisen lap (plate cake)

This is the traditional Welsh plate cake. It used to be baked on an enamel plate, but it can be put into a shallow cake tin. In some parts of Wales the dough is rolled out, cut into rounds and cooked on the bakestone (griddle).

METRIC	IMPERIAL
225 g plain flour	8 oz plain flour
2 teaspoons baking powder	2 teaspoons baking powder
½ teaspoon grated nutmeg	½ teaspoon grated nutmeg
50 g butter	2 oz butter
50 g lard	2 oz lard
100 g soft brown sugar	4 oz soft brown sugar
100 g mixed dried fruit	4 oz mixed dried fruit
2 eggs, beaten	2 eggs, beaten
approx. 150 ml cream or buttermilk	approx. ¼ pint cream or buttermilk

Sift the flour, baking powder and nutmeg into a mixing bowl. Cut the fat into the flour and rub in to a breadcrumb consistency. Mix in the sugar and dried fruit. Stir in the eggs and sufficient cream or buttermilk to make a soft dough. Put into a shallow greased 20-23 cm/8-9 inch tin. Bake in a preheated moderate oven at 180°C/350°F, Gas Mark 4 for 20 to 30 minutes until risen and set. Lower the heat to 140°C/275°F, Gas Mark 1 for a further 40 minutes or until a skewer inserted comes out clean.

If cooking on the bakestone, make the dough slightly firmer, roll out to 2.5 cm/1 inch thick, cut into 6 cm/2½ inch rounds. Cook on a warmed greased bakestone for about 15 minutes on each side.

Teisen tel (honey cake)

This honey cake with its meringue topping can be served for tea or as a dessert for lunch.

METRIC	IMPERIAL
225 g plain flour	8 oz plain flour
½ teaspoon bicarbonate of soda	½ teaspoon bicarbonate of soda
1 teaspoon ground cinnamon	1 teaspoon ground cinnamon
100 g butter	4 oz butter
100 g soft brown sugar	4 oz soft brown sugar
3 eggs, separated	3 eggs, separated
100 g honey, warmed	4 oz honey, warmed
approx. 2 tablespoons warm water	approx. 2 tablespoons warm water
TOPPING:	TOPPING:
50 g caster sugar	2 oz caster sugar
1 tablespoon warm honey	1 tablespoon warm honey

Sift the flour with the bicarbonate of soda and cinnamon. Cream the butter and sugar together until light and fluffy. Beat in the egg yolks gradually and then the warmed honey. Fold in the flour adding a little warm water if the mixture gets too stiff. Beat one egg white until stiff but not too dry and fold it in lightly.

Turn the mixture into a greased 20 cm/8 inch round cake tin with a loose bottom. Bake in a preheated moderately hot oven at 200°C/400°F, Gas Mark 6 for 15 minutes. Lower the heat to 185°C/375°F, Gas Mark 5 for a further 15 to 20 minutes. Remove from the oven and allow it to shrink slightly before turning it out. Beat the remaining 2 egg whites until stiff. Fold in the sifted sugar quickly and lightly. Put the cake on a baking sheet and brush it all over with warmed honey. Swirl the meringue over with a palette knife, drawing it up in points. Return to a preheated moderate oven at 160°C/325°F, Gas Mark 3 for 15 minutes or until the meringue is set and delicately coloured. Serve cold.

Welsh cakes

These popular griddle cakes have long since crossed the Welsh border into England. They are served hot for tea with butter, sprinkled with cinnamon sugar, or cold spread with jam or honey. They travel up the Welsh mountains in the haversack of a shepherd or a hiker, to be eaten for lunch, partnered by a chunk of Caerphilly cheese.

METRIC	IMPERIAL
225 g plain flour	8 oz plain flour
1 teaspoon baking powder	1 teaspoon baking powder
¼ teaspoon mixed spice	¼ teaspoon mixed spice
50 g butter or margarine	2 oz butter or margarine
50 g lard	2 oz lard
75 g caster sugar	3 oz caster sugar
50 g currants	2 oz currants
1 egg, beaten	1 egg, beaten
2-3 tablespoons milk	2-3 tablespoons milk

Sift the flour, baking powder and spice into a mixing bowl. Cut the fat into the flour and rub in to a breadcrumb consistency, then mix in the sugar and currants. Mix in the egg and sufficient milk to make a stiff dough. Roll out on a floured board to ½ cm/¼ inch thick. Cut into 7.5 cm/3 inch rounds. Bake on a hot greased griddle until golden brown, about 4 minutes on each side.

Teisen dinca

Make up the Welsh Cake dough adding 175 g/6 oz peeled and grated cooking apples before adding the egg. Mix to a stiff dough, adding milk if necessary. Roll out, cut into rounds and cook on the griddle like Welsh Cakes. Serve hot with butter, golden syrup or honey.

Above: Welsh cakes

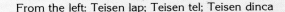

From the left: Teisen lap; Teisen tel; Teisen dinca

Ireland

Porter cake

This is a good moist fruit cake which keeps well. It is
quick and easy to mix and you can make it into a
Christmas cake by increasing the dried fruit and using a
larger tin. It is named after the type of stout which was
traditionally used.

METRIC	IMPERIAL
350 g plain flour	*12 oz plain flour*
¼ teaspoon mixed spice	*¼ teaspoon mixed spice*
175 g butter or margarine	*6 oz butter or margarine*
275 g soft brown sugar	*10 oz soft brown sugar*
450 g mixed dried fruit	*1 lb mixed dried fruit*
50 g glacé cherries, chopped	*2 oz glacé cherries, chopped*
50 g walnuts, chopped	*2 oz walnuts, chopped*
or	*or*
50 g blanched almonds,	*2 oz blanched almonds,*
shredded	*shredded*
grated rind of 1 lemon	*grated rind of 1 lemon*
½ teaspoon bicarbonate of	*½ teaspoon bicarbonate of*
soda	*soda*
150 ml warm stout	*¼ pint warm stout*
3 eggs, beaten	*3 eggs, beaten*

Line and grease a 20 cm/8 inch round cake tin (p.49) and
tie a band of brown paper round the outside of the tin and
5 cm/2 inches above it to protect the top of the cake during
baking. Sift the flour and mixed spice into a mixing bowl.
Cut the fat into the flour and rub in to a breadcrumb
consistency. Stir in the sugar, fruit, nuts and grated lemon
rind and mix well. Dissolve the bicarbonate of soda in the
warm stout and add to the beaten eggs. Stir this into the
dry ingredients and mix well.

Pour into the prepared tin and bake in the centre of a
preheated cool oven at 140°C/275°F, Gas Mark 1 for 2
hours or until set. Reduce the heat to 120°C/250°F, Gas
Mark ½ for a further hour or until a skewer inserted comes
out clean.

Allow to cool in the tin before turning out. Do not cut the
same day. It is best if kept to mature in an airtight tin.

Left: Porter cake

Below: Barm brack; Apple and potato cake

Barm brack

This fruited yeast bread is traditionally served in Ireland on Hallowe'en. A ring is baked in it and whoever gets it is supposed to be married within the year.

METRIC	IMPERIAL
15 g fresh yeast	*½ oz fresh yeast*
or	*or*
10 g dried yeast with	*¼ oz dried yeast with*
1 teaspoon sugar	*1 teaspoon sugar*
150 ml tepid milk or water	*¼ pint tepid milk or water*
225 g strong white flour	*8 oz strong white flour*
½ teaspoon salt	*½ teaspoon salt*
¼ teaspoon ground	*¼ teaspoon ground*
cinnamon	*cinnamon*
¼ teaspoon ground nutmeg	*¼ teaspoon ground nutmeg*
50 g butter or lard	*2 oz butter or lard*
40 g soft brown sugar	*1½ oz soft brown sugar*
1 egg, beaten	*1 egg, beaten*
50 g currants	*2 oz currants*
100 g sultanas	*4 oz sultanas*
25 g candied peel	*1 oz candied peel*
TO GLAZE:	*TO GLAZE:*
melted butter or 1	*melted butter or*
tablespoon sugar	*1 tablespoon sugar*
dissolved in 1 tablespoon	*dissolved in 1 tablespoon*
hot water	*hot water*

Dissolve the yeast in half the warm milk or water, adding the teaspoon of sugar if using dried yeast, and leave to froth. Sift the flour, salt and spices into a warm mixing bowl. Cut the fat into the flour and rub in to a breadcrumb consistency and mix in the sugar. Add the remaining warm milk with the beaten egg to the yeast liquid, and stir into the flour.
Beat to a soft dough, then fold in the fruit and peel. Cover and leave in a warm place to rise until doubled in bulk. Knock back the dough (p.15) and shape into a rounded loaf. Put into a well greased shallow 18 cm/7 inch round cake tin. Bake in a preheated moderate oven at 180°C/350°F, Gas Mark 4 for 50 to 60 minutes or until a skewer inserted comes out clean. While still hot, brush with melted butter or sugar and water glaze.

Apple and potato cake

This is a splendid winter warmer for high tea on a cold day. The potatoes must be hot and floury. You can use either Bramley apples which go fluffy when cooked, or dessert apples which keep their shape.

METRIC	IMPERIAL
750 g floury potatoes,	*1½ lb floury potatoes,*
peeled	*peeled*
3 teaspoons salt	*3 teaspoons salt*
50 g butter or margarine	*2 oz butter or margarine*
approx. 4 tablespoons	*approx. 4 tablespoons*
self-raising flour, sifted	*self-raising flour, sifted*
2-3 dessert apples, peeled,	*2-3 dessert apples, peeled,*
cored and chopped	*cored and chopped*
TO FINISH:	*TO FINISH:*
2 tablespoons caster sugar	*2 tablespoons caster sugar*
2-3 tablespoons softened	*2-3 tablespoons softened*
butter	*butter*

Boil the potatoes in well salted water. Drain and cover with a clean cloth until dry and fluffy, but still very hot. Sieve through a mouli-legumes or wire sieve and weigh off 500 g/1 lb.
Put the sieved potato in a warm mixing bowl and beat in the fat. Work in sufficient flour to make the dough manageable, adding salt to taste.
Divide the dough in half and pat or roll out into 2 rounds of equal size just over 1.5 cm/½ inch thick. Place one round on a warmed and greased griddle and spread with the chopped apple. Cover with the other round of dough and pinch the edges together.
Bake on the griddle over moderate heat until brown underneath. Slide the greased base of a cake tin underneath, turn the cake over and cook the other side. Slide the cake on to a hot serving dish, fold back one half of the top, sprinkle the apples with sugar and spread with softened butter. Repeat with the other half of the cake and serve at once dredged with caster sugar.
If no griddle is available, the cake can be cooked in a preheated moderately hot oven at 200°C/400°F, Gas Mark 6 for about 30 minutes without turning.

English counties

Richmond maids of honour (Surrey)

There are varying stories about the origin of these cakes. Some say they were popular with the Maids of Honour who attended the ill-fated Anne Boleyn at Richmond Palace, others say they were a favourite delicacy of Queen Elizabeth. The recipes also vary, some mixing floury baked potato with the ground almonds, others using clotted cream. Some people use curd cheese instead of making fresh curds with milk, which must drain overnight. Rennet is obtainable from chemists and some delicatessens. Plain junket tablets can also be used, following the instructions on the packet.

METRIC	IMPERIAL
1.2 litres milk	2 pints milk
1 teaspoon rennet	1 teaspoon rennet
75 g butter	3 oz butter
2 egg yolks	2 egg yolks
75 g caster sugar	3 oz caster sugar
1 tablespoon brandy (optional)	1 tablespoon brandy (optional)
25 g ground almonds	1 oz ground almonds
50 g floury cooked potato, sieved or cake crumbs	3 oz floury cooked potato, sieved or cake crumbs
¼ teaspoon grated nutmeg	¼ teaspoon grated nutmeg
grated rind and juice of 1 lemon	grated rind and juice of 1 lemon
225 g Flaky Pastry (p.88)	8 oz Flaky Pastry (p.88)

MAKES ABOUT 30

To make the curd, warm the milk, stir in the rennet and leave in a warm place until set. Tie the curd in a piece of muslin, and hang over a bowl to drain overnight.
Sieve the drained curd, which will weigh about 100 g/4 oz, with the butter. Beat together the yolks, sugar and brandy (if using). Add the ground almonds, sieved potato or cake crumbs, nutmeg and lemon rind and juice. Blend the mixture into the curd and butter. Roll out the pastry very thinly to 3 mm/⅛ inch thick. Cut into rounds and line about 30 patty tins (p.81). Prick the bottom and two-thirds fill with the mixture. Bake in a preheated moderate oven at 180°C/350°F, Gas Mark 4 for 25 to 30 minutes or until set and golden brown. Cool on a wire tray.

Richmond maids of honour

Kentish cake

This little cake with its unusual mixture of coconut, almonds and chocolate has an attractive flavour.

METRIC	IMPERIAL
100 g butter	4 oz butter
100 g caster sugar	4 oz caster sugar
3 eggs, beaten	3 eggs, beaten
100 g self-raising flour	4 oz self-raising flour
25 g cocoa	1 oz cocoa
25 g desiccated coconut	1 oz desiccated coconut
25 g ground almonds	1 oz ground almonds
1 tablespoon golden syrup, warmed	1 tablespoon golden syrup, warmed
¼ teaspoon vanilla essence	¼ teaspoon vanilla essence

MAKES ONE 15 CM/6 INCH CAKE

Cream the butter and sugar until light and fluffy. Beat in the eggs gradually. Sift the flour and cocoa and mix in the coconut and almonds, then fold into the creamed mixture with the warmed golden syrup and flavour with vanilla. Turn the mixture into a greased 15 cm/6 inch cake tin. Bake in the centre of a preheated moderately hot oven at 190°C/375°F, Gas Mark 5 for 50 minutes or until a skewer inserted comes out clean. Allow to shrink slightly before turning out on to a wire tray to cool.

Apple cheese cakes (Sussex)

Country housewives in pre-freezer days often preserved surplus fruit for the winter by cooking it into a thick well-flavoured purée called a cheese — apple and damsons were particular favourites. These fruit cheeses are very handy for making cakes and pastries.

METRIC	IMPERIAL
225 g apples	8 oz apples
4-5 tablespoons water	4-5 tablespoons water
thinly peeled rind of ½ lemon	thinly peeled rind of ½ lemon
2-3 cloves	2-3 cloves
½ stick cinnamon or pinch of ground cinnamon	½ stick cinnamon or pinch of ground cinnamon
1-2 tablespoons sugar	1-2 tablespoons sugar
25 g butter	1 oz butter
scant 25 g cake or fresh breadcrumbs	scant 1 oz cake or fresh breadcrumbs
2 egg yolks or 1 whole egg, beaten	2 egg yolks or 1 whole egg, beaten
100 g Sweet Shortcrust Pastry (p.79)	4 oz Sweet Shortcrust Pastry (p.79)
caster sugar for sprinkling	caster sugar for sprinkling

MAKES 12 TO 15

Wash the apples and cut into small chunks, remove the stem and 'eye', but do not peel. Cover the base of a pan with water, add the apples, lemon rind, cloves, cinnamon and sugar. Cover and cook until softened. Remove the lid and continue cooking into a thick pulp, stirring frequently so it does not stick. Remove the cinnamon stick, if using. Sieve the pulp and return to the pan over gentle heat. Add the butter and when melted remove the pan from the heat. Cool slightly, then stir in the crumbs and egg. Leave until cold.

Roll out the pastry thinly and line 12 to 15 patty tins (p.81). Prick the bottom and 3 parts fill with the apple mixture. Bake in a preheated moderately hot oven at 200°C/400°F, Gas Mark 6 for 15 minutes or until the pastry is crisp and the filling set. Remove from the tins and cool on a wire tray. When cold, sprinkle generously with caster sugar.

Kentish cake; Apple cheese cakes

Chelsea buns (Middlesex)

These sticky fruit buns with their distinctive square shape, were one of the delicacies for which the Chelsea Bun House was specially famed. The Bun House flourished under royal patronage from the days of the Hanoverians until it was finally demolished in 1839.

METRIC	IMPERIAL
225 g strong white flour	8 oz strong white flour
15 g fresh yeast	½ oz fresh yeast
or	or
1½ teaspoons dried yeast with 1 teaspoon sugar	1½ teaspoons dried yeast with 1 teaspoon sugar
½ teaspoon salt	½ teaspoon salt
100 ml warm milk	4 fl oz warm milk
25 g butter or lard	1 oz butter or lard
1 egg, beaten	1 egg, beaten
40 g butter, melted	1½ oz butter, melted
75 g mixed dried fruit (sultanas, currants, raisins)	3 oz mixed dried fruit (sultanas, currants, raisins)
2 tablespoons chopped mixed peel	2 tablespoons chopped mixed peel
50 g soft brown sugar	2 oz soft brown sugar
¼ teaspoon ground cinnamon or nutmeg	¼ teaspoon ground cinnamon or nutmeg
caster sugar for sprinkling	caster sugar for sprinkling
TO GLAZE:	TO GLAZE:
2 tablespoons clear honey, warmed or Sweet Milk Glaze (p.16)	2 tablespoons clear honey, warmed or Sweet Milk Glaze (p.16)

MAKES 9

Grease and warm an 18 cm/7 inch square cake tin. Put 50 g/2 oz of the flour into a warm mixing bowl, add the yeast (with the sugar if using dried yeast) and blend in the milk smoothly. Leave in a warm place for 10 to 20 minutes or until frothy. Sift the rest of the flour with the salt into another bowl and rub in the hard fat. Mix into the yeast batter with the beaten egg. Beat until the dough leaves the sides of the bowl. Turn on to a floured board and knead into a smooth dough (p.14). Cover and leave to rise until doubled in bulk.

Knock back the dough (p.15) and roll out into a 30 x 23 cm/12 x 9 inch rectangle. Brush with melted butter and cover with dried fruit, chopped peel and brown sugar, mixed with the spice. Trickle over the remaining butter. Roll up the dough like a Swiss roll and cut into nine 2.5 cm/1 inch slices. Place, cut side down, in the greased tin. Prove for about 30 minutes until the dough is puffy and the buns are just touching.

Sprinkle with caster sugar and bake in a preheated hot oven at 220°C/425°F, Gas Mark 7 for 15 to 20 minutes. Remove from the oven and brush with warm honey or Sweet Milk Glaze while still hot. Allow to cool slightly before separating the buns.

Chelsea buns; London buns

London buns

This traditional London version of the old 'Penny Buns' is flavoured with candied orange peel and caraway seeds instead of currants. They should be eaten freshly baked or split, toasted and buttered.

METRIC	IMPERIAL
450 g strong or plain flour	*1 lb strong or plain flour*
2 teaspoons salt	*2 teaspoons salt*
¼ teaspoon grated nutmeg	*¼ teaspoon grated nutmeg*
15 g fresh yeast	*½ oz fresh yeast*
or	*or*
1½ teaspoons dried yeast	*1½ teaspoons dried yeast*
50 g caster sugar	*2 oz caster sugar*
120 ml warm milk	*4 fl oz warm milk*
50 g butter	*2 oz butter*
25 g candied orange peel, chopped	*1 oz candied orange peel, chopped*
½ teaspoon caraway seeds	*½ teaspoon caraway seeds*
1 egg, beaten	*1 egg, beaten*
Sugar Syrup (p.16)	*Sugar Syrup (p.16)*
MAKES 12	

Sift the flour, salt and nutmeg into a warm bowl. Dissolve the yeast and sugar in the warm milk and leave to froth. Add the butter to melt it, then mix in the beaten egg. Make a well in the flour, stir in the liquid and mix to a smooth dough, with the candied orange peel and caraway seeds. Knead thoroughly (p.14), cover and leave in a warm place to rise until doubled in bulk. Knock back the dough (p.15) and shape into 12 round or oval buns. Place on a greased baking sheet, cover and prove until doubled in size. Bake in a preheated hot oven at 220°C/425°F, Gas Mark 7 for 15 minutes or until a skewer inserted comes out clean. Glaze while still hot and cool on a wire tray.

Cherry bumpers

Cherry bumpers (Buckinghamshire)

These cherry-filled turnovers are traditional at the end of the cherry picking season in August when they are made 'bumper' size for the pickers. In winter canned cherries can be used.

METRIC	IMPERIAL
500 g cherries, stalked and stoned	*1 lb cherries, stalked and stoned*
50-75 g brown sugar	*2-3 oz brown sugar*
450 g Flaky Pastry (p.88) or Sweet Shortcrust Pastry (p.79)	*1 lb Flaky Pastry (p.88) or Sweet Shortcrust Pastry (p.79)*
TO GLAZE:	*TO GLAZE:*
milk	*milk*
caster sugar	*caster sugar*
MAKES 8	

Roll out the pastry to 5 mm/¼ inch thick. Cut out rounds using a medium saucer. Cover one half of each round with cherries, leaving a border of 1 cm/½ inch and sprinkle liberally with brown sugar. Damp the border, fold over the other half of the pastry, press the edges together and pinch into flutes. Brush with milk and sprinkle with caster sugar. Bake in a preheated hot oven at 220°C/425°F, Gas Mark 7 for 20 minutes or until well risen and golden brown. Serve hot or cold, preferably with cream.

Sally lunns (Somerset)

There are various versions of this famous English tea cake, both of the recipe and the origin of the name. Some say they are named after a woman in Bath who is reputed to have baked them for the Prince Regent. Others maintain that the name is a corruption of the French *soleillune* — sun and moon cakes.

METRIC	IMPERIAL
450 g strong white flour	*1 lb strong white flour*
1 teaspoon salt	*1 teaspoon salt*
15 g fresh yeast	*½ oz fresh yeast*
or	*or*
1½ teaspoons dried yeast	*1½ teaspoons dried yeast*
1 teaspoon sugar	*1 teaspoon sugar*
50 ml warm water	*2 fl oz warm water*
125 ml single cream or milk	*5 fl oz single cream or milk*
50 g butter	*2 oz butter*
2 eggs, beaten	*2 eggs, beaten*
Sweet Milk Glaze (p.16)	*Sweet Milk Glaze (p.16)*
MAKES 2	

Grease and warm two 15 cm/6 inch round cake tins. Sift the flour and salt into a warm bowl. Dissolve the yeast with the sugar in the water and leave to froth. Warm the cream or milk, dissolve the butter in it and allow to cool slightly. Mix in the beaten eggs and add to the yeast. Make a well in the flour and stir in the liquid. Mix to a smooth soft dough. Cover and leave in a warm place until doubled in bulk. Turn on to a floured board and knead carefully (p.14). Divide the dough in half and round up each half into a ball. Put a ball into each tin, cover and leave until it has risen again and fills the tins.

Bake in the centre of a preheated hot oven at 220°C/425°F, Gas Mark 7 for 20 minutes or until golden and a skewer inserted will come out clean. Bring the hot glaze to the boil and brush over the cakes while still in the tin. Allow to shrink before turning out. Cut horizontally into 2 or 3 rounds and spread generously with butter or clotted cream. Reform and serve hot cut into wedges. Alternatively, toast the slices and spread with butter. This is very good on the second day.

Sally lunn; Bath buns

Bath buns (Somerset)

These are another speciality of Somerset which are now found all over Britain. The original recipe produced a light rich dough, but the contemporary buns are more solid and the amount of butter varies in different recipes.

METRIC	IMPERIAL
450 g strong white flour	*1 lb strong white flour*
1 teaspoon salt	*1 teaspoon salt*
25 g fresh yeast	*1 oz fresh yeast*
or	*or*
15 g dried yeast	*½ oz dried yeast*
2 teaspoons sugar	*2 teaspoons sugar*
4 tablespoons warm water	*4 tablespoons warm water*
175 g butter	*6 oz butter*
150 ml warm milk	*5 fl oz warm milk*
2 eggs, beaten	*2 eggs, beaten*
175 g sultanas	*6 oz sultanas*
2-3 tablespoons chopped mixed peel	*2-3 tablespoons chopped mixed peel*
Sweet Milk Glaze (p.16)	*Sweet Milk Glaze (p.16)*
approx. 100 g cube sugar, crushed	*approx. 4 oz cube sugar, crushed*
MAKES 12	

Sift the flour and salt into a warm mixing bowl. Dissolve the yeast with the sugar in the warm water and leave to froth. Melt the butter in the milk and add to the yeast with the beaten eggs. Blend into the flour with the sultanas and peel to make a fairly soft dough.

Turn on to a floured board and knead (p.14). Cover and leave in a warm place until doubled in bulk. Shape roughly into 12 buns. Set them well apart on a greased baking tray. Cover and leave to prove until puffy.

Bring the glaze to the boil and brush it over the buns. Sprinkle with the crushed cube sugar. Bake in a preheated hot oven at 220°C/425°F, Gas Mark 7 for 20 to 25 minutes or until golden and cooked through. Cool on a wire tray. Serve with butter.

Lardy cake (Wiltshire)

These were made as celebration cakes at harvest time and for other festivals in various parts of England. The richness of the recipe varies according to the region. In Suffolk they have a recipe which contains only a small quantity of lard and which is called, rather strangely, 'Brotherly Love'.

METRIC	IMPERIAL
350 g strong white flour	*12 oz strong white flour*
1 teaspoon salt	*1 teaspoon salt*
10 g lard	*¼ oz lard*
10 g fresh yeast	*¼ fresh yeast*
250 ml water	*8 fl oz water*
FILLING:	*FILLING:*
100 g lard	*4 oz lard*
75 g sultanas	*3 oz sultanas*
25 g chopped mixed peel	*1 oz chopped mixed peel*
100 g sugar	*4 oz sugar*
TO GLAZE:	*TO GLAZE:*
milk	*milk*
caster sugar	*caster sugar*

Make the dough according to the recipe for Basic White Bread Dough (p.16). Knead well, cover and leave in a warm place to rise until doubled in bulk. Turn on to a well floured board and knock back the dough (p.15). Roll it out thinly to about 1.5 cm/½ inch, then cut an 18 x 46 cm/7 x 18 inch rectangle. Mark across into 3 equal sections. Dot the top two thirds with half the lard and sprinkle with half the fruit, peel and sugar.

Fold up the bottom third of the dough, then fold over the top third. Seal the edges with the rolling pin, give a quarter turn and roll out again into a rectangle as for Flaky Pastry (p.88). Repeat with the rest of the lard, fruit and sugar; fold and turn. Roll and fold once again.

Line a roasting tin, approximately 25 x 20 cm/18 x 8 inches with foil and grease it. Put in the dough and leave in a warm place for 30 minutes or until risen and doubled in bulk. Brush with milk and sprinkle with sugar. Mark into squares with the back of a knife and bake in a preheated moderately hot oven at 200°C/400°F, Gas Mark 6 for 35 to 40 minutes.

Leave in the tin for the cake to soak up any fat which has leaked out. For a crisper under crust, cool on a wire tray.

Lardy cake

Cornish pasties (Cornwall)

Originally these pasties (called Tiddy Oggy) were made 'man sized' to make a satisfying packed meal for a farm worker. They were put on the kitchen table, each one with its own pastry initial on the side and collected as the men went out to work. In hard times the filling had a high proportion of vegetables, in prosperous times more meat.

METRIC	IMPERIAL
450 g topside of beef, minced	1 lb topside of beef, minced
100 g cooked potato or turnip, diced	4 oz cooked potato or turnip, diced
100 g onion, peeled and finely chopped	4 oz onion, peeled and finely chopped
2 tablespoons chopped fresh parsley	2 tablespoons chopped fresh parsley
¼ teaspoon mixed dried herbs	¼ teaspoon mixed dried herbs
salt	salt
freshly ground black pepper	freshly ground black pepper
450 g Plain Shortcrust Pastry (p.74)	1 lb Plain Shortcrust Pastry (p.74)
1 egg, beaten	1 egg, beaten

MAKES 8

Mix the meat with the vegetables, parsley and dried herbs. Season well with salt and pepper.

Roll out the pastry to 5 mm/¼ inch thick and cut into 15 cm/6 inch rounds, using a small plate. The trimmings can be worked up and re-rolled.

Divide the filling between the pastry rounds, placing it in the centre of each round. Brush the edges with water and draw them up to meet on top of the filling. Press firmly together, crimp with a fork and pinch into flutes.

Place on a greased baking tray and brush all over with beaten egg. Roll some pastry scraps into a thick 'cord', shape into initials and press on the side of the pasties. Brush with beaten egg. Cut 2 slits in each side of the pasties to let the steam escape.

Bake in a preheated moderately hot oven at 200°C/400°F, Gas Mark 6 for 15 minutes, then lower the heat to 180°C/350°F, Gas Mark 4 and cook for a further 35 to 50 minutes or until golden. Serve hot or allow to cool and store in an airtight container.

Many home cooks make pasties with chopped cooked meat left over from the Sunday roast, in which case the filling should be moistened with gravy and the pastry baked for not more than 25 to 30 minutes.

Apple cake (Dorset)

Apple cakes are made in the various West Country counties and are eaten hot or cold with clotted cream or butter.

METRIC	IMPERIAL
225 g self-raising flour	8 oz self-raising flour
1 teaspoon salt	1 teaspoon salt
100 g butter	4 oz butter
500 g cooking or dessert apples, peeled, cored and chopped	1 lb cooking or dessert apples, peeled, cored and chopped
100 g caster sugar	4 oz caster sugar
2 eggs, beaten	2 eggs, beaten
25 g soft brown sugar	1 oz soft brown sugar

Sift the flour and salt into a mixing bowl. Cut the fat into the flour and rub in to a breadcrumb consistency. Mix in the apples, caster sugar and eggs. Turn into a greased 20-23 cm/8-9 inch cake tin. Level off the top and sprinkle with the brown sugar. Bake in a preheated moderately hot oven at 200°C/400°F, Gas Mark 6 for 30 to 40 minutes. Allow to shrink slightly before turning out.
Serve hot with clotted cream, or split and buttered. If eating cold, cool on a wire tray and serve with butter.

Saffron cake (Cornwall)

Saffron has been used for its distinctive flavour and bright yellow colouring in English cooking since early days. It is the stigma of the autumn crocus and can be bought ground or in threads or filaments. Saffron is expensive but it is so potent that it is sold by the grain and only a minute quantity is needed. The filaments must be infused in water or milk and the liquid used to flavour and colour the mixture.

METRIC	IMPERIAL
½ teaspoon saffron threads	½ teaspoon saffron threads
150 ml milk	6 fl oz milk
15 g fresh yeast	½ oz fresh yeast
or	or
1½ teaspoons dried yeast with 1 teaspoon sugar	1½ teaspoons dried yeast with 1 teaspoon sugar
450 g plain flour	1 lb plain flour
pinch of salt	pinch of salt
¼ teaspoon ground cinnamon	¼ teaspoon ground cinnamon
¼ teaspoon ground nutmeg	¼ teaspoon ground nutmeg
¼ teaspoon mixed spice	¼ teaspoon mixed spice
50 g caster sugar	2 oz caster sugar
150 ml cream or 100 g butter, softened	5 fl oz cream or 4 oz butter, softened
1 tablespoon citron peel, chopped	1 tablespoon citron peel, chopped
50 g currants	2 oz currants
50 g sultanas	2 oz sultanas
Sweet Milk Glaze (p.16)	Sweet Milk Glaze (p.16)

MAKES ONE 18-20 CM/7-8 INCH CAKE

Crumble the saffron threads into a cup. Heat half the milk to boiling point and pour 3 tablespoons on to the saffron, leave for at least 10 minutes to infuse. Add the cold milk to the hot to cool it, add the yeast (with the sugar if using dried yeast) and mix until smooth.
Sift the flour, salt and spices into a warm mixing bowl and mix in the sugar. Stir in the cream, add the saffron liquid and the remainder of the milk and beat into a soft dough. Add a little warm water if necessary. Mix in the peel and dried fruit. Cover and leave in a warm place until doubled in bulk.
Knock back the dough (p.15), put it into a warmed and greased 18-20 cm/7-8 inch cake tin and leave in a warm place until doubled in bulk. Bake in the centre of a preheated moderately hot oven at 200°C/400°F, Gas Mark 6 for 15 minutes, then reduce the heat to 190°C/375°F, Gas Mark 5 or put the cake on a lower shelf for a further 15 to 20 minutes. A skewer inserted will come out clean when the cake is cooked. Allow to shrink slightly before turning out on to a wire tray to cool. Brush with hot glaze while still warm.

Cornish pasties: Saffron cake; Apple cake

Banbury cakes (Oxfordshire)

Banbury cake was originally made as one large very rich cake but by the 18th century the spicy fruit filling was encased in a crisp flaky crust. The pastries were kept hot in a cloth.

METRIC	IMPERIAL
100 g butter	4 oz butter
½ tablespoon honey	½ tablespoon honey
1 teaspoon ground cinnamon	1 teaspoon ground cinnamon
1 teaspoon ground allspice	1 teaspoon ground allspice
225 g currants	8 oz currants
100 g candied orange and lemon peel, chopped	4 oz candied orange and lemon peel, chopped
225 g Flaky Pastry (p.88) or Rough Puff Pastry (p.86)	8 oz Flaky Pastry (p.88) or Rough Puff Pastry (p.86)
TO GLAZE:	TO GLAZE:
1 egg white, beaten	1 egg white, beaten
2 tablespoons caster sugar	2 tablespoons caster sugar
MAKES ABOUT 6	

Cream the butter with the honey and spices. Blend in the currants and peel. Roll out the pastry thinly and cut into 10 cm/4 inch rounds. Put a spoonful of the filling in the centre of each round, damp the edges of the pastry and draw them together over the filling. Squeeze together, turn the pastry over and shape into an oval. Roll lightly to flatten slightly and cut 2 slits to let out the steam. Brush with beaten egg white and sprinkle with caster sugar. Use the trimmings to make more cakes.

Put on a baking sheet and bake in a preheated hot oven at 230°C/450°F, Gas Mark 8 for 15 minutes or until well risen and golden. Serve hot.

Coventry cakes (Warwickshire)

The long triangular shape of these cakes is traditional. At Christmas time they are often filled with mincemeat instead of jam, and are known locally as Coventry God Cakes.

METRIC	IMPERIAL
225 g Rough Puff Pastry (p.86) or Flaky Pastry (p.88)	8 oz Rough Puff Pastry (p.86) or Flaky Pastry (p.88)
225 g jam or mincemeat	8 oz jam or mincemeat
TO GLAZE:	TO GLAZE:
1 egg white, beaten	1 egg white, beaten
caster sugar	caster sugar
MAKES ABOUT 8	

Roll out the pastry very thinly to 3 mm/⅛ inch. Cut out 15 x 6.5 cm/6 x 2½ inch ovals. Put 2 teaspoons of jam or mincemeat on the top half of the pastry and brush the edges with water. Fold up the lower half leaving 2.5 cm/1 inch of the bottom pastry extending beyond the top. Fold over the bottom pastry edges neatly and firmly to enclose the filling. Turn the cake over and roll lightly with the rolling pin, keeping the long shape. Make 3 diagonal slits on top to allow steam to escape.

Place on a baking sheet, brush with beaten egg white and sprinkle with caster sugar. Bake in a preheated hot oven at 230°C/450°F, Gas Mark 8 for 10 minutes. Reduce the heat to 200°C/400°F, Gas Mark 6 and continue cooking for 15 minutes or until golden and crisp. Cool on a wire tray.

Banbury cakes; Coventry cakes; Derby cakes; Northamptonshire cheesecakes

Derby cakes

These cakes are quick and easy to make. They are more like biscuits and keep just as well in an airtight tin. Some people add a good pinch of mixed spice or ground coriander to the mixture.

METRIC	IMPERIAL
225 g plain flour	8 oz plain flour
pinch of salt	pinch of salt
100 g butter or margarine	4 oz butter or margarine
100 g soft brown sugar	4 oz soft brown sugar
100 g currants	4 oz currants
1 egg yolk, beaten	1 egg yolk, beaten
approx. 50 ml milk	approx. 2 fl oz milk

MAKES ABOUT 16

Sift the flour and salt into a mixing bowl. Cut the fat into the flour and rub in to a breadcrumb consistency. Mix in the sugar and currants. Stir in the egg yolk and sufficient milk to make a stiff dough. Knead until smooth.

Roll out on a floured board to just over 1 cm/¼ inch thick. Cut into 5 cm/2 inch rounds. Place on a greased baking tray. Work up, roll and cut out the scraps. Prick well and bake in a preheated moderate oven at 180°C/350°F, Gas Mark 4 for 15 minutes or until set and golden. Cool on a wire tray and store in an airtight tin.

Northamptonshire cheesecakes

These little tarts are filled with fresh curd made in the same way as for Richmond Maids of Honour (p.118). In this Northampton version the filling is warmed and currants are added.

METRIC	IMPERIAL
100 g drained fresh curds (p.118)	4 oz drained fresh curds (p.118)
50 g butter	2 oz butter
2 eggs, beaten	2 eggs, beaten
75 g caster sugar	3 oz caster sugar
100 g currants	4 oz currants
3-4 teaspoons grated lemon rind	3-4 teaspoons grated lemon rind
few drops of almond essence	few drops of almond essence
225 g Rich Shortcrust Pastry (p.77)	8 oz Rich Shortcrust Pastry (p.77)
grated nutmeg to sprinkle	grated nutmeg to sprinkle

MAKES 16

Press the curds through a wire sieve with a wooden spoon. Heat the butter, eggs and sugar over very low heat (or the mixture will curdle) until thickened. Remove from the heat and stir in the sieved curd, currants and grated lemon rind. Flavour to taste with a few drops of almond essence. Roll out the pastry to 5 mm/¼ inch thick and line sixteen 7.5/3 cm diameter tins. Prick the bottom of the tarts and spoon in the curd mixture so they are three-quarters filled. Grate a little nutmeg over the filling.

Cut the pastry trimmings into narrow strips and lay 2 crosswise over each tart, sealing the ends on to the pastry edge with water.

Bake in a preheated moderate oven at 180°C/350°F, Gas Mark 4 for 25 to 30 minutes until the filling is set and the pastry golden. Remove from oven, lift out of the tins and cool on a wire tray.

Manx bun loaf (Isle of Man)

Much of the baking on the island reflects, like this recipe, a Scottish influence. This is a richly fruited scone loaf made with bicarbonate of soda instead of yeast.

METRIC	IMPERIAL
225 g plain flour	8 oz plain flour
pinch of salt	pinch of salt
pinch of mixed spice	pinch of mixed spice
pinch of ground nutmeg	pinch of ground nutmeg
1 teaspoon bicarbonate soda	1 teaspoon bicarbonate soda
100 g lard or butter	4 oz lard or butter
100 g soft brown sugar	4 oz soft brown sugar
225 g sultanas	8 oz sultanas
100 g currants	4 oz currants
225 g raisins	8 oz raisins
25 g chopped mixed peel	1 oz chopped mixed peel
1 tablespoon black treacle	1 tablespoon black treacle
250 ml buttermilk or milk soured with 2 teaspoons lemon juice	8 fl oz buttermilk or milk soured with 2 teaspoons lemon juice

MAKES ONE 500 G/1 LB LOAF

Line the base and grease an 800 g/2 lb loaf tin. Sift the flour, salt, spice, nutmeg and bicarbonate of soda into a mixing bowl. Cut the fat into the flour and rub in to a breadcrumb consistency. Mix in the sugar and dried fruit and peel. Dissolve the treacle in the buttermilk and stir it in. Put into the loaf tin and bake in a preheated moderate oven at 180°C/350°F, Gas Mark 4 for about 1½ hours. A skewer inserted will come out clean when the loaf is cooked. Allow to shrink slightly before turning out on to a wire rack to cool.

Eccles cakes (Lancashire)

These are similar to Banbury Cakes but without any candied peel in the filling and they are round instead of oval.

METRIC	IMPERIAL
100 g currants	4 oz currants
50 g butter, melted	2 oz butter, melted
50 g soft brown sugar	2 oz soft brown sugar
pinch of grated nutmeg	pinch of grated nutmeg
225 g Flaky Pastry (p.88)	8 oz Flaky Pastry (p.88)
TO GLAZE:	TO GLAZE:
1 egg white, beaten	1 egg white, beaten
caster sugar	caster sugar

MAKES 8 TO 10

Mix together the currants, butter, brown sugar and nutmeg. Roll out the pastry to 5 mm/¼ inch thick and cut into 10 cm/4 inch rounds. Put a teaspoonful of filling in the centre of each round and damp the border. Pull the pastry together over the filling and squeeze together (see picture below). Turn the pastries over and roll out until the fruit begins to show through. Score the top with a sharp knife into a diamond pattern. Brush with egg white and sprinkle with caster sugar. Bake in a preheated hot oven at 230°C/450°F, Gas Mark 8 for 15 minutes or until well risen and golden brown. Serve hot or cold.

From the left: Manx bun loaves; Eccles cakes; Rum nicky; Ripon cheesecakes

Rum nicky (Cumberland)

Cumberland rum butter is a Christmas treat much appreciated in other parts of the country. It is a delicious hard sauce made with butter, brown sugar and rum and is served with Christmas pudding and mince pies instead of brandy butter. In this sweet pie a similar mixture is used to flavour the unusual date and ginger filling.

METRIC	IMPERIAL
100 g stoned dates, chopped	*4 oz stoned dates, chopped*
50 g preserved ginger, chopped	*2 oz preserved ginger, chopped*
1 cooking apple, peeled, cored and chopped	*1 cooking apple, peeled, cored and chopped*
50 g butter	*2 oz butter*
25 g soft brown sugar	*1 oz soft brown sugar*
2 teaspoons grated lemon rind	*2 teaspoons grated lemon rind*
2 tablespoons rum	*2 tablespoons rum*
225 g Sweet Shortcrust Pastry (p.79)	*8 oz Sweet Shortcrust Pastry (p.79)*
icing sugar to finish	*icing sugar to finish*

Mix together the chopped dates, ginger and apple. Cream the butter with the sugar and lemon rind and gradually beat in the rum. Grease the base of a 20 cm/8 inch shallow round pie dish and damp the lip.
Divide the pastry in half and roll out one half thinly and line the pie dish (see Double Crust Pie p.76). Cover the base with the mixed dates, ginger and apple. Spread the creamed mixture over the filling. Roll out the remaining pastry and cover the top. Knock back the edge of the pastry (p.75) and pinch into flutes. Cut V-shaped slits in the top of the pie to allow the steam to escape.
Bake in a preheated hot oven at 220°C/425°F, Gas Mark 7 for 10 to 15 minutes. Reduce the heat to 190°C/375°F, Gas Mark 5 and cook for a further 20 minutes or until the pastry is crisp and golden. Remove from the oven and dust with sieved icing sugar. This pie is usually served hot.

Ripon cheesecakes (Yorkshire)

There are many varieties of cheese cakes and although few of them today have any cheese in the filling, they are still called 'cheesecakes'. Some of them are made with fresh curds, like Richmond Maids of Honour (p.118), others have breadcrumbs and/or ground almonds. In Ripon, cheesecakes are traditionally served during the first week in August called Wilfra Week, commemorating St. Wilfred.

METRIC	IMPERIAL
300 ml milk	*½ pint milk*
25 g fresh white breadcrumbs	*1 oz fresh white breadcrumbs*
100 g butter, cut up	*4 oz butter, cut up*
50 g ground almonds	*2 oz ground almonds*
25 g caster sugar	*1 oz caster sugar*
finely grated rind of 1 lemon	*finely grated rind of 1 lemon*
3 eggs, beaten	*3 eggs, beaten*
225 g Rich Shortcrust Pastry (p.77)	*8 oz Rich Shortcrust Pastry (p.77)*

MAKES 16

Bring the milk to the boil and pour it over the breadcrumbs. Leave for 10 minutes for the crumbs to swell. Stir in the butter with the ground almonds, sugar and lemon rind. When thoroughly mixed gradually stir in the beaten eggs. Leave to cool.
Roll out the pastry to 3 mm/⅛ inch thick and line 16 greased patty tins (p.81). Prick the bottom and nearly fill with the mixture. Bake in a preheated moderate oven at 180°C/350°F, Gas Mark 4 for 20 to 25 minutes or until set. Allow to shrink in the tins, then lift out of the tins to cool on a wire tray.

Foreign baking

On the continent recipes have crossed many frontiers, sometimes in their original form, sometimes to be modified to national customs and taste or adjusted to use such ingredients as are regionally available. These recipes have been chosen because they are popular, not only in their own country, but with us as well. There is a wide choice of cakes, pastries and breads — from the rich Danish pastries (p.148), Austrian Apple Strudel (p.136) and Hungarian Nut Torte (p.138) — to the familiar breakfast time French brioches and croissants (p.142), and flat breads from northern Sweden (p.149) which have become popular as crispbreads in other countries. Baking styles in America are as varied as the diverse nationalities who have settled in that country, bringing their own traditions and tastes. On Thanksgiving Day, corn bread and pumpkin pie are traditional American fare, but at Christmas time many families revive the customs of their country of origin and the descendants of German and Austrian immigrants bake Stollen (p.139), the Italians bake their Panetone (p.141) and the Dutch their Christmas Kranz (p.147).

America

Fresh strawberry shortcake

This American favourite is quick and easy to make, either as individual shortcakes for tea, or one large one as a lunch time dessert. It is also excellent filled with fresh raspberries.

METRIC	IMPERIAL
225 g plain flour	8 oz plain flour
pinch of salt	pinch of salt
3 teaspoons baking powder	3 teaspoons baking powder
75 g butter	3 oz butter
75 g caster sugar	3 oz caster sugar
approx. 75 ml milk	approx. 3 fl oz milk
40 g butter, melted	1½ oz butter, melted
350 g fresh strawberries, hulled	12 oz fresh strawberries, hulled
1-2 tablespoons caster sugar	1-2 tablespoons caster sugar
150 ml whipping or double cream, whipped	6 fl oz whipping or double cream, whipped

Above: Hot apple muffins. Right: Popovers

Sift the flour, salt and baking powder into a mixing bowl. Cut the fat into the flour and rub in to a breadcrumb consistency. Add the caster sugar and mix to a soft dough with the milk. Turn on to a floured board and knead for about 1 minute. Divide in half and roll each half into a round on a greased baking sheet, brush one round with melted butter and place the other round on top. Bake in the centre of a preheated hot oven at 220°C/425°F, Gas Mark 7 for 20 to 30 minutes or until firm and golden brown. Separate the two rounds and cool on a wire tray. Put aside 9 even-sized strawberries for decoration.

Slice the remaining strawberries in half.
When the shortcake is cold, spread the sliced berries on the bottom layer, sprinkle with sugar and replace the top. Spread the cream over the top of the shortcake and ruffle it up. Decorate with the selected strawberries.
To make small shortcakes, cut the rolled dough into 7.5 cm/3 inch rounds and then follow the same method, baking for about 20 minutes.

Hot apple muffins

These American muffins are quite different from the English variety being raised with baking powder, but they are quite delicious, split and buttered for breakfast and very quick and easy to make. They are served hot and can conveniently be reheated by putting on a baking tray and covering loosely with foil in a hot oven at 220°C/425°F, Gas Mark 7 for 5 to 6 minutes.

METRIC	IMPERIAL
225 g plain flour	8 oz plain flour
1 teaspoon salt	1 teaspoon salt
3 teaspoons baking powder	3 teaspoons baking powder
50 g caster sugar	2 oz caster sugar
2 eggs, beaten	2 eggs, beaten
150 ml milk	¼ pint milk
50 g butter, melted	2 oz butter, melted
225 g cooking or dessert apples, peeled, cored and chopped fairly small	8 oz cooking or dessert apples, peeled, cored and chopped fairly small

MAKES 24

Grease 24 5 cm/2 inch muffin or bun tins. Sift the dry ingredients into a mixing bowl. In a small bowl beat the eggs with the milk and mix in the melted butter.
Stir the liquid quickly into the flour mixture. Speed is essential once the liquid is added to the baking powder, so do not beat the mixture or bother about any lumps. Fold in the chopped apples. Spoon the mixture into the greased bun tins so they are one-third full. Bake in a preheated hot oven at 220°C/425°F, Gas Mark 7 for 15 to 20 minutes or until well risen and golden brown. Turn out of the tins and serve hot.

Popovers

These crispy batter puffs are well named as in the hot oven they rise like balloons and literally 'pop over'. They are ideal served straight from the oven with grilled gammon or sausages for high tea or supper, or with roast meat instead of Yorkshire puddings.

METRIC	IMPERIAL
100 g plain flour	4 oz plain flour
½ teaspoon salt	½ teaspoon salt
2 eggs	2 eggs
175 ml milk	6 fl oz milk
25 g butter, melted	1 oz butter, melted

MAKES 8 TO 10

Brush dariole moulds or individual Yorkshire pudding tins with oil. Pour off any surplus as, if it mixes with the batter, the popovers will be heavy. Put the moulds on a baking sheet and heat in a hot oven at 230°C/450°F, Gas Mark 8.
Sift the flour and salt into a mixing bowl and make a well in the centre. Beat the eggs until frothy and stir them into the flour with half the milk. Beat or whisk into a smooth batter, then whisk in the rest of the milk and the melted butter. Pour into the heated tins so they are one-third full. Bake in the oven for 15 minutes, then reduce the heat to 180°C/350°F, Gas Mark 4 or put on a lower shelf and cook for a further 15 to 20 minutes or until crisp. Remove from the oven and pierce with a skewer to let the steam escape. Serve hot.

Cheese popovers

Make the batter as above and season well with salt and paprika. Oil and heat the tins, put 2 tablespoons batter in each one and cover with 1 teaspoon grated cheese and cover with another tablespoon of batter. Bake in a preheated hot oven at 230°C/450°F, Gas Mark 8 for 20 minutes or until well risen and golden. Reduce the heat as above and cook until crisp. Serve hot.

Left: Fresh strawberry shortcake

Devil's food chocolate cake

This is a rich dark cake with fluffy, crisp white frosting, decorated with melted chocolate.

METRIC	IMPERIAL
100 g plain chocolate, broken up	4 oz plain chocolate, broken up
125 g butter	5 oz butter
100 g dark brown sugar	4 oz dark brown sugar
1 tablespoon golden syrup	1 tablespoon golden syrup
200 g plain flour	7 oz plain flour
25 g cocoa	1 oz cocoa
1 teaspoon bicarbonate of soda	1 teaspoon bicarbonate of soda
2 eggs, beaten	2 eggs, beaten
100 ml milk	4 fl oz milk
TO FINISH:	TO FINISH:
450 g American Frosting	1 lb American Frosting
50 g plain chocolate	2 oz plain chocolate
2 tablespoons water	2 tablespoons water

MAKES ONE 20 CM/8 INCH CAKE

Syrup at the thread stage for American frosting

Line the base and grease 2 straight-sided 20 cm/8 inch layer cake tins (p.49). Heat the chocolate in a saucepan with the butter, sugar and syrup until just melted.
Sift the flour, cocoa and bicarbonate of soda into a mixing bowl. Make a well in the centre and stir in the cooled melted ingredients. Stir in the eggs and beat well, then mix in the milk. Pour the mixture into the prepared tins and bake in a preheated moderate oven at 180°C/350°F, Gas Mark 4 for 30 minutes or until set. Allow to cool in the tins before turning out on to a wire tray to cool.
When cold sandwich together with some of the American Frosting and coat the top and sides with the rest, swirling it with a palette knife, working quickly before it sets.
When the frosting has set, melt the chocolate with the water in a bowl over a pan of hot water. Stir until smooth and trickle it across the top of the cake from the tip of a spoon in a lattice pattern.

American frosting

This is the traditional icing for a Devil's Food Chocolate Cake and is also known as white mountain snow because of its appearance. The cake is iced before a chocolate topping is added.

METRIC	IMPERIAL
450 g granulated sugar	1 lb granulated sugar
250 ml water	8 fl oz water
2 egg whites	2 egg whites
¼ teaspoon vanilla essence	¼ teaspoon vanilla essence
or	or
2 teaspoons coffee essence	2 teaspoons coffee essence
or	or
2 teaspoons lemon juice	2 teaspoons lemon juice

Dissolve the sugar in the water over gentle heat, stirring. Do not allow to boil until the syrup is clear. When dissolved, raise the heat and boil rapidly, without stirring, to 120°C/240°F, until it forms a 'thread' when trickled off a spoon. If not hot enough, the frosting will not set, if overboiled it will set hard too soon.

Meanwhile whisk the egg whites in a large bowl until stiff and dry. When the syrup is ready, remove from the heat and allow the bubbles to subside. Holding the saucepan well above the bowl, pour the syrup in a thin stream over the egg whites, beating continuously with a wooden spoon. Add the flavouring and continue beating until the frosting loses its shiny appearance and *begins* to look like cotton wool. Use immediately before it sets.

Chocolate sour cream frosting

This frosting remains soft and creamy.

METRIC	IMPERIAL
75 g plain chocolate, broken into pieces	3 oz plain chocolate, broken into pieces
2 tablespoons water	2 tablespoons water
225 g icing sugar	8 oz icing sugar
approx. 75 ml soured cream	approx. 3 fl oz soured cream

Put the chocolate in a bowl with the water over a saucepan of simmering water. The hot water must not touch the bottom of the bowl. When soft, stir until smooth and creamy. Sift the icing sugar into a bowl and gradually stir in 2 tablespoons soured cream. Mix in the melted chocolate and add a little more soured cream to give a thick coating consistency.

Devil's food chocolate cake; White walnut cake

White walnut cake

This is traditionally a very sweet cake and if preferred the smaller quantity of sugar may be used.

METRIC	IMPERIAL
225 g butter or soft (tub) margarine	8 oz butter or soft (tub) margarine
275-350 g caster sugar	10-12 oz caster sugar
225 g plain flour	8 oz plain flour
3 teaspoons baking powder	3 teaspoons baking powder
pinch of salt	pinch of salt
250 ml milk	8 fl oz milk
4 egg whites	4 egg whites
75-100 g walnuts, chopped	3-4 oz walnuts, chopped
1/4 teaspoon vanilla essence (optional)	1/4 teaspoon vanilla essence (optional)
TO FINISH:	TO FINISH:
Chocolate Sour Cream Frosting or American Frosting (opposite)	Chocolate Sour Cream Frosting or American Frosting (opposite)
9 walnut halves	9 walnut halves

MAKES ONE 18-20 CM/7-8 INCH CAKE

Line and grease three 18 cm/7 inch sandwich tins or one 20 cm/8 inch round cake tin (p.49). Cream the fat and sugar together until light and fluffy. Sift together the flour, baking powder and salt and mix them in alternately with the milk, a third at a time. Whisk the egg whites until stiff but still moist, and fold into the mixture, alternating with the chopped nuts. Flavour with the vanilla if liked. Pour the mixture into the tin(s) and bake in a preheated moderate oven at 180°C/350°F, Gas Mark 4 for about 30 minutes for 3 tins or 1 hour for 1, or until springy to the touch. Split the large cake into 3 when cold.

Spread the layers with Chocolate Sour Cream Frosting, sandwich together and swirl the remainder over the top and sides of the cake. Alternatively fill and frost with American Frosting. Decorate with walnut halves.

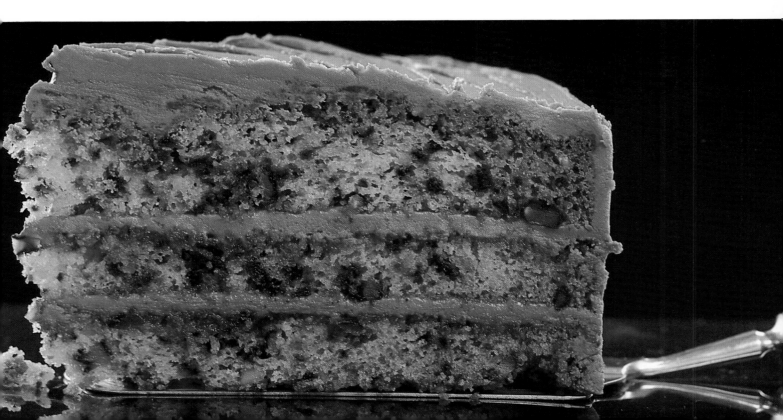

Austria

Raspberry Linzer torte; Apple strudel

Raspberry Linzer torte

This open tart, which is a speciality of the town of Linz, is made with a spiced pastry. It is commonly filled with raspberry jam but it is even more delicious made with fresh raspberries and served with Schlagsahne (p.152).

METRIC	IMPERIAL
125 g plain flour	5 oz plain flour
½ teaspoon ground cinnamon	½ teaspoon ground cinnamon
1 teaspoon instant coffee powder	1 teaspoon instant coffee powder
50 g ground hazelnuts	2 oz ground hazelnuts
75 g butter	3 oz butter
65 g caster sugar	2½ oz caster sugar
finely grated rind of ½ lemon	finely grated rind of ½ lemon
2 egg yolks or 1 whole egg, beaten	2 egg yolks or 1 whole egg, beaten
FILLING:	FILLING:
approx. 5 heaped tablespoons (275 g) raspberry jam or fresh raspberries with 2 tablespoons sugar	approx. 5 heaped tablespoons (10 oz) raspberry jam or fresh raspberries with 2 tablespoons sugar
TO GLAZE:	TO GLAZE:
1 egg white, beaten	1 egg white, beaten
caster sugar	caster sugar

Sift the flour, cinnamon and coffee into a mixing bowl and mix in the ground nuts. Cut the fat into the flour and rub in to a breadcrumb consistency. Mix in the sugar and lemon rind.

Stir in the beaten egg and knead into a soft dough. Chill for at least 30 minutes. Grease an 18-20 cm/7-8 inch pie plate. Roll out the dough into a round, put into the plate and with floured fingers work it out until it lines the plate, about ½ cm/¼ inch thick. Trim the edges neatly. Work up the trimmings and roll out to ½ cm/¼ inch thick and cut into narrow strips.

Prick the bottom of the pie and spread with raspberry jam or crushed fresh raspberries sweetened with caster sugar. Lay the strips of pastry across the filling in a lattice pattern. Trim the ends and press them into the edge of the pie. Brush the pastry with beaten egg white and dust with caster sugar. Bake in a preheated moderate oven at 180°C/350°F, Gas Mark 4 for 40 minutes or until set. Serve cold in the pie plate or lift out when cold.

Apple strudel

A strudel can be made with a sweet or savoury filling and one of the most popular is spiced apple, though a cherry filling is also a favourite. It requires practice to stretch the dough really wafer thin and it is much easier if you use oil instead of melted butter, which stiffens the dough as it cools. This feather-light pastry is rewarding to make and a delight to eat.

METRIC	IMPERIAL
100 g plain flour	4 oz plain flour
2 tablespoons corn oil	2 tablespoons corn oil
warm water to mix	warm water to mix
oil for brushing	oil for brushing
FILLING:	FILLING:
50 g butter	2 oz butter
50 g fresh white breadcrumbs	2 oz fresh white breadcrumbs
450 g sharp apples, peeled and coarsely grated	1 lb sharp apples, peeled and coarsely grated
grated rind and juice of ½ lemon	grated rind and juice of ½ lemon
50 g sultanas	2 oz sultanas
50 g walnuts or almonds, chopped	2 oz walnuts or almonds, chopped
½ teaspoon ground cinnamon	½ teaspoon ground cinnamon
50 g caster sugar	2 oz caster sugar
25 g butter, melted	1 oz butter, melted
icing sugar for dredging	icing sugar for dredging

SERVES 6 TO 8

Sift the flour into a warm mixing bowl and make a well in the centre. Add 3 tablespoons warm water to the oil, mix together and stir into the flour. Work into a soft, but not sticky dough, adding a little more warm water if necessary. Knead well, then roll into a long sausage shape. Hold the 'sausage' by one end and bang it on a floured board. Repeat the lifting and banging process which will lengthen the sausage, for several minutes, holding it by alternate ends until little bubbles appear under the surface of the dough. Knead it into a ball and leave it to relax for 30 minutes under an inverted bowl. Meanwhile prepare the filling. Heat the butter and fry the breadcrumbs in it until crisp.

Mix the grated apples with the lemon rind. Spread a large clean teacloth on the table and flour it. Roll out the dough on the cloth as thin as possible into a rectangle. Brush the surface of the dough with warm oil to make it pliable. Place your hands, palms downwards under the dough and stretch it over your knuckles, working from the centre outwards until it is paper thin and the pattern of the cloth shows through. An Austrian would say 'until you can read your love letters through it'.

Trim off the uneven edges to give a neat rectangle. Sprinkle the dough with the fried breadcrumbs, the apples, sultanas and chopped nuts and the cinnamon mixed with the sugar.

Lift up the edge of the cloth nearest you and roll up the strüdel away from you. Seal the edge with water and seal the two ends. Using the cloth, roll the strüdel on to a greased baking sheet, join underneath. Bend into a horseshoe shape and brush with melted butter.

Bake in a preheated moderately hot oven at 200°C/400°F, Gas Mark 6 for about 30 minutes or until crisp and golden. Dredge with icing sugar and serve sliced, hot or cold with Schlagsahne (p.152).

Strudel dough is stretched over the knuckles until paper thin

Hungary

Nut torte

This continental torte is made like a whisked sponge but with ground nuts instead of flour and has a crisp caramel topping instead of frosting. You can use walnuts, almonds, hazel or cashew nuts or a mixture of two or more kinds.

METRIC	IMPERIAL
50 g unblanched almonds	2 oz unblanched almonds
50 g walnuts	2 oz walnuts
4 eggs, separated	4 eggs, separated
125 g caster sugar	5 oz caster sugar
Mocha Butter Cream	Mocha Butter Cream
(½ quantity p.151)	(½ quantity, p.151)
CARAMEL TOPPING:	CARAMEL TOPPING:
75 g sugar	3 oz sugar
3 tablespoons water	3 tablespoons water
25 g walnut halves	1 oz walnut halves
SERVES 8	

Line the base and grease two 18 cm/7 inch sandwich tins (p.49). Mince the nuts in a mouli grater or electric grinder. Whisk together the egg yolks and caster sugar in a mixing bowl until a pale lemon colour. Whisk the whites until stiff but not too dry. Using a concave spatula or large cooking spoon, fold the whites and nuts into the egg yolks and sugar until well blended, but do not overfold. Pour into the sandwich tins and level off. Bake on the same shelf in the centre of a preheated moderate oven at 180°C/350°F, Gas Mark 4 for 30 minutes or until set. The top should spring back when gently pressed. Remove from the oven and allow to shrink slightly before turning out on to a wire tray to cool. When cold, place one half of the torte on a large serving plate, spread with Mocha Butter Cream and put the other one on top.

Caramel topping: oil the edge of the plate so any drips of caramel can be easily removed. Dissolve the sugar in the water in a small saucepan over a low heat. Stir until the syrup is clear, but do not allow to boil. When clear, raise the heat and boil rapidly without stirring until a rich caramel colour. Use immediately or the caramel will burn and turn too dark and make the torte bitter. Pour the caramel on top of the torte, spreading it with an oiled palette knife neatly to the edge. Arrange the walnuts on top quickly before the caramel gets hard. Press the back of a knife into the caramel marking it into 8 portions to make it easier to cut when serving. When the remaining caramel in the pan has cooled slightly, dip the end of the knife in it and draw it up in threads and trickle them over the nuts, or pull into spun sugar.

If you are not planning to serve the torte until the following day, it is advisable to delay making the caramel until then as it absorbs moisture in the air and loses its crispiness.

Nut torte

Germany

Dresden Christmas stollen

Stollen is a fruited yeast bread made in many parts of Germany. At Christmas time most families prefer the Dresden version which is rich and is decorated with colourful candied fruits for the occasion.

METRIC	IMPERIAL
75 g sultanas	3 oz sultanas
75 g raisins	3 oz raisins
25 g flaked almonds, toasted	1 oz flaked almonds, toasted
25 g glacé cherries, halved	1 oz glacé cherries, halved
50 g candied lemon peel, chopped	2 oz candied lemon peel, chopped
grated rind of 1 lemon	grated rind of 1 lemon
25 ml rum or brandy	1 fl oz rum or brandy
450 g plain flour	1 lb plain flour
pinch of salt	pinch of salt
¼ teaspoon ground mace or grated nutmeg	¼ teaspoon ground mace or grated nutmeg
25 g fresh yeast	1 oz fresh yeast
or	or
15 g dried yeast	½ oz dried yeast
50 ml warm milk	2 fl oz warm milk
100 ml warm water	4 fl oz warm water
50 g sugar	2 oz sugar
100 g butter, softened	4 oz butter, softened
approx. 40 g butter, melted	approx. 1½ oz butter, melted
CHRISTMAS DECORATION:	CHRISTMAS DECORATION:
mixed candied fruits, slices of orange, lemon and citron peel, glacé cherries and angelica	mixed candied fruits, slices of orange, lemon and citron peel, glacé cherries and angelica
icing sugar, sifted	icing sugar, sifted
TO GLAZE:	TO GLAZE:
4 tablespoons sugar	4 tablespoons sugar
4 tablespoons water	4 tablespoons water

Put the fruit, nuts, peel and grated lemon rind in a bowl and pour over the rum or brandy. Leave to soak, preferably overnight, until the spirit is absorbed. Sift the flour, salt and spice into a warm mixing bowl. Mix the yeast with the warm milk and water and a teaspoon of the sugar, sprinkle with flour and leave in a warm place until the crust cracks. Stir the yeast mixture into the flour with the remaining sugar and mix into a dough. Beat in the softened butter. Turn the dough on to a floured board and knead for 10 minutes (p.14) until smooth and no longer sticky. Cover the dough and leave in a warm place for 30 minutes or until doubled in bulk. Knock it back, (p.15) and work in the fruit, one-third at a time. Do this quickly or the dough will discolour. Shape into an oval. Roll out to about 2.5 cm/1 inch thick. Make a dent lengthwise with the rolling pin, slightly off centre. Fold over on to the wide side so the bottom edge of the dough extends beyond the top like a Parker House Roll (p.28) and press down. Place the stollen on a greased baking sheet, cover and leave in a warm place to prove for about 20 minutes or until puffy. Brush with melted butter and bake in a preheated hot oven at 230°C/450°F, Gas Mark 8 for 30 minutes. Reduce the heat to 200°C/400°F, Gas Mark 6 and continue baking for a further 20 to 30 minutes. A skewer inserted will come out clean when the stollen is cooked. Meanwhile dissolve the sugar in the water for the glaze. While the stollen is still hot, brush with the sugar glaze. When decorating for Christmas, arrange mixed candied fruits on top of the Stollen and brush again with the sugar glaze or cover the top generously with sifted icing sugar. Stollen keeps well and can also be sliced and toasted.

Dresden Christmas stollen

Italy

Amaretti

These macaroons are made in various sizes and in Italy are used in many ways — small ones for petit fours and decoration, larger ones crushed and incorporated with ices and dessert creams.

METRIC	IMPERIAL
100 g ground almonds	4 oz ground almonds
15 g ground rice or rice flour	½ oz ground rice or rice flour
225 g caster sugar	8 oz caster sugar
¼ teaspoon ratafia essence	¼ teaspoon ratafia essence
2 egg whites	2 egg whites
2 sheets of rice paper	2 sheets of rice paper
12 blanched almonds, split	12 blanched almonds, split
1 egg white, beaten for glazing	1 egg white, beaten for glazing
MAKES 24	

Mix together the almonds, rice or flour and caster sugar. Add the ratafia essence to the unbeaten egg whites and mix into the dry ingredients. Cream to a smooth paste (an electric blender will save much time). Put the mixture into a forcing bag with a plain 1.5 cm/½ inch nozzle. Rule the rice paper into 5 cm/1½ inch squares. Pipe the mixture into the centre of each square making biscuits 2.5 cm/1 inch in diameter and flatten slightly.
Press a split almond in the centre of each macaroon. Brush lightly with beaten egg white. Bake in a preheated moderate oven at 180°C/350°F, Gas Mark 4 for about 20 minutes or until golden brown. Cool on a wire tray and cut off the rice paper round each macaroon. Store in an airtight tin.

Frangipane barquettes

Frangipane has an interesting history. The word means 'broken bread' and refers to the crushed biscuits in the creamy filling. It is said that the Italian family who invented it, made Communion wafers and that the recipe was introduced into France by Catherine de Medici. In turn, Mary Queen of Scots brought it to Scotland when it became known as Edinburgh cream tart.

METRIC	IMPERIAL
225 g Sweet Shortcrust Pastry (p.79)	8 oz Sweet Shortcrust Pastry (p.79)
70 g unsalted butter	2½ oz unsalted butter
40 g plain flour	1½ oz plain flour
150 ml milk	¼ pint milk
1 egg plus 1 yolk, beaten	1 egg plus 1 yolk, beaten
25 g caster sugar	1 oz caster sugar
2 teaspoons finely grated lemon rind	2 teaspoons finely grated lemon rind
25-50 g Amaretti or ratafia biscuits, coarsely crushed	1-2 oz Amaretti or ratafia biscuits, coarsely crushed
1 tablespoon rum or sweet sherry	1 tablespoon rum or sweet sherry
¼ teaspoon vanilla essence	¼ teaspoon vanilla essence
4 tablespoons raspberry or apricot jam	4 tablespoons raspberry or apricot jam
TO DECORATE:	TO DECORATE:
about 120 ml double or whipping cream, whipped	about 4 fl oz double or whipping cream, whipped
chopped pistachio nuts or glacé fruits	chopped pistachio nuts or glacé fruits
MAKES ABOUT 12	

Roll out the pastry and line 12 or more boat shaped tins and bake blind (see Ricotta Barquettes p.83).
Meanwhile make the filling. Melt 40 g/1½ oz of the butter in a small saucepan. Remove from the heat and blend in the flour then the milk. Gradually stir in the beaten eggs, sugar and grated lemon rind. Cook, stirring continuously, until the mixture thickens and leaves the side of the pan. If it is not cooked, the filling will taste of raw flour. Heat the remaining butter in a small pan, until it turns nut brown, and stir it into the mixture. This 'beurre noisette' gives the frangipane its characteristic flavour. Stir the Amaretti or ratafias into the mixture and flavour with the rum or sherry and vanilla. Spread a little jam on the bottom of each pastry case. Spoon or pipe in the filling. When cold, decorate with piped whipped cream and chopped pistachio nuts or glacé fruits.

Panetone

This sweet yeast cake is a traditional part of the Christmas fare in Italy, but it is served with coffee and for breakfast throughout the year in many regions. Panetone keeps well in an airtight container and can be reheated whole.

METRIC	IMPERIAL
approx. 350 g plain flour	*approx. 12 oz plain flour*
¼ teaspoon salt	*¼ teaspoon salt*
15 g fresh yeast	*½ oz fresh yeast*
or	*or*
1½ teaspoons dried yeast	*1½ teaspoons dried yeast*
50 g caster sugar	*2 oz caster sugar*
4 tablespoons warm water	*4 tablespoons warm water*
3 eggs or 6 egg yolks	*3 eggs or 6 egg yolks*
¼ teaspoon vanilla essence	*¼ teaspoon vanilla essence*
2 teaspoons finely grated lemon rind	*2 teaspoons finely grated lemon rind*
100 g butter, softened	*4 oz butter, softened*
75 g sultanas	*3 oz sultanas*
40 g candied citron peel, chopped	*1½ oz candied citron peel, chopped*
25 g butter, melted	*1 oz butter, melted*

Sift about 225 g/8 oz of the flour and salt into a bowl and put to warm. Dissolve the yeast in the warm water, with a teaspoon of the sugar and leave in a warm place to froth. Mix the rest of the sugar into the flour. Beat the eggs with the vanilla essence and lemon rind. Stir into the flour, a third at a time and mix into a soft dough, which can be gathered into a ball. Gradually beat in the softened butter. Add a little more flour, working the dough with your hands into a manageable ball. Turn it on to a floured board and knead for about 10 minutes (p.14) until smooth and silky. Put into a warm bowl, cover, and leave for about 45 minutes to 1 hour or until doubled in bulk.

Knock back the dough (p.15) and knead in the sultanas and peel. Shape the dough into a ball, put into a greased and lined 18 cm/7 inch round cake tin and cut a cross in the top. Leave in a warm place for about 15 to 20 minutes or until doubled in bulk.

Brush the top of the panetone with melted butter and bake in the centre of a preheated moderately hot oven at 200°C/400°F, Gas Mark 6 for 10 minutes. Brush again with melted butter and reduce the heat to 180°C/350°F, Gas Mark 4 for a further 40 minutes or until the top is crisp and golden and a skewer inserted comes out clean. Cool on a wire tray. Serve cut into thick wedges.

Amaretti; Frangipane barquettes; Panetone

France

Croissants

Hot croissants and coffee for breakfast are one of the first
pleasures for visitors to France.

METRIC	IMPERIAL
225 g strong white flour	8 oz strong white flour
1 teaspoon salt	1 teaspoon salt
15 g lard	½ oz lard
15 g fresh yeast	½ oz fresh yeast
or	or
1½ teaspoons dried yeast	1½ teaspoons dried yeast
100 ml warm water	4 fl oz warm water
1 teaspoon sugar	1 teaspoon sugar
1 egg, beaten	1 egg, beaten
75 g butter	3 oz butter
1 egg, beaten with	1 egg, beaten with
1 teaspoon caster sugar	1 teaspoon caster sugar
to glaze	to glaze

MAKES 6

Sift the flour and salt into a warm mixing bowl. Rub in the
lard. Dissolve the yeast in the warm water with the sugar.
Leave to froth, then mix in the beaten egg. Make a well in
the centre of the flour, add the yeast mixture and gradually
work into a dough. Beat vigorously until it leaves the sides
of the bowl clean. Turn on to a floured board and knead for
10 minutes (p.14) until smooth. Cream the butter with a
rounded knife and divide into 3 equal portions.
*Roll out the dough into a strip about 18 cm/7 inches wide
and 5 mm/¼ inch thick. Keep the sides straight and the
corners neat. Mark the dough across into 3 equal sections.
With a palette knife flake one-third of the butter on to the
top of the dough leaving a border of 1 cm/½ inch. Fold the
bottom third up and the top third down, incorporating as
much air as possible and seal the edges with the rolling
pin as for Flaky Pastry (p.88). Give the dough a quarter
turn.
Repeat from * twice more, flaking on a third of the butter
each time. Work quickly or the butter may melt and make
the dough sticky. Put the folded dough in a polythene bag
and refrigerate for 30 minutes. Repeat the rolling, folding
and turning 3 more times without adding any butter.
Replace in the bag and refrigerate again for 30 minutes.
To shape the croissants, roll out the dough into a neat
strip 56 x 15 cm/22 x 6 inches and trim the edges. Turn the
long side towards you and working from the left, notch the
nearest edge at 15 cm/6 inch intervals, leaving 7.5 cm/3
inches over at the right hand end. Notch the further edge
at 15 cm/6 inch intervals working from the right. Cut
diagonally across the pastry from notch to notch into
triangles measuring 15 cm/6 inches at the base. Set aside
the half triangles at each end to cut into Fleurons (p.90).
Brush the triangles with the egg and sugar glaze. Roll up
loosely from the base, finish with the tip underneath, then
curve into a crescent shape. Place the croissants on a clean
baking tray, well apart. Cover with a clean cloth and leave
in a warm place for 30 minutes or until puffy. Brush
lightly with the egg and sugar glaze and bake in a
preheated hot oven at 220°C/425°F, Gas Mark 7 for 20
minutes or until well risen and golden. Serve warm with
butter and preserves or reheat before serving.

Brioches; Croissants

Brioches

In many French homes these sweet yeast sponges are
'dunked' into the breakfast bowls of café au lait (milky
coffee). They can also be served with butter and preserves.

METRIC	IMPERIAL
225 g strong white flour	8 oz strong white flour
½ teaspoon salt	½ teaspoon salt
1 tablespoon caster sugar	1 tablespoon caster sugar
15 g fresh yeast	½ oz fresh yeast
or	or
1½ teaspoons dried yeast	1½ teaspoons dried yeast
with 1 teaspoon sugar	with 1 teaspoon sugar
2 tablespoons warm water	2 tablespoons warm water
2 eggs, beaten	2 eggs, beaten
50 g butter, melted	2 oz butter, melted
TO GLAZE:	TO GLAZE:
1 tablespoon sugar	1 tablespoon sugar
2 tablespoons milk	2 tablespoons milk

MAKES 12

Sift the flour and salt into a warm mixing bowl, mix in the
sugar and make a well in the centre. Dissolve the yeast in
the warm water, with the sugar if using dried yeast. Leave
to froth, then pour into the flour. Mix in, gradually adding

Rum babas

METRIC	IMPERIAL
100 g plain flour	4 oz plain flour
pinch of salt	pinch of salt
15 g fresh yeast	½ oz fresh yeast
or	or
1½ teaspoons dried yeast	1½ teaspoons dried yeast
2 tablespoons caster sugar	2 tablespoons caster sugar
50 ml warm water	2 fl oz warm water
2 eggs, beaten	2 eggs, beaten
65 g butter, creamed	2½ oz butter, creamed
RUM SYRUP:	RUM SYRUP:
100 g caster sugar	4 oz caster sugar
175 ml water	6 fl oz water
4 tablespoons rum	4 tablespoons rum
150 ml double or whipping cream, whipped	¼ pint double or whipping cream, whipped
maraschino or glacé cherries, to decorate	maraschino or glacé cherries, to decorate

MAKES 8

Grease and warm eight 10 cm/4 inch ring moulds. Sift the flour and salt into a warm mixing bowl. Cream the fresh yeast with the sugar, add the water and beaten eggs. If using dried yeast, dissolve it with the sugar in the water and let it froth before adding the eggs.

Make a well in the centre of the flour, stir in the yeast liquid and eggs and beat with a wooden spoon into a smooth batter. Cover the bowl and leave in a warm place to prove for 45 minutes or until doubled in bulk. Beat in the creamed butter gradually and spoon or pipe the batter into the prepared moulds until they are half full. Place on a baking tray, cover and leave in a warm place until the dough rises to the rim of the tins. Bake in a preheated moderately hot oven at 200°C/400°F, Gas Mark 6 for 15 minutes or until well risen and golden brown. Meanwhile, prepare the rum syrup by dissolving the sugar in the water, then boiling briskly to a syrup consistency. Cool slightly and add the rum. When cooked, remove the babas from the oven and allow to shrink slightly before turning out into a shallow tin. While they are still hot, spoon over the rum syrup and leave them to soak it up. When ready to serve, put into paper cases and fill the centres with a swirl of whipped cream. Top with a maraschino or glacé cherry.

the beaten eggs and melted butter. Beat with a wooden spoon until the dough leaves the sides of the bowl clean. Knead the dough on a floured board for 5 minutes (p.14). Put into an oiled polythene bag and leave in a warm place for 1 hour or until the dough has doubled in bulk. Knock back the dough (p.15) then shape into a thick sausage shape and divide into 12 equal portions. Oil some brioche tins or fluted bun tins, 6 cm/2½ inches wide. Pinch off a quarter of each piece of dough and shape into a ball. Roll the rest of the piece into a larger ball and put into a bun tin. Make a hole in the centre with the floured handle of the wooden spoon, pressing it down to the bottom of the tin and rotating it to widen the top of the hole. Insert the smaller ball in the hole and press it in gently but firmly. Place the tins on a baking tray, cover and leave in a warm place or until doubled in bulk. Mix the sugar with the milk for the glaze, then brush over the brioche. Bake in the centre of a preheated hot oven at 220°C/450°F, Gas Mark 8 for 10 minutes or until well risen and golden brown. Cool on a wire tray.

Rum babas

Gâteau jalousie

The name of this gâteau has nothing to do with jealousy as might be thought. The wooden shutters you see on most French houses are known as jalousies and the pastry top on this gateau is cut across at regular intervals to resemble the slats of the wooden shutters.

METRIC	IMPERIAL
225 g Flaky Pastry (p.88) or puff pastry	8 oz Flaky Pastry (p.88) or puff pastry
approx. 225 g apricot jam	approx. 8 oz apricot jam
50 g mixed crystallized and glacé fruits, chopped	2 oz mixed crystallized and glacé fruits, chopped
TO GLAZE:	TO GLAZE:
1 egg, beaten	1 egg, beaten
caster sugar	caster sugar

Roll out the pastry to 3 mm/⅛ inch thick into a large rectangle and cut out a 30 cm/12 inch square. Cut in half to make two strips 15 cm/6 inches wide. Place one piece on a damp baking sheet and prick all over. Leaving a border all round of 2.5 cm/1 inch, spread over the jam evenly and fairly thickly. Scatter over the chopped fruits. Sprinkle the other piece of pastry lightly with flour and fold it in half lengthwise. With a sharp knife cut through the folded edge to a depth of 5 cm/2 inches, at regular 1 cm/⅜ inch intervals, leaving a border all round of 2.5 cm/1 inch, uncut. Unfold the pastry carefully and brush off any loose flour. (If the pastry has softened in the warm kitchen, it will be difficult to lift after slitting, so refrigerate it for 20 minutes or until stiffened.)
Brush the border of the bottom piece of pastry with water, lift on the slashed top carefully and press the borders together with your finger tips. Knock back the outside edges with the back of a knife (p.75) and scallop them. Mark the top of the border with criss-cross lines. Leave the gâteau to relax for 20 to 30 minutes in a cool place, not the refrigerator.
Bake in a preheated hot oven at 230°C/450°F, Gas Mark 8 for 25 minutes. Brush the top with the beaten egg and dredge with caster sugar, then continue baking for a further 5 minutes or until the pastry has a golden glaze. Lift the gâteau carefully on to a wire tray to cool.
When cold, cut across into 6 or 8 slices and serve with Chantilly Cream (p.152).

Cutting folded pastry for Gâteau jalousie

Gâteau jalousie with apple filling

Spread the pastry base with quince jelly and cover with thick apple purée sweetened to taste. Finish and bake as above.

Gâteau jalousie with cream filling

Spread the pastry base thinly with redcurrant jelly instead of apricot jam and cover with thick cold Pastry Cream flavoured with vanilla or almond essence (p.152). Finish and bake as above.

Gâteau jalousie; Chestnut meringue gâteau

Chestnut meringue gâteau

This gâteau is a lovely party piece for sweet-toothed people. For very special occasions it can be decorated with halved marrons glacés.

METRIC	IMPERIAL
3 egg whites	3 egg whites
175 g caster sugar	6 oz caster sugar

Cover 2 baking sheets with parchment or greaseproof paper and draw 2 circles on each, 18 cm/7 inches in diameter. Lightly oil the greaseproof paper if using. Beat the egg whites until stiff and dry, sift in 50 g/2 oz of the sugar and whisk again until thick and glossy. Sift and fold in the remaining sugar, half at a time. Spoon the meringue into a large piping bag with a large rose nozzle. Pipe 9 small rosettes on to the baking sheets outside the circles. Divide the remaining meringue equally between the 4

circles and spread it out evenly about 1.5 cm/½ inch thick into 4 flat biscuits. Bake in a preheated cool oven at 140°C/275°F, Gas Mark 1 for about 1 hour or until crisp. Meanwhile make the Chestnut Meringue Cream and Praline.

Remove the meringues to a pastry board. Cut the parchment or paper between the circles. Turn upside down and peel off the paper. If a little sticky return to the oven for a few minutes to dry out.

Divide the Chestnut Meringue Cream into 4 equal portions. Spread one portion over each of 3 meringue rounds and place on top of each other with the plain one on top. Spread most of the remaining Chestnut Meringue Cream round the sides.

Spread the crushed Praline on a sheet of greaseproof paper and holding the gâteau sideways between two hands, roll it in the praline until the sides are evenly coated.

Place the gâteau on a plate and arrange the meringue rosettes on top, fixing each one with a dab of Chestnut Meringue Cream. Refrigerate until required, preferably overnight, which will make it easier to cut.

Chestnut meringue cream

METRIC	IMPERIAL
1 large egg white	1 large egg white
100 g icing sugar	4 oz icing sugar
175 g unsalted butter	6 oz unsalted butter
4 tablespoons sweetened chestnut purée	4 tablespoons sweetened chestnut purée
¼ teaspoon vanilla essence	¼ teaspoon vanilla essence
approx. 2 teaspoons lemon juice	approx. 2 teaspoons lemon juice

Put the egg white and icing sugar in a bowl over a saucepan of simmering water and whisk until it will form soft peaks. Remove from the saucepan and continue whisking until cool.

Cream the butter with the chestnut purée and gradually beat into the cooled meringue. If the meringue is hot, the butter will turn oily. Flavour with vanilla essence and lemon juice to taste.

Praline

METRIC	IMPERIAL
75 g caster sugar	3 oz caster sugar
3 tablespoons water	3 tablespoons water
75 g whole unblanched almonds	3 oz whole unblanched almonds

Lightly oil a tin. Put the sugar and water in a heavy-based saucepan and stir over gentle heat until thoroughly dissolved. Tip in the almonds, stir once and not again. Bring to the boil and bubble briskly until the syrup is caramel coloured and smells of toffee. The oil comes out of the almond skins and darkens the syrup before it caramelizes so be careful, or it will not set properly. Pour the praline into the tin and spread with an oiled palette knife. When quite cold chop coarsely. It can be stored very satisfactorily in a completely airtight jar or tin.

Holland

Christmas tree cookies

These rich and decorative cookies are made to hang on the Christmas tree so they have a little hole in the top for a narrow ribbon or tinsel cord to go through. They are coated with coloured coffee sugar crystals or iced and decorated with silver balls or sugar strands. They are very popular with children at birthday parties.

METRIC	IMPERIAL
250 g plain flour	*9 oz plain flour*
1 teaspoon baking powder	*1 teaspoon baking powder*
pinch of salt	*pinch of salt*
165 g caster sugar	*5½ oz caster sugar*
1 teaspoon finely grated	*1 teaspoon finely grated*
* lemon rind*	* lemon rind*
165 g unsalted butter	*5½ oz unsalted butter*
approx. 1 tablespoon milk	*approx. 1 tablespoon milk*
TO DECORATE:	*TO DECORATE:*
1 egg white, beaten	*1 egg white, beaten*
4-5 tablespoons coloured	*4-5 tablespoons coloured*
* coffee sugar crystals*	* coffee sugar crystals*
Lemon Glacé Icing (p.150)	*Lemon Glacé Icing (p.150)*
silver and red balls, sugar	*silver and red balls, sugar*
* strands, etc.*	* strands, etc.*

MAKES ABOUT 30 TO 36

Sift the flour, baking powder and salt into a mixing bowl. Mix in the sugar and grated lemon rind. Cut the fat into the flour then rub in to a breadcrumb consistency and knead into a soft dough, adding a little milk if needed. Shape into a ball and set aside in a cool place for at least 1 hour before rolling out. Turn the dough on to a floured board and roll out to 3 mm/⅛ inch thick.

Using biscuit cutters, cut out a variety of shapes — Christmas trees, stars, rings and animals. Work up and re-roll the trimmings to make more cookies. With a thick skewer, pierce a hole in the top of each one. Leaving the other shapes plain, brush one side of the Christmas trees and stars sparingly with egg white, then dip into the coffee sugar before baking. Bake all the shapes in a preheated moderate oven at 180°C/350°F, Gas Mark 4 for 15 to 20 minutes or until set and golden. Cool on a wire tray.

Stick silver and red sugar balls on the points of the Christmas trees and stars with a dot of Glacé Icing. Spread the other biscuits with Glacé Icing and coat with sugar strands — chocolate, pink, green, etc. When set, thread a narrow red or green ribbon or a tinsel cord through the hole in each cookie and hang on the Christmas tree or fir boughs.

Dutch Christmas ring (kerstkranz)

This is an attractive cake for the Christmas table, especially when a decorative candle is put in the centre of the ring with some sprigs of holly and fir. It is a good idea to make the almond filling in advance and store it in an airtight container until required.

METRIC	IMPERIAL
225 g Danish Pastry dough (p. 148)	*8 oz Danish Pastry dough (p. 148)*
1 egg, beaten	*1 egg, beaten*
FILLING:	FILLING:
120 g ground almonds	*4½ oz ground almonds*
120 g caster sugar	*4½ oz caster sugar*
finely grated rind of 1 lemon	*finely grated rind of 1 lemon*
1 small egg, beaten	*1 small egg, beaten*
6 glacé cherries, halved	*6 glacé cherries, halved*
TO DECORATE:	TO DECORATE:
3-4 tablespoons apricot jam	*3-4 tablespoons apricot jam*
1 tablespoon water	*1 tablespoon water*
2 angelica 'leaves'	*2 angelica 'leaves'*
100 g thin Lemon Glacé Icing (p.150)	*4 oz thin Lemon Glacé Icing (p.150)*
6 glacé cherries, halved	*6 glacé cherries, halved*

Mix the almonds and sugar with the grated lemon rind. Work in sufficient beaten egg to make a soft but not sticky paste. Knead into a ball.

Roll out the pastry into a strip 10 x 53 cm/4 x 21 inches and 3 mm/⅛ inch thick. Roll the almond paste into a thin roll 48 cm/19 inches long. Press the cherry halves deep into it at equal intervals. Place the almond paste roll over the pastry strip, just above centre. Fold the upper edge of the pastry down over the roll. Damp the lower edge with water, curl it up over the roll to just overlap the first pastry flap and press the edges firmly together.

Place a 15 cm/6 inch saucepan lid on a baking sheet. Lift the pastry on to it with the join underneath and curl it round the lid. Remove the lid. Damp one end of the pastry roll with water and insert it in the other end. Press the join firmly and neatly together. Cover and leave to rise for 15 to 20 minutes. Glaze with beaten egg and bake in a preheated hot oven at 230°C/450°F, Gas Mark 8 for 20 to 25 minutes or until well risen and golden brown.

Meanwhile, heat the apricot jam with the water and sieve it. Brush the pastry with it and arrange the cherry halves in pairs with the angelica leaves in the middle, round the ring. Coat while hot, with very thin Lemon Glacé Icing.

Dutch Christmas ring;
Christmas tree cookies

Scandinavia

Danish pastries

The fame of these delicious pastries has travelled far beyond the borders of their own country. They are rich yeast-leavened pastries which can be shaped in various ways, and contain a variety of fillings, marzipan, custard, lemon curd, and fruit and nuts. In the following recipe marzipan is used. It can be home made using half quantities of the recipe on page 98, or ready made.

METRIC	IMPERIAL
225 g plain flour	*8 oz plain flour*
pinch of salt	*pinch of salt*
25 g butter or lard	*1 oz butter or lard*
15 g fresh yeast	*½ oz fresh yeast*
or	*or*
1½ teaspoons dried yeast	*1½ teaspoons dried yeast*
15 g caster sugar	*½ oz caster sugar*
5 tablespoons warm water	*5 tablespoons warm water*
1 egg, beaten	*1 egg, beaten*
125 g butter	*5 oz butter*
225 g Marzipan (p.98), finished weight	*8 oz Marzipan (p.98), finished weight*
thin Glacé Icing (p.150) for glazing	*thin Glacé Icing (p.150) for glazing*

MAKES 14

Sift the flour and salt into a warm mixing bowl and rub in the lard. Blend the yeast with the sugar and water. Leave for 10 minutes to froth if using dried yeast. Stir into the flour with the beaten egg and mix to a soft dough. Turn on to a floured board and knead lightly for about 5 minutes until smooth (p.14). Put in an oiled polythene bag and refrigerate for 10 minutes.

Cream the butter with a palette knife and shape into a 'brick'. Roll out the dough into a rectangle 1 cm/½ inch thick. Spread the butter evenly over half the dough leaving a border 2.5 cm/1 inch round the edge. Fold over the other half of the dough, seal the edges with a rolling pin and give the pastry a quarter turn. Re-roll, fold, seal and quarter turn as for Rough Puff Pastry (p.86). Repeat three times, chilling for 10 minutes between each rolling. Put in the polythene bag and chill for at least 30 minutes before shaping.

Roll out the dough slightly and divide in half. Roll one half into a rectangle 30 x 20 cm/12 x 8 inches. Cut into 6 10 cm/4 inch squares.

Divide the marzipan into 14 pieces, roll 6 into little balls and flatten slightly. Place one in the centre of each square and brush with beaten egg. Draw up the corners together in the centre like an envelope and seal with the beaten egg. Place the pastries on a baking sheet, cover and leave in a warm place for about 20 minutes until puffy. Brush with beaten egg and bake in a preheated hot oven at 220°C/425°F, Gas Mark 7 for 15 to 20 minutes or until crisp and golden. Brush with Glacé Icing and cool on a wire tray.

Roll the second half of the pastry into a 25 cm/10 inch square and divide into 4 quarters. Cut each square diagonally making 8 triangles. Roll the remaining pieces of Marzipan into tiny sausage shapes. Place in the centre of the long side of each triangle. Brush the pastry edges with beaten egg and roll up with the point underneath. Curve into a crescent shape. Place on a baking sheet. Prove, glaze and bake as for the pastry envelopes.

Danish pastries

Swedish flat bread; Norwegian hole cake

Norwegian hole cake

This is really a flat rye bread with a hole cut in the centre, which will fit over the wooden rod in the centre of the Scandinavian bread boards made for ring crispbreads.

METRIC	IMPERIAL
40 g fresh yeast	1½ oz fresh yeast
or	or
20 g dried yeast with 1 teaspoon sugar	¾ oz dried yeast with 1 teaspoon sugar
approx. 300 ml milk	approx. ½ pint milk
65 g butter or margarine, melted	2½ oz butter or margarine, melted
1 teaspoon salt	1 teaspoon salt
100 g treacle	4 oz treacle
2 teaspoons ground aniseed or ground fennel seeds	2 teaspoons ground aniseed or ground fennel seeds
750 g rye flour and strong white flour, mixed	1½ lb rye flour and strong white flour, mixed
225 g plain flour	8 oz plain flour

Cream the fresh yeast with a little milk in a bowl. If using dried yeast, dissolve it in 4 tablespoons milk with the sugar and leave to froth.
Warm the rest of the milk, add the melted fat and pour into the yeast. Stir in the salt, treacle and ground spice. Sift and gradually mix in the flours and work into a dough, adding a little extra warm water if necessary. Beat until it leaves the sides of the bowl. Cover and leave in a warm place until doubled in bulk.
Knock the dough back (p.15) and knead until smooth. Divide the dough into 4 equal pieces and roll out into 20 cm/8 inch rounds. With a tumbler, cut out a hole in the centre of each cake. Place the cakes on a greased baking sheet, cover and leave in a warm place to rise. (The cut out circles can be made into scones or worked up into another flat cake.)
Prick the cakes all over and bake in a preheated moderately hot oven at 200°C/400°F, Gas Mark 6 for about 35 minutes. Brush with salted water and cool on a wire tray.

Swedish flat bread

These thin crispbreads have become very popular outside Scandinavia. They are baked on a griddle (p.44) but a frying pan with a thick base will do very well.

METRIC	IMPERIAL
225 g stone ground wholemeal flour	8 oz stone ground wholemeal flour
225 g rye or barley flour	8 oz rye or barley flour
1 teaspoon salt	1 teaspoon salt
250-350 ml lukewarm water	8-12 fl oz lukewarm water

Blend the flours together with the salt. Mix in sufficient water to bind into a dough — the quantity will depend on the types of flour used. Beat until dough leaves the sides of the bowl, then turn on to a floured board and knead thoroughly (p.14). Heat the griddle over moderate heat and grease it. Divide the dough into four and roll out one quarter into a round as thin as possible. Using a plate about 20 cm/8 inches wide, trim the edges into a neat circle. Prick all over to prevent the dough bubbling during cooking.
Transfer to the griddle and cook over moderate heat for about 15 minutes or until slightly coloured, then turn and cook the other side. Repeat with the rest of the dough, working up the trimmings for re-rolling and baking. Cool on a wire tray. When cold, store in an airtight container.

Toppings and fillings

Basic glacé icing

METRIC
approx. 1 tablespoon water
100 g icing sugar, sifted

IMPERIAL
approx. 1 tablespoon water
4 oz icing sugar, sifted

Stir the water into the icing sugar very gradually, and mix to a spreading consistency, adding a little more water if necessary. Beat until smooth.
For a thinner icing, mix to a pouring consistency, adding ½ teaspoon water at a time.
For a very thin, transparent icing continue adding the water very carefully. Flavour and colour to taste.

Chocolate

Sift 1 tablespoon cocoa with the icing sugar and mix with black coffee or water.

Coffee

Sift 2 teaspoons instant coffee powder with the icing sugar and mix with black coffee instead of water.

Lemon

Mix with strained lemon juice instead of water. Tint pale yellow with a few drops of yellow colouring, or leave white.

Lemon curd

Beat 3-4 teaspoons lemon curd with the basic mixture.

Orange

Use orange juice instead of water to mix and tint with a few drops of orange colouring.

Peppermint

Add a few drops of peppermint oil to the basic mixture and tint a delicate green.

Vanilla

Add a few drops of vanilla essence to the basic mixture and tint pink with a few drops of cochineal if liked.

From the left: Peppermint, orange, vanilla, chocolate and coffee glacé icing

Basic butter cream mixture

METRIC
100 g unsalted butter
175 g icing sugar, sifted

IMPERIAL
4 oz unsalted butter
6 oz icing sugar, sifted

Cream the butter and gradually beat in the icing sugar until smooth. Flavour and colour as required in one of the following ways:

Chocolate

Sift 1 tablespoon cocoa with the icing sugar and add ¼ teaspoon vanilla essence or a little rum.

Coffee

Sift 1-2 teaspoons instant coffee powder with the icing sugar.

Lemon

Cream the finely grated rind of 1 lemon with the butter and add 1-2 teaspoons lemon juice to the butter cream. Tint with a few drops of yellow colouring.

Lemon curd

Beat 2 tablespoons lemon curd with the basic mixture.

Mocha

Sift 2 teaspoons instant coffee powder and 1 tablespoon cocoa with the icing sugar.

Orange

Cream the finely grated rind of 1 orange with the butter and add 1 tablespoon orange juice to the butter cream. Tint with a few drops of orange colouring.

Raspberry

Beat 2-3 tablespoons raspberry jam into the basic mixture and sharpen to taste with lemon juice. Tint pink with a few drops of cochineal.

Walnut

Beat 2-3 tablespoons ground walnuts into the basic mixture.

Mocha, walnut, coffee, lemon and raspberry butter cream

Chantilly cream

METRIC	IMPERIAL
120 ml double cream with 3 tablespoons single cream	4 fl oz double cream with 3 tablespoons single cream
or	or
175 ml whipping cream	6 fl oz whipping cream
1-2 teaspoons caster sugar	1-2 teaspoons caster sugar
few drops of vanilla essence	few drops of vanilla essence

Whip the cream until beginning to thicken, then add the sugar and vanilla essence and continue whipping until the cream just holds its shape. In hot weather be careful not to over whip.

Schlagsahne (fluffy whipped cream)

In Germany and Austria this is served with gâteau and desserts. Make like Chantilly Cream, then fold in a stiffly beaten egg white.

Pastry cream

METRIC	IMPERIAL
1 egg plus 1 egg yolk	1 egg plus 1 egg yolk
50 g caster sugar	2 oz caster sugar
40 g flour	1½ oz flour
300 ml milk	½ pint milk
¼ teaspoon vanilla or almond essence	¼ teaspoon vanilla or almond essence

Whisk the eggs and sugar together until smooth and nearly white. Gradually stir in the flour and then the milk. Pour into a small saucepan and bring to the boil, stirring steadily. Simmer for 3 to 5 minutes, stirring, to cook the flour thoroughly.
If a thick cream is required, as for Gâteau Jalousie (p.144), cook for a few minutes longer to reduce the liquid.
Flavour to taste with vanilla or almond essence and pour into a cold dish to cool. Stir from time to time to prevent a skin forming.
Flavourings: Pastry Cream can also be flavoured with 1 to 2 tablespoons of fresh lemon juice or sweet sherry instead of vanilla or almond essence.

Apricot glaze

METRIC	IMPERIAL
100 g apricot jam	4 oz apricot jam
1 tablespoon lemon juice	1 tablespoon lemon juice
2 tablespoons water or syrup from canned fruit	2 tablespoons water or syrup from canned fruit

Dissolve the jam thoroughly with the lemon juice and water or fruit syrup in a small saucepan over a gently heat. When dissolved, boil until it drops off the edge of a wooden spoon in flakes. If the glaze is too liquid, it will not set and if it is overcooked it will be chewy. Using a wooden spoon strain it through a wire sieve over the fruit.

Red currant glaze

Use red currant jelly instead of apricot jam. Do not overboil as it sets very quickly. It does not require sieving.

Left: Folding in the stiffly beaten egg white for Schlagsahne. Below: Chantilly cream, pastry cream and red currant glaze

Index

Acknowledgements

Photography by Bryce Attwell: 12-24, 26-33, 35, 36-37, 56-57, 66-67, 70-73, 75-85, 86, 87, 88-89, 94-97, 148-149; Melvin Grey: 88; Gina Harris: Endpapers, 4-11, 25, 34-35, 38-39, 44-45 (top), 45, 46-47, 52-53, 62-65, 68-69, 74-75, 85, 98-109, 118-127, 130-131, 134-147, 148, 150-153; Roger Phillips: 40-45, 48-52, 54-55, 58-61, 90-93, 110-117, 128-129, 132, 133.

Notes

Notes

Notes

Notes